it's Too Too LATE

TO DIE YOUNG

NOW

MISADVENTURES IN ROCK AND ROLL

F
Foruli
Codex

Published by Foruli Codex

FIRST EDITION

ISBN 978-1-905792-56-6

Cover by Andy Vella at Velladesign (www.velladesign.com)

Printed by Lightning Source

Foruli Codex is an imprint of Foruli Ltd, London

www.forulicodex.com

ANDREW MUELLER

it's Too Late

TO DIE YOUNG

NOW

MISADVENTURES IN ROCK AND ROLL

Also by Andrew Mueller

I Wouldn't Start From Here
Rock & Hard Places

Andrew Mueller was born in Wagga Wagga, Australia, and lives in London, England. He is a Contributing Editor at *Monocle*, regularly broadcasts on Monocle 24, and also writes for the *Guardian*, *Uncut* and the *New Humanist*, among many others, on a wide variety of subjects, even if the only things he really cares about are country music and the Geelong Football Club.

He is the author of two other books of only slightly self-aggrandising non-fiction, *I Wouldn't Start From Here* and *Rock & Hard Places*, and is at least partially responsible for two albums: *I'll Leave Quietly*, with his band The Blazing Zoos, and *The North Sea Scrolls*, a musical historiography composed in cahoots with Luke Haines and Cathal Coughlan.

Mr Mueller can be contacted/hired/propositioned/insulted via his website at www.andrewmueller.net. He will not reply to emails containing spelling errors or misplaced apostrophes. 'Now get out,' he adds, 'you said this would only take five minutes.'

For Sebastian,
who'd better not grow up to be like his uncle

CONTENTS

Overture   In which the author considers his reasons
            for toasting a camel   **12**

Chapter 1   In which the author is kicked in the shin
            by the drummer from a well-loved British
            ska band   **23**

Chapter 2   In which the author goes to a pub to
            watch a band, still unaware that this
            could be a job description   **35**

Chapter 3   In which the author is abused by masked
            Melburnians   **41**

Chapter 4   In which the author flounders in the gulf
            between ambition and ability   **57**

Chapter 5   In which the author's mother takes
            messages from Run-DMC and Dwight
            Yoakam   **71**

Chapter 6   In which the author gets a guitar lesson
            from Billy Bragg   **81**

Chapter 7   In which the Hoodoo Gurus take umbrage   **91**

Chapter 8   In which the author questions Johnny
            Rotten's sartorial choices   **97**

Chapter 9   In which the author makes up things
            for a scurrilous scandal sheet   **113**

CONTENTS

Chapter 10   For which the author fails to think of a less clichéd subtitle than 'London Calling'   **123**

Chapter 11   In which the author mans the home front   **139**

Chapter 12   In which the author attempts rock journalism in the least rock'n'roll city in America   **153**

Chapter 13   In which the monkey becomes zookeeper   **173**

Chapter 14   In which the author re-examines, and partially recants, some impetuous youthful judgements   **187**

Chapter 15   In which the author gets hit with a grunge icon's hat   **209**

Chapter 16   In which the author enjoys a fifteen-second career as a stadium rock god   **231**

Chapter 17   In which the author learns from his elders and betters   **243**

Chapter 18   In which the author is unable to avoid noticing that things, on a number of levels, are not what they once were   **255**

Chapter 19   In which the author quits, then unquits   **271**

Chapter 20   In which the author enjoys interviewing the uncool   **291**

Chapter 21   In which the author contributes nothing to the biggest rock story of the decade   **303**

Chapter 22   In which the author goes to the worst thing ever   **315**

Chapter 23 In which the author does little to
improve *Melody Maker*'s chances of ever
interviewing Morrissey again   **331**

Chapter 24 In which the author endures a brief turn
as spokesidiot for a generation   **345**

Chapter 25 In which the author elicits a remarkable
. confession from The Jesus & Mary Chain **355**

Chapter 26 In which the author is handed the
regimental revolver and instructed to take
a walk in the woods   **375**

Chapter 27 In which the author toys with the 'And
then I woke up, and discovered it had all
been a dream' closing gambit   **385**

Epilogue   **395**

Acknowledgements   **396**

'Rock and Roll means well
But it can't help telling young boys lies.'

– Drive-By Truckers, 'Marry Me'

OVERTURE

IN WHICH THE AUTHOR
CONSIDERS HIS REASONS FOR
TOASTING A CAMEL

It's a stock question beloved of lazy hacks trying to prod an intimate revelation from their subject: what would they save if their house caught fire? (I've never asked it myself, to the best of my recollection.) A common answer, assuming family and pets are accounted for, is photo albums (or, I guess, the digital equivalent). But does anybody ever look at them?

I hadn't, not for twenty years, give or take, until *It's Too Late to Die Young Now* began gestating. After I'd burrowed into the dankest recesses of the office closet to retrieve them, actual blowing of dust off musty volumes was required – as was rather less romantic sponging away of tenacious mould, and a brief stand-off with one of the emaciated arachnids that pass as spiders in Britain. He proved no match for the April–August 1992 volume.

The images in these albums are either of, or by, someone I know very well, yet barely recognise: me, as a young man. They're taken in places I recall with varying degrees of reliability – Paris, New York, Los Angeles, Berlin, Chicago, Toronto, Dublin, Seattle, Belfast, Manchester, dozens more. They feature musicians, roadies, fans, photographers, journalists and a woman in the street in Hartford, Connecticut, who was wearing antennae on her head, and giant foam bricks as shoes; I daresay she had her reasons.

One picture struck me as especially resonant. It was taken in Tangiers, Morocco, in October 1995. Notwithstanding my forbidding expression – I always feel awkward smiling in photos, on top of which I suspect I may have had a few, this particular evening – it is a portrait of someone living his dream, such as it is.

The subject is wearing a T-shirt clearly sent to him by some favour-currying record company (in this case, whoever had released the most recent album by Tindersticks). Around his neck is draped a black lanyard bearing a laminated silver pass emblazoned with the word 'Press', which no doubt admits him to some glamorous sanctum off-limits to the riffraff. In his right hand, tilted gently towards the camera, is a bottle of pricey-looking French plonk which, judging by his insouciant grip, was paid for by someone else.

Behind him, serving as affirmation of the exoticness of the location, are a pair of camels. Out of shot, but not by much, are an extremely famous rock'n'roll band.[1]

*

---

1   Def Leppard, as it happened. They were in Morocco on the first leg of an attempt – successful, as far as I remember or care – to play three shows on three continents in one calendar day, leaping time zones in order to perform in Morocco, Britain and Canada, beginning shortly after midnight with an acoustic set in a cave complex outside Tangiers. Def Leppard's record company hired a plane to take several dozen hacks along for the ride, a goodly proportion of whom, by the time the Lep mounted the stage, had gotten lost, hidden beneath one of the buffet tables, or passed out, their souvenir fezzes lending their dishevelment an unexpected but potent melancholy.

Whatever station you've reached in life, lofty or lowly or neither, you've arrived at it via an incalculable route of junctions, roundabouts and forks. You can amuse or terrify yourself endlessly by speculating on the consequences of your choices, how things may have worked out better or worse or just differently if you had or hadn't made that call, replied to that email, shown up at that thing, shot that man in Reno just to watch him die, and so forth. Just as there was evidently a sequence of decisions that delivered one young Australian to a few yards downwind of Moroccan camels and an extremely famous rock'n'roll band, so there are uncountable roads he didn't travel, many of which might have led to responsible adulthood and steady employment. This book is the story of a lucky escape.

It's also a retracing of a route now all but washed away. The music press once rivalled the armed forces as a means by which feckless youths with limited financial resources could see the world and terrorise the natives, but without the early starts and with less danger of getting shot at (though this wasn't unheard of). It's all gone now, pretty much. The British music press – the proper, old-school, every-Wednesday music press – used to support three titles, *NME*, *Melody Maker* and *Sounds*, two of which I worked for. Only *NME* still exists, and both it and its readership are a dwindling diminishment of what they were. There was never really much of a future in rock journalism; there's now barely a present.

Though several greater tragedies have befallen mankind, the current decrepitude of the music press is a shame nonetheless. Before *Melody Maker* in particular opened up the world to me, it opened up worlds to me. Though I started writing – at least, typing – about music in 1987, I didn't really understand what rock journalism could be until 1988, when I purchased my first copy of *Melody Maker*. Rather incredibly, it was the issue which featured on its cover hapless grebo time-wasters Gaye Bykers on Acid – even more incredibly, that much considered, I bought the following week's paper as well. This became a habit, and working for *Melody Maker* became a consuming ambition. It was an unlikely aspiration for a teenager from Sydney to entertain, but perhaps for that reason, it came off. In 1989, I began contributing to *Melody Maker*, filing features and reviews from Sydney. In 1990, I moved to London. In 1991, I became *Melody Maker*'s reviews editor. In 1993, I quit. In 1994, I rejoined. In 1996, I got sacked.

It's Too Late to Die Young Now is set in this period – the last period, it turned out, in which the music press would ever matter, to the extent that it ever did. I'm not saying that its terminal decline corresponds precisely with my departure, but the reader may make of the coincidence what they will.

*

Music fans in their late thirties or older are the last of a kind.

They – we – are the last music fans who bought albums, who subscribed to music magazines, who had to work, in any sense of the word, to enjoy the music they enjoyed. Music was once something that people saved up and paid for, and subsequently displayed with alphabetically indexed pride on their shelves, and had to make time to listen to. It is now regarded as something that all but comes out of the tap.

People my age are supposed to think that modern music and its attendant culture are crass, fatuous and annoying, and indeed I do. But the generation gap which rock'n'roll mined so profitably for so long now operates precisely in reverse to the way it did as recently (or as long ago, I can't decide) as when I pushed my carefully accumulated pocket money over the counter in exchange for my first seven-inch single.

Middle-aged people no longer find modern music discomfiting or threatening, but tedious and limp.

I don't think it's untoward grandstanding to argue that the demise of the music press is part of the reason for the pallid, paint-by-numbers grimness of so much modern music. At its best, the rock press – the British rock press in particular – served not just as critics, but curators, encouraging musicians and fans alike to think, to learn, to experiment, to demand more. Most musicians would, of course, deny that any such symbiotic relationship existed – but they all grew up avidly reading *Melody Maker* and *NME*. Indeed, were it not for *Melody Maker*'s classifieds, many bands would never have met.

It's Too Late to Die Young Now is not an anthology, though it does contain excerpts of original journalism, or at least those portions of my youthful scribblings that I can reread without wanting to grow a beard and go to sea under a picturesque alias. I also harbour some hope that my reflections on those scrawlings from two decades further down the trails of writing and living might resonate beyond the admittedly insular world of music journalism, speaking to everyone who has ever wondered how they'd feel now if they met the younger version of themselves. At the risk of giving away the ending, it's a deeply weird combination of wanting to hug them, and wanting to slap them.

*

On an afternoon in the recent past, I'm walking through London. In the right-hand pocket of my jacket is my iPod, which is set to shuffle; I'm taking a ride on the random rollercoaster of memories and emotions improvised by the whims of the device. I'm scarcely alone in this, of course. All over the world, buses, trains, planes and footpaths are crowded with people whose psychological landscapes must be lurching back and forth across the spectrum from Munch's *The Scream* to the signature scenes of *Singin' in the Rain*. It cannot be doing any of us any good.

Anyway, the song that has popped up as you join me is 'The Sixteen Days' by Ed Kuepper. It's the fourth track on side one of *Rooms of the Magnificent*, the second solo album by the former Saints guitarist and Laughing Clowns frontman, released in 1986. 'The Sixteen Days' is one of my favourite Ed Kuepper cuts, and *Rooms of the Magnificent* is my favourite Ed Kuepper album (the necessary qualification to this declaration is that I haven't heard all of Ed Kuepper's solo albums, as Kuepper's solo career has been so bewilderingly prolific that it feels like there are many more Ed Kuepper albums than there is the time left for a man in his mid-forties to listen to them).

Rooms of the Magnificent seemed to me then, and seems to me now, a pretty definitive statement of Kuepper's formidable talent, and 'The Sixteen Days' is a compelling summary of those qualities: the brilliant shimmer of twelve-string acoustic guitar carrying the rhythm part, the urgent ferocity of Kuepper's electric lead, the characteristically opaque lyrics, the insidious, irresistible hook in the chorus, the languid drawl of one of those male rock voices which manages to make a virtue of its limitations, like Neil Young's or Lou Reed's or Robert Smith's, although Kuepper sounds like none of them.

It's twenty-five years, give or take, since I first heard this song. I might have heard it the first time on the ABC's alternative radio station 2JJJ FM (now officially known as Triple J) or *Rage*, the midnight-till-dawn music program that ran on ABC-TV at weekends, but as 'The Sixteen Days' was never a single, it's more likely I first heard it on the record player in my tiny bedroom in my family's house in the George's Heights military base on Sydney's lower North Shore. I would have toted the album home by ferry and by bus, flat on my lap so as not to bend the vinyl, after buying it at Phantom or Waterfront or Redeye, all much-loved independent record stores in the city centre. And though I can't be precisely certain, it's a reasonable bet that the money with which I bought *Rooms of the Magnificent* was earnt working in another record shop, in Crows Nest, in North Sydney – Music Plus, a suburban high street sort of record shop, with precisely none of the kudos of Phantom or Waterfront or Redeye, but one in which I'd nevertheless persuaded the owner to let me establish a rack for independent releases, so I'd occasionally get the chance to talk to other people who knew who Ed Kuepper was.

Though it is difficult to imagine that there are six subjects about which Kuepper himself could care less, he occupies a crucial role in the ensuing narrative. The first thing I was ever paid money for writing, in June 1987, was a review of a gig at the pub up the street, the Mosman Hotel, by Kuepper and his then backing band, The Yard Goes On Forever (they were named, though I can't imagine I knew this at the time, after one of the entrancingly deranged albums that Richard Harris made with Jimmy Webb in the late 1960s). This review ran in a free Sydney listings paper called *On the Street*. It started like this:

There is no doubting that Ed Kuepper has mellowed with age. From his days as part of the vanguard of Australian punk with The Saints, to the at-times-cacophonic aural assault of The Laughing Clowns, Kuepper's music has evolved into melodic, acoustic rock. This newer musical direction perfectly complements his droning vocal style and esoteric lyrics to produce a sound that on record is as captivating and challenging as any of his previous ventures.

I've read worse, I suppose. I've sure as hell written worse. I went on to note the material from which Kuepper's shirt was made (silk – though Kuepper was a definitively diffident outsider, loftily disdainful of fashion, it was nevertheless technically the eighties) and (pointlessly) the resemblance borne by drummer Mark Dawson to satirist Patrick Cook. I also drew a hilariously – and, given that I doubt I'd heard of Kuepper myself twelve months before, outrageously – pious distinction between the 'genuine' fans who knew the words to every song on Kuepper's first solo album, 1985's *Electrical Storm*, and those bandwagon-overcrowding come-latelys who appeared to have been enticed by *Rooms of the Magnificent*.

I tapped out the review on my mother's typewriter, and posted it to the address listed in *On the Street*'s masthead. One Wednesday a couple of weeks later, I picked up the new issue of the paper from the pile inside the front door of Redeye Records. In neither hope nor expectation, I leafed through to the pages which contained the live reviews. There, I beheld a stock photo of Ed Kuepper, and a review of his recent performance at the Mosman Hotel. Balls, I thought. They'd already had a writer covering it. Then I noticed the by-line and gradually absorbed that the correspondent in question had a name indistinguishable from mine.

I've a vague memory of subsequently walking very quickly a few blocks in a direction I had no need to take, and then walking back to where I'd started. There was, probably, a degree of pacing in small circles and breathing too quickly. On the ferry and the bus home, I repeatedly re-read the words I'd last seen being folded into an envelope in my bedroom, as if frightened they'd fade from the page if not watched very, very carefully.

·ₐ·

The journey chronicled in the following pages is defined to an extent by how odd all of the above sounds in a modern-day context. The hearing of new music for the first time on the radio. The journey into town to the record store. The exchange of money – and probably, by the standards of the day, a hefty whack thereof – for a vulnerable vinyl album, on which most of the songs were unfamiliar. The idea of the album having two sides, and possibly some semblance of thematic semi-coherence uniting them. The record player. The typewriter. The filing of copy by post. It was all only a quarter of a century ago.

It's Too Late to Die Young Now is partly, though not exclusively, a book about being a music journalist during this period. And it's somewhat, if not altogether, a work of music criticism, reflecting a little of the background noise of those times – a pretty gripping soundtrack, as it happened, dominated successively by Manchester, Seattle and, finally, a resurgent, swaggering London. And it's very much, but not entirely, a memoir – of a time in one man's life, and of the time in every man's life, during which it is pretty much decided, by himself and by extraneous factors over which he exerts varying degrees of control, who and what he will spend the rest of his time here being.

And what I am is a rock journalist. I mean, I'm also – or have been – a travel writer, a foreign correspondent, a book reviewer, a film critic, a sports reporter, an op-ed columnist, a radio anchor, a television presenter and pretty much every other sort of journalist bar an agony aunt (and that's only because nobody ever asked). But though I've done all those sorts of journalism, and even done some of them reasonably well, I am at heart and in outlook a rock journalist, a denizen of that least-esteemed sub-strata of hackery, a species of scrivener taken seriously by nobody, least of all ourselves. Rock journalists stay rock journalists, whatever else we might go on to do. The vocation has something in common with the titular hostelry of a song routinely – and quite rightly – vilified by myself and my kind: you can check out any time you like, but you can never leave.

ANDREW MUELLER

1

IN WHICH THE AUTHOR IS KICKED IN THE SHIN BY THE DRUMMER FROM A WELL-LOVED BRITISH SKA BAND

Everybody alive in the post-World War II world, in which music became commodified and efficiently distributed, can plot – and revisit at will – a soundtrack to their lives.

The first musical memories are usually those imposed by the record collections of their parents. These will include the first pop song to which they can remember knowing some or all of the words (for me, this was B.J. Thomas's 1969 hit 'Raindrops Keep Fallin' on My Head'),[1] and the first record they can recall deliberately, voluntarily listening to (the 1968 Original Broadway Cast recording of *Hair*, a favourite of my mother, the fervour of whose hopes that I didn't understand a word of it can only be wondered at).

Then there will be the first artist or group about whom they're pretty sure they consciously thought, 'I like this artist

---

1   This was written by Hal David and Burt Bacharach for the soundtrack of *Butch Cassidy & The Sundance Kid*. I would meet Bacharach nearly thirty years later, in 1998, when I interviewed him and Elvis Costello about the album (*Painted From Memory*) they'd just made together. I decided, I think correctly, to spare him the revelation of his role in my personal discography, anticipating that it would prompt complete nonplussedness.

or group.' This will almost certainly be someone who just happens to be big enough to be on the radio a lot in your parents' car, and in the cars of the parents of the other kids at your primary school (almost nobody discovers individuality before high school, as almost nobody turns into a desperate, insecure solipsist – and therefore a rampaging snob – before they're a teenager). This will also almost certainly be an artist or group who play songs with tunes, as children like tunes because they haven't yet turned into desperate, insecure solipsists – and therefore rampaging snobs – and parents like tunes because they're too tired to like anything else. So: Abba.

There will be, possibly around the age of ten, the first single purchased with your own pocket money (Blondie's 'Heart of Glass', a choice so preposterously precocious that I wouldn't dare invent it; I cheerfully and candidly balance this implicit boast with the confession that I subsequently saved pocket money for no end of inexplicable drivel, up to and including at least two singles by Racey).[2] And the first video that made

---

2 One of which was definitely 'Some Girls' – a song which, I learnt many years later, was initially offered by its composers, Nicky Chinn and Mike Chapman, to Blondie, who turned it down. Racey's rendering is a tinny glam shimmy in the vein of such inescapable wedding DJ favourites as Mud's 'Tiger Feet' or Sweet's 'Ballroom Blitz' (both also Chinn/Chapman productions). Mike Chapman went on to produce, among much else, most of Blondie's albums, which means, of course, that he produced 'Heart of Glass'; something about his works clearly resonated at this point (I also remember buying Exile's 'How Could This Go Wrong?', another Chapman composition, and The Knack's 'My Sharona', a Chapman production). Our affinity had limits, however, which is to say that civilised countries no longer countenance punishments appropriate to having been an accessory to the perpetration of Tina Turner's 'The Best', anthem for the global diaspora of people who carry their mobile phones in little holsters on their belts. Legendary as quite the tyrannical perfectionist, Chapman once appeared on the cover of BAM magazine dressed as General George S. Patton. He was born in Queensland.

music look like it might be more than lyrics and a tune, that it might be a life, a world, more interesting and dangerous – and/or stupider and sillier – than yours. I don't know exactly what this was, but I do know where I saw it, as does every Australian of a certain age – on *Countdown*, a weekly music program hosted by a mumbling man in a cowboy hat. This was Ian 'Molly' Meldrum, who now enjoys, through a combination of career longevity, nostalgia and (in fairness) seeming a basically decent egg, near universal affection in Australia. Indeed, a serious domestic accident in 2011, and his spirited recovery from same, almost certainly qualifies Meldrum for modern Australia's highest national honour, only conferred upon well-loved celebrities following the overcoming of tribulation. This is, of course, the Our (see also Our Kylie, Our Delta, etc). While it would be churlish to deny that *Countdown* introduced some great international artists – Blondie not least among them – its local content was, overwhelmingly, inane provincial mediocrity. Though such is the dialectical nature of pop, and such was the dominance of *Countdown*, this may have been the reason that the Australian underground of the 70s and 80s was so vibrant. So thanks, Our Molly.

Around that time, there will also have been the first artist or group you got properly into via your own peer group, heedless of the tastes of your parents, and the appeal of whom was probably related to the degree to which your parents found them baffling, repellent, obnoxious, tuneless and witless (Kiss). The first artist or group whose poster you affixed to your wall (Kiss – the staggeringly crass photograph in which they are depicted, bloodied and bandaged, in a pastiche of a portrait of wounded Civil War veterans). The first album you asked a friend to record for you onto cassette (Kiss's *Double Platinum*). The first album you successfully pestered your mother into buying for you (Kiss's

Kiss Unmasked). The first album towards which you experienced vague but discernible stirrings of disappointment and dissatisfaction (Kiss's *Kiss Unmasked* again – although this landmark may be peculiar to the evolution of that chronically querulous stripe of person destined to become a rock journalist). The first artist or group whose name on a magazine cover enticed you to purchase said edition (Kiss, again – the issue of *Juke* which claimed to contain photographs of Kiss *sans* makeup).

I should state for the record that my views on Kiss today are broadly congruent with those held by my parents at the time, and that I'm therefore grateful – yet mildly reproachful – that the folks didn't restrict my rations to gruel and pond water and dispatch me to the doghouse until I stopped bringing this rubbish into their home, and started listening to proper rock'n'roll like AC/DC instead.

*

At some slightly later point, usually in mid-adolescence, the meaning of music changes. It develops from merely being words and notes arranged in an order you happen to find pleasing into a keystone of your personal culture, a constitution of codes and rituals to which you ally yourself as a means of joining some sort of community, and as a way of representing yourself to anyone who cares to take an interest. This is also usually happenstance, based largely on where you happen to go to school in your mid-teens.

I went to a lot of schools, as children of military personnel do. The primary schools I attended – one in Sydney, one in Point Lonsdale, two in Canberra – were okay, I guess. The first secondary school I attended, Holder High School in Canberra, presented a forbidding brutalist concrete visage which earned it the nickname 'Holditz'. The prevailing musical tastes were standard-issue suburban, which is to say that the girls listened to Duran Duran and other such blouses in blouses, and the boys listened to Midnight Oil. I didn't much care for Duran Duran, and I did like Midnight Oil, but I don't recall possessing any especially militant opinions about these, or about music in general.

The second secondary school I attended, for third and fourth form, was the Catholic boys' high school St Paul's College, at the top of Darley Road overlooking Manly, in Sydney. It wasn't anybody's first choice – it was just the only school within walking distance of our new home inside the barracks of the School of Artillery on North Head, where Dad had been appointed commanding officer. St Paul's was the only single-sex school I attended, the only private school I attended, and the only religious school I attended. Not coincidentally, I hated it.

My difficulties at St Paul's were not, when measured against the lurid pageant of human suffering, noteworthy – probably no more or less than might be expected for the new kid, the (at the time) quite short kid, the lippy and sarcastic kid, the kid who was a calamitous liability to any sports team encumbered with him, the kid who wouldn't kneel during church services (I've never understood why this refusal so upsets the religious, just as I've never understood the inability of people who are dancing to leave alone those who are not. My theory is that both the worshippers and the rug-cutters fear that they appear ridiculous, and that this concern will be assuaged if they can compel everyone else to participate in their nonsense.)

With a few treasurable exceptions, my classmates – and, I'm sure, not a few of the teachers – thought I was an insufferable smartarse, and I thought they – and quite a few of the teachers – were a herd of oafish dimwits. An impartial observer would probably have concluded that everybody was at least half right. It was, however, at St Paul's that my hitherto altogether normal interest in music – which is to say the sort of interest most people have, where they like the sort of thing they like, and regard everything else with amiable indifference – began metastasising into something more consuming.

*

Noel Coward cannot have known how right he would be proven when he made his famous quip about the strange potency of cheap music. One of the charms of working as an itinerant hack in an age dominated by the popular culture of the West has been witnessing the radiant hybrids that occur as accelerating technology wafts assorted cultural pollen over ever greater distances, sprinkling seeds upon incongruous landscapes.

I have, in my time, sipped Guinness with the singer of an Irish-style folk band in Belgrade,[3] watched an Abba tribute act from Russia conduct singalonging revellers in a park in Ulan Bator, listened to Seattlesque grunge outfits rehearsing in sandbagged basements beneath the ruins of Sarajevo, and quaffed bootleg grappa with members of an XTC-influenced

---

3 The Orthodox Celts, whose singer, Aleksandar Petrovic, I met while on assignment in Serbia for *The Face* in late 2000, shortly after the revolution that had dismantled the squalid gangsters' paradise presided over by Slobodan Milosevic. 'When the parliament was on fire,' said Petrovic, 'I thought the destruction was bad – it is an old and beautiful building. But I remember thinking of the Easter Rising and the Post Office in Dublin. It was the same picture – a burning building with police and army in front of it. So it was a kind of Easter Rising for us, but it ended happily.' Petrovic had gleaned an impressive knowledge of Irish history from the works of The Dubliners, The Wolfe Tones and The Pogues, among others of that ilk. You can get pretty much anybody to listen to a lecture on pretty much anything, so long as you set it to a tune.

rock group in Tehran.[4] None of which seems any weirder than the fact that, in 1983 and 1984, at a Catholic boys' high school in a beachside suburb of Sydney, a goodly proportion of at least one form were besotted with the ska scene which had flourished in the United Kingdom a few years earlier.

I never figured out how this happened. It's possible that the phenomenon gestated in tapes sent home from London by someone's travelling older sibling, but that doesn't account for the half-decade time delay. It could be that someone in my form liked Madness, who'd had actual hits in Australia and been shown on *Countdown*, and wondered if there was more like that where they came from – though I can't imagine how they'd have found out, given that Australia barely had a music press to speak of, and British music magazines, usually months-old sea-mail copies, were generally only to be found in bigger newsagents in the city (although at this point I didn't know that, either). 2JJJ is another potential culprit – but that wouldn't explain why I didn't know of any other school in Sydney at the time where kids were reporting for roll-call sporting Terry Hall-style flat-top haircuts, incorporating crepe-soled suede shoes into their uniforms and even, in a couple of cases, rocking checked porkpie hats until instructed to desist by bemused teachers.

I don't remember when I first heard any of this 'ska' stuff, but I do remember vividly how I felt when I did: relieved.

---

4 127 Band, who enjoy the dubious privilege of getting to practise their art in a place where rock'n'roll is still perceived as a threat. 'Somewhere in this city,' singer Sohrab Mohebbi told me in 2007, outlining the bureaucracy that burdened all Iranian artists, 'there's a grown man, who gets dressed in the morning, kisses his wife goodbye, and goes and sits in an office and gets paid to decide that my band can't play in front of thirty of our friends.' This remains about as heartbreaking an illustration of the dreariness and stupidity of tyranny as I've heard.

Relieved because I actually, genuinely liked it – and there-fore probably hoped, as a result, to be spared at least some of the (half-arsed and low-level, but nonetheless debilitating and tedious) bullying inflicted by the flat-tops-and-crepes faction. I wasn't, of course – the flat-tops-and-crepes faction merely adjusted their opinion of me from annoying dweeb to craven parvenu, and continued breaking eggs in my school-bag. Though I'd prefer not to think that the passion for music which has since nourished my soul and provided part of my living might be a lingering symptom of some adolescent outbreak of Stockholm syndrome, the first album I ever paid for with my own money, four years after its release, was The Specials' 1979 self-titled debut, *The Specials*.

This was swiftly followed into the corner of my parents' record cabinet that I'd annexed by The Specials' audaciously titled 1980 follow-up, *More Specials*, Madness's *Complete Madness*, The Selecter's *Too Much Pressure*, The Beat's *What is Beat?* and a couple of 2 Tone label compilations, all purchased from a Manly record shop clearly attuned to the quirks of its market. Even though there seemed little prospect of it ever being any real concern of mine, I was disappointed that Adrian Thrills' sleeve notes on the *This Are Two Tone* compilation referred to the ska scene in the past tense. It was some consolation that at least one local band refused to admit this: I also bought *D-D-D-Dance*, the debut album by Sydney ska band The Allniters, and a T-shirt flaunting their name.

I had no idea that I wanted to be a journalist, still less a rock journalist – I doubt I had any idea that such a thing as a rock journalist existed. I hadn't the blurriest notion who Adrian Thrills was, and no way of finding out, other than perhaps approaching strangers in the streets of Sydney's hipper districts, wherever they were, and asking, 'Excuse me, have you the blurriest notion who Adrian Thrills is?' (He wrote for the *NME*, but I didn't know what that was, either.) I wanted to be a doctor or a fighter pilot – ideally, a surgeon who also flew F-111s for the Royal Australian Air Force and on Saturdays played centre half-forward for Geelong, except during the summer, when I batted number four for Australia.

It is probably an unsolvable problem, but it cannot be beneficial to humanity that every man is an aching disappointment to his teenage self.

*

I still have a lot of those ska records, or digital representations thereof. Most of them, I think, have held up splendidly, at least the British ones. A twenty-first-century reacquaintance, via YouTube, with The Allniters' breezy version of Bobby Bloom's 'Montego Bay' – specifically, with the sound of white Australians affecting Caribbean accents – prompted a curling of the toes which may require surgical correction.

Those two Specials albums in particular are nigh flawless. The first, produced by Elvis Costello, is a bracingly articulate expression of young manhood, strutting awkwardly, preening uncertainly, radiating terrified bravado as it grapples with those questions which young men quaintly suppose have answers, specifically: i) why women are weird, ii) why people are unpleasant, and iii) why stuff just isn't fair. The second, one of the great lost classics of the post-punk era, released just twelve months later, sounds like the work of people who have grown up vertiginously quickly: a clammy, queasy hallucination of apocalypse, topped and tailed with readings of the cheesy standard 'Enjoy Yourself', the first defiant and exuberant, the last possibly the most sarcastic 107 seconds of popular song ever recorded.

I'm not certain what aspects of these albums I related to. My experience of fleeing, as fast as two-inch soles permitted, from National Front skinheads through the mean streets of Coventry was limited. I'd never even sought admission to a nightclub, still less the sort of place that would be spelled 'Nite Klub'. I didn't know any girls who'd done too much, much too young – chance, indeed, would have been a fine thing. And while I'd received some instruction in the atomic paranoia which was the style at the time, from a couple of sandal-shod teachers and the recordings of Midnight Oil – the cover of whose 1984 album, *Red Sails in the Sunset*, depicted Sydney Harbour immediately following a nuclear missile strike – the likelihood of the beautiful view from our kitchen window being reduced to irradiated aridity never struck me as significant. The simplest explanation that fits the facts, where The Specials were concerned, was that I thought their records were riddled with belting tunes, and that the group looked imperishably cool on the sleeves: two judgements I stand by.

*

My discovery that I enjoyed post-punk English ska may not have impressed my dullard tormentors at St Paul's, but it did amount to the first steps on the path chronicled in this book. Roughly ten years later, during a regular Sunday afternoon social soccer match in Regent's Park in London, I would be – during one of my rare and fleeting interludes in possession of the ball – enthusiastically (though not maliciously) clattered by Madness drummer Woody. If only, I thought, as I subsequently pursued him down the wing bent on barbarous vengeance, shattered shin guard flapping from one sock, they could see me now.

IT'S TOO LATE TO DIE YOUNG NOW

ANDREW MUELLER

2

IN WHICH THE AUTHOR GOES TO THE PUB TO WATCH A BAND, STILL UNAWARE THAT THIS COULD BE A JOB DESCRIPTION

In 1985, the Australian Army ordered us across Sydney Harbour, from North Head to Middle Head, to a house which, while smaller, had an even better view – an even better view, indeed, than just about any house in Sydney, which meant a better view than just about any house in the world. To walk out of our front door was to be slapped across the eyes with a life-size postcard of Sydney Harbour. A short walk up Middle Head Road lay an even more giddying prospect: a school I liked, and which appeared to like me.

If St Paul's turned me into a music fan, Mosman High turned me into – the tentative, primordial beginnings of – a writer. Every school should be like Mosman High, and I'd been to enough that weren't anything like Mosman High to appreciate it. By miraculous luck or good management, a culture of easygoing encouragement and uncontrived respect existed among staff and students. Accomplishment was ungrudgingly applauded, failure constructively discussed. The teachers seemed to be motivated principally by a conviction that their subject was an enthralling hoot: classes felt less like lessons than the guilelessly enthusiastic gushings of gung-ho hobbyists. It said everything about Mosman High's English department that for the creative writing section of our final trial exams, they set the question 'Take your least favourite character from any of this year's texts, and dispose of them in whatever fashion seems appropriate'. (Such terrible revenges were inflicted on Pip from *Great Expectations* that most of us, a few years later, would yawn through *American Psycho*.) And I began to understand what, at base, most writing – and certainly any worthwhile journalism – is: the writer's attempt to explain something to himself.

School uniforms were disdained in favour of a regimen of pseudo-bohemian dishevelment, except by one classmate who recognised – correctly – that the most revolutionary and individualistic statement he could make in the circumstances was to uphold the official dress code to the letter, even to the extent of wearing what may have been the only Mosman High tie sold since World War II. He may also have understood that, as is always the case, everyone was essentially wearing some sort of uniform anyway. The most hapless ethnographer – myself, for example – would have had little difficulty classifying punks, hippies, surfers, stoners, geeks and goths, among other standard playground fauna.

Unusually, however, there was no intertribal rancour, which promoted a culturally unencumbered exchange of music. You were allowed to enjoy The Cramps even if you didn't put glue in your hair. And if you did put glue in your hair, it was nevertheless considered perfectly acceptable to like The Smiths. People with suntans listened to The Cure. People who probably couldn't see themselves in mirrors listened to Hoodoo Gurus. Absolutely everybody listened to Violent Femmes. Not only did I hear things I'd never heard before, I heard things I wouldn't have heard anywhere else, on the grounds that they wouldn't have been suggested to a new kid with a somewhat incongruous collection of band logos inked onto his disposals store satchel.

By the time we moved to Mosman, my record collection had outgrown its corner of my parents' cabinet, and now leant between the amplifier and speakers of my first stereo. My ska records had been joined by evidence of a regard for Australian folk, probably inculcated by a parental affection for same. Our family had acquired, somewhere in our peregrinations, a supermarket compendium of traditional bush ballads, brayed in absurdly overplayed rural accents by session musicians who must have spent the time between takes weeping with laughter and/or self-loathing. I think Mum liked this stuff because it was, after a fashion, the music of where she'd come from – the countryside of New South Wales, descended in part from people who had doubtless preferred to style themselves wild colonial boys, but who were more likely a rabble of hapless petty miscreants that Britain had been understandably happy to see the back of. Dad, of honest South Australian immigrant stock, just used to like listening to it – often interspersed with the world's national anthems, by the band of the Coldstream Guards – after he'd had a few.

So, alongside the alumni of 2 Tone, I was also listening to The Bushwhackers, an indefatigable institution who recast Australian folk tunes as beer-flecked pub rock, and Redgum, who clearly had no fear of the clichés of their genre, flaunting beards, cardigans, acoustic guitars and pious left-wing cant with earnest, unselfconscious vigour (I'd still argue that their 1983 chart-topper 'I Was Only 19' is worthy of being covered by Steve Earle, but the recollection of some of their more purse-lipped homilies on the evils of the western world leaves me retrospectively astounded that I didn't spend more of my teens campaigning in favour of the unnecessary damming of wild rivers, just to annoy Redgum).

Between my new classmates, 2JJJ and some exemplary music television programming (*Rock Arena* and *Rage* on the ABC, *Rock Around the World* on SBS), my tastes broadened quickly. The time in your life during which you properly discover music is an unrepeatably thrilling period, an agog roam through a vault of glittering treasures, antique and modern, foreign and local. I can't say whether it's just as exciting to the neophyte when everything is available on demand as soon as you flip open your laptop: I hope so. It is possible that there would have been a given month in which I heard, for the first time, The Clash, Bruce Springsteen, The Byrds, Jimi Hendrix, Elvis Costello, The Triffids, Al Green, The Velvet Underground, Paul Kelly, Lynyrd Skynyrd, R.E.M., Hunters & Collectors, Green on Red, The Pogues and choice excerpts of the outputs of Motown, Def Jam and 4AD. If that sounds a suspiciously unimpeachable list, I can only retort that my classmates had rarefied taste – certainly, none of them were to blame for my decision to queue over-night for tickets to see Dire Straits on their twenty-one-night stand at Sydney Entertainment Centre. (I will still argue, however, that Dire Straits' 1980 album *Making Movies* is a neglected classic, apart from its closing track, 'Les Boys', which is the worst song ever written by anybody, ever, with the obvious exception of John Lennon's 'Imagine'.)

At some stage during this period, I would have attended my first gig, as such. This may have been a performance by the covers band formed by school friends, who regularly played rock standards at a hotel bar in Cremorne which had either a progressive attitude to underage drinking or blind door staff. Or it may have been, with entrance secured by flashing the bouncer a copy of a university-going friend's birth certificate, a show at the Mosman Hotel, a short walk uphill from school.

Though I'd nothing to measure the experience against, any Sydney gig-goer of the late 1980s was enormously blessed in both the quantity of venues and the quality of music. Of the bands who might plausibly have been the first I ever saw, I can say that I'd pay to see any of them again: Ups & Downs, a troupe of lank-fringed Queenslanders with a delirious line in Byrdsian jangle; The Happy Hate-Me-Nots, muscular punkers in cheerfully deep hock to Hüsker Dü; The Warumpi Band, a part-Aboriginal group from Papunya, Northern Territory, as far from Sydney as Moscow is from London, who set tales of their homeland to a raw, dry, rhythm and blues; John Kennedy's Love Gone Wrong, who sang of hearts broken in Sydney's inner suburbs, pioneering a sub-genre of country: urban and western.

I found out about these shows, and read a little about these artists, in *On the Street*, which was dropped off in bundles every Wednesday at Sydney pubs, bars and record shops. *On the Street* performed its core task brilliantly – it told its readers who would be playing where, and when. It did a lot else really pretty badly. Its editorial was mostly either vacuous boosterism or witless sneering.

My writing would fit in perfectly.

ANDREW MUELLER

3

IN WHICH THE AUTHOR IS ABUSED BY MASKED MELBURNIANS

My relationship with *On the Street* was, for the first couple of months, oddly detached. Just as nobody had called to tell me that the first thing I'd submitted – my review of Ed Kuepper at the Mosman Hotel – was going to run, nobody called to tell me that I'd be welcome to send more, or even to find out who the heck I thought I was anyway. As far as *On the Street* knew, I could have been a Soviet agent transmitting coded treasons through maladroit similes, a chapter of Freemasons conniving to promote Lodge brothers under a pseudonym, Ed Kuepper's cousin – the coincidence of Germanic surnames might have raised one or two questions – or, indeed, an adolescent army brat who still hadn't left home.

If no encouragement was offered, none was required. I went to the gigs I had already planned to attend, wrote whatever quantity of words I thought reasonable, posted the reviews in, and grew progressively twitchier as each Wednesday drew nearer. Almost none of what I wrote warranted publication – very little of it, indeed, didn't warrant a briskly phrased suggestion that I spend more time at the university lectures I'd been avoiding – but my scrapbook began to fill gratifyingly. I reviewed, among other occurrences, a double bill of The Lime Spiders and Painters & Dockers at the Hotel Manly, a triple bill of Wall of Voodoo, Ed Kuepper and The Yard Goes on Forever and Love Gone Wrong at Sydney University, and a show played by the utterly unheard-of band of some friends in the sunroom of someone's house on Palm Beach. Reading this crap a quarter-century later, I am ecstatic with gratitude for the non-existence, at this point, of an online arena, wherein my inane drivellings would have been quickly – and quite rightly – dismembered by hooting vigilantes, along with my altogether unearned confidence, perhaps crushing my larval writerly ambitions and thereby compelling me to spend adulthood working for a living.

Eventually, *On the Street* – in the person of its editor, Margaret Cott – called me. The conversation set the pattern for the rest of our association, in that Margaret was kinder about my abilities than I deserved, and offered to pay me a quantity of money which, while negligible, was certainly more than my nonsense merited. She asked me to drop by the office, then situated on York Street, in Sydney's centre, so that I might collect what I was owed for the gig reviews *On the Street* had already printed – twenty-five dollars a shot – and pick up some vinyl to write about, if I fancied so doing. I suppressed palpitations as I processed what she was proposing: that I be paid to go to gigs, that I be given records, that I be permitted space in which to express my opinions about these, and that I be endowed, as a consequence, with a certain power to shape tastes – to make, verily, and to break. If anyone had pointed out the very good reasons to temper my glee – i.e. that I couldn't write a lick, and had absolutely no idea about anything – I'd have been whooping too loudly to hear them.

Equipped with commissions and the attendant places on guest lists, and burdened with consequent hubris, I breezily and obliviously set about reducing mercifully undemonstrative multitudes of *On the Street* readers to (I am in hindsight certain) weekly agonies of will-to-live-sapping despair. I was trivial, gaily sharing details of where my friends and I had been for a drink beforehand (Paul Kelly solo at the Hip Hop Club). I was pompous, presuming to publicly scold persons far more talented than myself on subjects about which I had no clue (The Verlaines at the Lansdowne Hotel, Suzanne Vega at Sydney Town Hall). I was crashingly unfunny, while clearly convinced I was being the precise opposite (Died Pretty, Mosman Hotel). I used exclamation marks in contexts other than reported speech or obviously sarcastic rhetoric, which should always be punishable by death, ideally administered with broadsword (Weddings Parties Anything, Lansdowne Hotel).

*

I dropped out of university. Or, rather, just found myself going less and less often, until one day I slouched guiltily into the English department to collect a gathering heap of ignored assignments, and had to explain to the receptionist that my tutor's name had escaped me. Mercifully, the record shop in Crows Nest which had employed me part-time for some months offered to pay me to come in every day.

Working in a record shop isn't – or, I suppose, the vocation having gone the way of lamplighters and chimney sweeps, wasn't – the toughest row to hoe. The hours were agreeable, my colleagues were affable and, if the owner wasn't in, we could listen to whatever we liked. In fact, only one thing stopped working in a record shop from being a thoroughly pleasant way to earn a buck, but that one thing was so dreadful that there were days when I contemplated the lot of coalminers and urinal-cake salesmen with wistful envy. I refer, of course, to the general public.

Whenever someone proclaims their all-embracing love of people, you can be reasonably sure that they're mad, and absolutely certain that they never worked in a record shop. No other occupation – aside, perhaps, from journalism – hangs you so often, by the fraying thread of your own sanity, above the fathomless abyss of human stupidity. People would come in and hum something they'd heard on the radio. They were always tone deaf, and after enduring thirty seconds of their drone, we'd send them away with a copy of Nick Cave's 'The Mercy Seat'; not one of them ever complained. Others would approach the counter with a description of a record so vague that it would scarcely have been less use to us if they'd pronounced it in Navajo. 'I don't know what it's called,' one idiot told us, 'or who it's by, but I know it has a green cover.' After considerable further interrogation – it was a slow afternoon – we deduced that what he wanted was The Smiths' *The Queen Is Dead*. And if he didn't want it, that's what he got.

Lest anyone think that all of the above is only what might be expected from consumers of rock music, the single most moronic enquiry I ever fielded was from someone browsing the classical section.

'I see you have *The Four Seasons* by Vivaldi,' she said.

Yes, I replied, fighting the urge to ask her if she could tell me why every person who bought it was, like her good self, a woman with stupid shoes and riotous hair who reeked of patchouli.

'Do you have it by anyone else?'

To this day, I regret very little as much as I regret not telling her no, but that I could heartily recommend Beethoven's Fifth by Tchaikovsky, or Bach's Toccata and Fugue in D Minor by Mahler. At moments like these, we availed ourselves of the only retribution available, a doorbell switch glued beneath the cash register, marked *Customer Eject Button*. Though it was not, sadly, actually connected to any apparatus capable of launching Tracy Chapman fans through the skylight, pressing it was a surprisingly effective psychological release.

Record store assistant by day, rock journalist by night – and DJ on weekends. The one connection to the University of Sydney I maintained was with Radio Skid Row, the community station housed in a basement on the campus, for whom I helmed the prestigious Sunday midnight until two am slot, broadcasting a show listened to by nobody at all except my mother and a lisping pervert in Dulwich Hill called Phil, who used to phone in an average of three or four imaginative propositions an hour, however many times I'd wearily invited him to fuck off the previous week. It was approximately as idyllic an existence as any eighteen-year-old could have enjoyed. If I hadn't been a spotty virgin who still lived with his parents, I could have gone very close to being pleased with myself.

*

I was assigned my first interview shortly before the end of 1987, and even more shortly before the purchase of my first tape recorder. My subjects were Melbourne rap duo Mighty Big Crime, recently signed by the local arm of Virgin, and preparing to release their debut single. This was a cover of Merle Travis's 'Sixteen Tons', a country standard which had been a hit for Tennessee Ernie Ford, among others, though if I knew this at the time it was only thanks to an unusually diligent press release. Mighty Big Crime's version of 'Sixteen Tons' was rendered in a cheerfully unsubtle approximation of the bratty sneering of The Beastie Boys, which was popular at around this time, and quite rightly – The Beastie Boys' 1986 hit '(You Gotta) Fight For Your Right (To Party!)' remains a hands-down champion in several important categories, specifically Best Use of Double Parentheses in a Song Title, and Greatest Opening Chord (the latter by half a head from The Ramones' 'Rock'n'Roll High School'). I met Mighty Big Crime, at what can only have been their insistence, at the Hungry Jack's outlet on George Street.

Mighty Big Crime presented as a pair of belligerent urchins wearing suspiciously freshly pressed skate-wear, and claiming to be called Tricky J and Gumpy. Their career was to be brief, and mentioned thirteen years hence in few if any reflections on the cultural highlights of the expiring millennium. Though it would be a stretch to describe this oblivion as unfair, Mighty Big Crime's idea, if their idea it was, of reworking country classics as hip hop jams displayed some understanding, advertently or otherwise, of the intricate cross-stitching of America's musical tapestry – and they delivered their 'Sixteen Tons' years before Ice-T acknowledged Johnny Cash's nihilist lament 'Folsom Prison Blues' as a cornerstone of gangsta rap, and before De La Soul named an album *3 Feet High and Rising* after a Johnny Cash song. Mighty Big Crime subsequently proceeded in short order to a second single – also a cover version, this time of Alice Cooper's 'School's Out' – and the knacker's yard.

Mighty Big Crime's only enduring purpose is as a benchmark for the changing attitudes of a music fan and music journalist, or at least of this music fan and music journalist. If a similar act broke now – and I'm certain a similar act is breaking now – I wouldn't notice. Five years ago, I might have noticed, but wouldn't have cared. Ten years ago, I might have cared, but would merely have rolled my eyes at yet another desperate act of major-label ambulance-chasing, barely worthy of the effort required to pound out a few lines of haughty derision. Fifteen, twenty years ago, I would have been aflame with self-righteous ire at this corporate hijacking of an organic underground movement, and might even, if gripped by an especially severe seizure of idiot liberal self-loathing, have perceived something faintly racist about the enterprise.

Twenty-five years ago, I was just plain awestruck. Mighty Big Crime were recording artists. Possibly not terribly famous and probably not terribly good, but recording artists nonetheless. They would have signed a contract. Inhabited a studio. Been asked to autograph the sleeves of their records. Most teenagers, knowing as little as they do, believe that all the world's wisdom is encoded in popular song; for the serious music fan, growing older is substantially a process of realising that this isn't the case, except to the heartening and terrifying extent that it is. I was aware that Mighty Big Crime were not, and were unlikely to become, residents of the pantheon of greats, but they did the same job as the people who were.

This could not be said for the second group I ever interviewed.

*

The second group I ever interviewed were the first group I ever interviewed of whom I'd heard. They were This is Serious Mum, generally known as TISM, a Melburnian phenomenon best imagined as a melange of the art-school obscurantism of The Residents and the absurdist surrealism of Monty Python, suffused with the zest for gleeful puerility that is so often the consequence of a respectable middle-class upbringing and a university education (titles on TISM's most recent EP, *Form And Meaning Reach Ultimate*

Communion, included 'Defecate on My Face', 'Kill Yourself Now and Avoid The Rush', 'Mistah Eliot – He Wanker' and 'I'm Into Led Zep'). TISM's records sounded like Devo jamming in a shed, and were lyrically given to morbid satire (a year later, they would have a hit album in Australia – a rarity for independent labels – with *Great Trucking Songs of the Renaissance*, trailed by a single entitled 'I'm Interested in Apathy'). TISM's members hid their identities behind Ku Klux Klan-ish disguises on stage, and pseudonyms on record: Marilyn Manson's conceit of amalgamating the names of well-loved cultural icons and mass murderers was predated by Ron Hitler Barassi.

TISM extended their creed of kamikaze contrarianism to their interactions with the press. They had, on one occasion, insisted on having questions yelled to them through megaphones from fifty metres away (the distance was kept with a precisely measured rope, held at each end by interviewer and subject, TISM refusing to answer if the twine slackened). For this interview, Margaret explained, TISM had declared that they would only communicate by fax: I was to type up my questions, dispatch them from *On the Street*'s office to a number in Melbourne, and await reply. It was terrifically exciting. I was actually interviewing a relatively well-known underground phenomenon in a fashion which suggested that I was being allowed in on the joke, if only as the butt of it. Plus, I'd never used a fax machine before.

My questions were mostly prosaic, if somewhat provocative – challenging TISM to reveal themselves, asking them what the point of it all was, that kind of thing. When TISM's response came back a few days later, they had replied to all of these enquiries with either 'Yes' or 'No'. They had engaged with only one question, a witheringly well-informed enquiry about their song 'The Back Upon Which Jezza

Jumped', which considered Collingwood ruckman Graeme 'Jerker' Jenkin and his unfortunate position in the mythology of Australian Rules football – it was Jenkin upon whom Carlton champion Alex Jesaulenko climbed to take an unforgettable mark in the 1970 grand final, creating a resonant image of Australian sport. TISM's song deployed Jenkin as a symbol of all the world's losers, an immortal avatar of the legion forgotten schlubs over whose backs the famous have clambered to reach the uplands of renown and prosperity. Unfair, I argued. By all accounts, Jenkin had been one of Collingwood's best on the day, dominating his opponent, the Carlton great John Nicholls, and certainly not at fault for his team's eventual capitulation. TISM claimed I'd misunderstood, and/or got the wrong game.

The rest of TISM's answer was a longish essay called 'TISM Guide to Creating an Avant-Garde'. This was mostly an attempt on TISM's part to stoke Melbourne–Sydney tensions prior to the imminent Sydney shows the interview was supposed to be promoting. TISM affected subscription to the view, held by many Melburnians, that their home city was a haven of genteel civilisation and espresso-sipping sophistication, while mine was a beer-sodden subtropical Gomorrah populated by sunscreen-smeared yobbos and shrieking homosexuals.

TISM's screed was at least self-aware. It began:

You Sydney people really go for us Melbourne avant-garde bands, don't you? You know, the sort of bands that are formed in rich private school dorms by the guys not good enough for football, not dumb enough to fail and not ugly enough for the debating team. I can only assume it's because all your rich young males are all lifeguards or too busy rendezvousing in spa baths that you haven't yet been able to manage the sort of baby-faced, angst-ridden, rich young snot-nosed galah that we seem to be able to throw up once every re-release of the works of Samuel Beckett.

This scabrous manifesto became gradually less coherent and more abusive, before finally suggesting that my fellow Sydneysiders 'stick to surfing or crawling up each other's arses. At least up in Sydney you've got a choice.' I typed it up as best I could, and it appeared over a full page of *On the Street*, accompanied by the press photograph *OTS* had been supplied, captioned 'TISM Congratulates the Worker', depicting a balaclavaed figure, presumably a member of TISM, shaking hands with a nonplussed factory operative. The assembly-line guy's perplexed expression was probably not far from that worn by my parents at this point, as they considered that their eldest son had tossed away a tertiary education to do . . . this.

*

At the end of 1987, I was asked, along with *On the Street*'s other writers, to name my favourite albums of the year for the magazine's Christmas issue. I assume I was asked to pick ten, as is usually the way of these things, but only eight appeared in print, either due to shortage of space or because I'd written something so fatheaded about the other two that it affronted even *OTS*'s indulgent editorial standards. These eight, and the place they occupied in my life then, and my views of them now, and in no particular order, were as follows.

The Go-Betweens, *Tallulah*
I had first heard of The Go-Betweens, probably via 2JJJ, around the release of their 1986 album *Liberty Belle & The*

Black Diamond Express, which I loved instantly – indeed, it remains my favourite work of art, and I'm prouder of few things than I am of my by-line beneath the sleeve notes on a 2004 reissue. *Tallulah* was a relatively uncertain, somewhat brooding affair, and hobbled by some specifically 1980s production misjudgements, but the songs were extraordinary: acute, astute meditations on heartbreak and desire, two subjects of which I had exactly no personal understanding at this point on the grounds that my heart had never been broken because nobody, as yet, found me all that desirable.

Paul Kelly and The Coloured Girls, *Under the Sun*

Kelly is now Australia's closest approximation of Bruce Springsteen, a universally respected yet approachable figure; sort of a national uncle. In 1987, Kelly was emerging from years of underground toil, beginning to get played on radio stations other than JJJ. *Under The Sun* contained what would become Kelly's signature song ('To Her Door'), a timely pre-empting of the jingoism scheduled to consume Australia in 1988 ('Bicentennial'), and the blossoming of an unusual ability to celebrate Australian mythology without actually or metaphorically donning a hat with corks swinging from it ('Bradman'). His backing band, named in homage to Lou Reed's 'Walk on the Wild Side', were eventually compelled to change their name by their American label. I finally interviewed Paul Kelly in 2012, backstage at London's Union Chapel. As it was a radio interview, he also played me a couple of songs. Despite some outrageous hint-dropping on my part, neither were 'To Her Door'.

Weddings Parties Anything, *Scorn of the Women*

Debut by Melburnians seeking to reclaim Australian folk from the clammy grip of heritage, and demonstrate that electric guitars and piano accordions were a congruous pairing. Though *Scorn of the Women* was an obvious attempt to field an antipodean response to The Pogues, it was a nonetheless compelling collection of rollicking drinking songs and wilfully maudlin laments. The title track was a bold inversion of the veterans' ballad template, war recalled by a man whose life had been ruined by the fact that he'd been physically unfit to serve.

Midnight Oil, *Diesel and Dust*

The Australian domination of my picks of 1987 was partly a consequence of the homeground umpiring that generally afflicts the Australian media. However, with due acknowledgement that everybody regards the culture of their own youth as a bountiful flowering unrivalled since fifteenth-century Florence, bliss it indeed was to be alive during the dawns of the late 1980s, if you were Australian and keen on thoughtful and intelligent rock'n'roll. Midnight Oil perpetrated a great subversive gesture with this expansive, compassionate survey of the hidden corners of Australia's actual and spiritual interior, ensuring that the dominant soundtrack of our coming bicentennial would be a record reminding Australians that the nation whose birth we were celebrating, whatever its manifold virtues, was founded on pillage and genocide.

The Smithereens, *Especially For You*

Superior college rock, riddled with brilliant tunes and smart lyrics about having one's heartstrings wrenched by the sort of women who might one day, I fondly imagined, talk to me. *Especially For You* was the first of many of the pleasant surprises peculiar to the rock critic, i.e. the record you would never have heard if an editor hadn't slung it across their desk and asked you to write something about it. The urge to share with others the joy of what you've discovered is one of humankind's more endearing instincts. It is also a mixed blessing, as will be understood by anyone who has spent a long flight sitting next to a Jehovah's Witness. Or next to a Smithereens fan.

Hüsker Dü, *Warehouse: Songs and Stories*

Hüsker Dü's previous album, *Candy Apple Grey*, had been an immense favourite at my school, something that can only have occurred via JJJ or *Rock Arena*, given the limited means by which a furious though exquisitely tuneful punk band from Minneapolis could be heard of in Sydney. *Warehouse* was a double album, and – like almost all double albums – would have packed a more resounding wallop if its filler had been excised from its killer, and it had been sold as a single record. I'm sure I was aware of its overreach and bloat but, especially at this early stage, was vulnerable to a common affliction of critics composing lists such as this: the desire to appear cool. Which is why nobody should ever believe anything they read in them.

Half Man Half Biscuit, *Back Again in the DHSS*

I'd been introduced to this obtuse gang of Liverpudlian satirists by a school friend who had an astounding knowledge of generally unhearable – and some unlistenable – music. I remember finding Half Man Half Biscuit funny. I just cannot now conceive why. This is not because I no longer think Half Man Half Biscuit funny – they are – but because I cannot have understood any of the jokes. I didn't know who Dickie Davies was ('Dickie Davies Eyes') or Dean Friedman ('The Bastard Son of Dean Friedman') or Nerys Hughes ('I Hate Nerys Hughes'). And as I neither knew nor cared much about

Eastern European soccer, I didn't know what the 'Honved' in 'I Was a Teenage Armchair Honved Fan' was, or what the narrator of 'All I Want For Christmas is a Dukla Prague Away Kit' was requesting. But rock music is an unusual art form in that a great deal of its appeal is rooted in aspiration, rather than empathy: it sings to what and where you wish you were, rather than what and where you happen to be. At some level, clearly, I wanted to be playing Subbuteo on Merseyside with a bunch of angry men who spent their days shouting at the television.

Biff Bang Pow!, *Oblivion*

I still listen, as the whims of my iPod dictate, to all the preceding seven albums, and would feel honoured to defend them in any court of opinion. I am therefore able to assert that fully 87.5% of my critical judgement has withstood the test of a quarter-century, a veritable dreadnought barely rusted by the tides of taste. I cannot, however, begin to account for my fondness for the milquetoast mimblings of Biff Bang Pow!, a group whose appearance on the mighty roster of the legendary Creation label was arguably not unrelated to the fact that Biff Bang Pow!'s singer was Creation boss Alan McGee. Many years later, McGee would dismiss – correctly – the works of Coldplay as 'music for bedwetters'. On the strength of this heart-stoppingly fey album, McGee's qualifications to make this judgement were unquestionable.

IT'S TOO LATE TO DIE YOUNG NOW

ANDREW MUELLER

4

IN WHICH THE AUTHOR FLOUNDERS IN THE GULF BETWEEN AMBITION AND ABILITY

I returned to university in 1988. I did this for the usual reason that people pursue full-time study of the arts, which is to say that I couldn't think of anything better to do. Not long afterwards, however, in the best tradition of rock'n'roll, I alighted on my true calling at a crossroads. In a key difference between my date with destiny and Robert Johnson's legendary rendezvous with a scarlet gentleman with horns, this did not occur at a moonlit junction in Mississippi – it was, more or less, the corner of Willoughby Road and Falcon Street in Crows Nest. And no bargain was struck with the Devil, unless the Lord of Darkness had assumed the form of a suburban newsagent. I was looking for something to read during my lunch break from the record shop, and I perceived amid the magazine racks an issue of something called *Melody Maker*. Twee name, I thought, unaware of *Melody Maker*'s origins as a chronicler of the British jazz scene of the 1920s.

It was the issue of 17 October 1987, a date that had been crossed off my own calendar about three months previously; this issue had arrived, as did most foreign journals, by sea mail. On the cover was a waifish young blond man in a red

T-shirt and a black cowboy hat, who I did not recognise, standing next to a pink and yellow logo which represented someone or something called Gaye Bykers on Acid, of whom or which I'd never heard. Elsewhere on the cover, more familiar names were advertised: Hothouse Flowers, Public Enemy, The Smiths, Echo & the Bunnymen. I purchased the thing, sat down in the park with my sandwich, and the world where I wanted to live fell into my lap.

I did not, at this point, require much in the way of distraction from my path. The effect of my first issue of *Melody Maker* was less like switching a speeding locomotive to another track, and more akin to tossing a stick across the sightline of an ambling labrador. I was already writing – to stretch a definition to its whimpering limits – about music, but I had no idea that music could be written about like this. *Melody Maker*'s writers ranted and rhapsodised, mocked and marvelled. They placed music, and the artists who made it, into wider contexts, some of which they took the trouble to invent themselves. And the places they went . . . That issue contained a review of a Michael Jackson concert in Tokyo, another of U2 and The Pogues in New York, a report from the joint New Order/Echo & the Bunnymen tour of the United States. Even the datelines on British gig reviews – London, Liverpool, Bath – seemed giddyingly exotic.

There was a four-page supplement, the seventh instalment of a part-work entitled 'Pop! The Glory Years', which appeared to be not so much a celebration and curation of the pantheon, but a calculated desecration, akin to charging around the rock'n'roll hall of fame in the unlit after-hours with spray-paint and a machete. Part seven discussed prog rock: of Pink Floyd, it recalled that 'when they appeared at Knebworth in 1975, their set climaxed with a Spitfire buzzing over the heads of the crowds and crashing in flames into the stage. Unfortunately, it missed the group.' Part seven – I mourned the likelihood that I would never locate parts one to six – also covered eighties rock like Dire Straits ('Listening to which made one imagine that the world's oceans had turned to dishwater') and classicist singer–songwriters including such titans as James Taylor ('An appalling example for legions of bleaters to follow'). Iconoclasm is always seductive to the young, on the grounds that they've little comprehension of the value of anything, though I'd already decided for myself that Pink Floyd were the worst group of all time, with the arguable exception of The Doors. I am still right about this.

It would be an exaggeration to report that I understood all of my first issue of *Melody Maker*. Parts of it might have been printed backwards for all the sense they made to me at the time. I loved music. I probably even thought about it a lot. But I'd never thought that 'Whenever left-inclined subcultural theorists encounter a black pop culture, they always follow the same syllogistic reasoning' (from someone called Simon Reynolds' intellectually expansive encounter with Public Enemy in New York, which elsewhere included learned reference to Miles Davis, Eldridge Cleaver and the Black Panthers, 1968-vintage Parisian Situationism, George Michael, Klaus Theweleit, Al Green and Colonel Gaddafi). Or that you were allowed to end a review of an album by an artist of the stature of Sting, as someone called Steve Sutherland did his gruff assessment of *Nothing Like the Sun*, with the exclamation 'Twerp!'

The thing that impressed me most, of the many things that impressed me, was that in the very issue in which Gaye Bykers on Acid were on *Melody Maker*'s front cover, and the subject of a three-page feature by someone called Carol Clerk, a live review of them by someone called Jon Wilde demanded to know what they were doing there. Wilde called the cover stars 'stupid and empty', 'slattern and cloddish' and, for good measure, a 'hoodlum racket'. Wilde was on all counts correct, as I'd learn when I eventually heard GBOA's stupid, empty, slattern, cloddish hoodlum racket (it was one of the retrospectively charming annoyances of the pre-internet world that I'd often read about artists in *Melody Maker* for weeks or months before I ever set ears on a note they'd recorded, and therefore had to imagine what they sounded like).

These people, it dawned on me, were making a living arguing about music, listening to records, going to gigs, talking to musicians, and travelling at what seemed to be someone else's expense. But they were a world away from where I was, professionally and geographically.

*

Australia spent 1988 commemorating the 200th anniversary of its invasion by Britain. I didn't have much of a problem with this. Though I – and millions of other Australians – had listened to *Diesel and Dust* enough to understand that there might be another side to our story, I'd also attracted hostile glares at Radio Skid Row when I'd reflexively articulated out loud my response to a fellow DJ complaining that the station's rugged policy of playing at least one Australian track every hour was 'tantamount to collaboration in these celebrations of genocide'. Though perhaps lacking in panache, the retort 'For fuck's sake' has served me well in subsequent encounters with self-loathing idiot relativists.

As Australia contemplated where it had come from, and pondered where it might be going, I had only one ambition (aside, obviously, from the acquisition of a girlfriend). That ambition was to write for *Melody Maker*. I had a vague idea of how I'd go about it – the same way I'd gone about getting hired by *On the Street*: by sending them some stuff I'd written. But I didn't do it, and I didn't do it because I wasn't good enough. I'd identified some favourite *Melody Maker* writers, the ones whose by-lines I'd stop by on my first eager leaf through each issue – Chris Roberts, Jon Wilde, Carol Clerk, the Stud Brothers, David Stubbs, Mat Smith, Simon Reynolds, Steve Sutherland, Allan Jones. I'd also identified a discrepancy in quality between their work and mine, a gulf so vast even a conceited nineteen-year-old couldn't fail to spot it. I was, after all, still unable to stop myself from using exclamation marks.

Such were the gnawing terrors that surfaced every week as I read, say, an appraisal as poised and perceptive as Steve Sutherland's review of Pixies' *Doolittle*:

> The savagery dormant in all Pixies songs is even more readily aroused when they broach sex. I always considered Black Francis's mewling revulsion on a par with a kid making a fuss about kissing an elderly, wrinkly relative, but as soon as 'Tame' degenerates into heavy breathing and we realise language has again deserted Francis in a crisis, we begin to worry, especially as his grunting is laced with Kim Deal's orgasmic coos, rendered with about as much passion as a child reciting its tables.

Or a case for the prosecution as perfectly summed up as David Stubbs' demolition of U2's *Rattle and Hum*:

> But one has to suspect that Bono, imagining he has found love in the voice of God, is merely in love with the sound of his own voice, echoing in the canyons, that the rain he seems to feel blowing refreshingly in

his hair is in fact the phlegm of his own bluster blowing
back in his face.

And then I'd read back something I'd written myself, and
become gripped by the desire to knock on every door in
Sydney until I'd retrieved every copy of that week's *On the
Street*, with a view to accumulating them into an enormous
pyre topped with an effigy of myself. *Melody Maker* was
for me what the Saturday afternoon broadcast of the Victorian Football League's match of the day must have been to
a teenage hopeful struggling to keep pace with the reserve
team of the Kickatinalong Koalas – both a gleaming beacon
of everything you want, and an agonising reminder of
everything you fear you're never going to get.

While I continued my nocturnal circuits of Sydney's teem-
ingly fecund live circuit, and tried to teach myself how to
say something interesting or funny about whichever records
Margaret assigned me, and attempted to compose questions
which might prompt interesting answers from gormless
Sydney rock groups to whom nobody was ever going to pay
attention, I read of Chris Roberts wandering New York with
Patti Smith or visiting the Los Angeles apartment of Jane's
Addiction's Perry Farrell, Allan Jones and Cowboy Junkies
snowbound in Washington State, Ted Mico riding through
Texas and Louisiana with That Petrol Emotion and Voice
of the Beehive, Ian Gittins on tour in Ireland with Happy
Mondays, Jon Wilde bickering with Shane MacGowan of
The Pogues in a restaurant in London.

It was wonderful. It was unbearable. With what I doubt
was intentional cruelty, Margaret assigned me my first ever
interview with an international artist. It was a telephone
conversation with someone professing to be called Rusty
Wing, of blood-congealingly unamusing British rap parody

group Morris Minor and the Majors, then promoting their dismal 'Fight For Your Right' send-up 'Stutter Rap', which had proved – almost interestingly, but mostly depressingly – nearly as popular in Australia as the Beastie Boys track it was attempting to lampoon.[1]

*

A hefty canon of cautionary wisdom counsels against ever meeting your heroes. It is balls. It stands to reason that if someone writes or sings or performs or builds something which profoundly moves you, the chances are decent that a degree of personal empathy might flourish between you, given the opportunity; while it is possible to stir something in someone's soul without meeting them, it is not possible to do it without, at some level, knowing them. I've met many of the people whose voices pour forth from my iPod most often. I got on fine with most of them. In no instance has this made what they create seem less exciting and inspiring – indeed, knowing them has often illuminated new depths to their work. Meeting your heroes is an excellent idea.

This observation is accompanied by the crucial rider that the person meeting the object of their veneration must be able to comport themselves like a confident grown-up, rather than

---

1   Some years later, the person chiefly responsible for Morris Minor and The Majors would enjoy another career as Tony Hawks, author of whimsical high-concept travel books which sold vastly more than any of mine, and the infuriating success of which prompted several publishers to suggest that maybe I should try pitching them a proposal about, say, beating every ambassador to the United Nations at air hockey, or teaching the banjo in Timbuktu, or riding a fucking spacehopper to Vladivostok. I do not know Tony Hawks, and will concede the theoretical possibility that he is a thoroughly pleasant chap who gives generously to charity, is kind to dogs and old ladies and never forgets anyone's birthday, but I nevertheless hope he suffers severely from piles.

a gibbering serf intoxicated by the chance to inhale from the same roomful of air. This was not an ability I had acquired by the point at which, with fewer than half a dozen notches on my tape recorder, Margaret asked me if I'd like to interview Roddy Frame of Aztec Camera. The idea of Roddy Frame phoning my house, where I lived, was allowed to dazzle only briefly before Margaret further explained that Frame was coming to Australia, to promote Aztec Camera's third album, *Love*, and that he'd be enduring journalists at Warner Brothers' offices in Crows Nest the following week, and that we – which was to say, I – had an hour of his time, if we wanted it.

A few years later, I'd get to know Roddy a bit, and we'd convene for the odd dinner in Soho, or occasionally watch his neurotic Weimaraner, Otto, capering about Kensington Park. This friendship was, at least from where I was sitting, founded substantially on an unspoken compact that our first meeting never be mentioned again: though Roddy is plausibly the least intimidating Glaswegian ever to draw breath, I would probably have been less completely terrified, at the moment of our initial handshake, by the prospect of sixty minutes shut in a room with a chainsaw-revving maniac in a hockey mask, a maternally defensive polar bear, ten evangelists and a jazz-funk ensemble.

It wasn't just that I was hopelessly besotted by Aztec Camera's albums. It was also that Roddy was barely older than me, twenty-three to my nineteen, but he seemed to have lived several extra lifetimes, even allowing for the vertiginous learning curve of early adulthood. He'd made three albums of gorgeous, precocious pop, lived in New York and London, toured the world, been touted by peers and critics as a freakish genius, acquired fame (though probably less than I imagined, given the teenage music nerd's habit of forgetting that most people, preoccupied as they are by work, family and existential despair, aren't all that interested) and fortune (again, probably less than I imagined, given the music industry newcomer's tendency to assume that anyone who has been on television holding a guitar is a billionaire). I, at roughly the age at which Roddy had been having his second album produced by Mark Knopfler, had interviewed Morris Minor and the Majors – and, to be honest, not done an especially good job of that.

Were some pantalooned apparition to emerge now from a fortuitously massaged teapot and offer me three wishes, the total erasure of this interview from my memory would be a contender. I did everything wrong, other than show up late, and if I'd shown up much earlier I'd have been locked in the night before. I stammered. I blathered. I realised far too late that I had thought of nothing to say to Roddy other than how much I liked his records, which was no help to anybody who might happen to read the story. Not only did I ask him to sign an album, which you should never do anyway, but I asked him even before I'd started failing to interview him (if you must ask an interviewee for an autograph – which, again, you should never do, as you're supposed to be there as a representative of your readers, not as some simpering courtier – then it must be the last thing you do).

Roddy was smart and funny, though I was too thick and too slow to follow most of it. Judging by the quotes I used, I must have mumbled something entrancingly predictable about the graduation from his indie rock roots that the polished soul of *Love* represented. Roddy's response was both astute and splendidly waspish. 'I was looking for a particular level of musicianship. I mean, who's going to pay, what, sixteen dollars, for a lot of feedback? You can do that at home with a twenty-quid amp.' He asserted that all the best records of the previous three years had been American mellow groove albums, and especially commended Anita Baker. Like the pious indie rock snob I was, I assumed he was joking.

Roddy knew enough not to be seduced by spurious notions of authenticity. Nodding at the posters of his label-mates hanging around the interview suite, he said, 'I think Tom Petty, Richard Clayderman, The Damned and Jackson Browne all do basically the same thing I do. It's just show business.'

Easy for Roddy to say. He sang like whichever cherub bisects the spectrum between imp and angel, played guitar like he had eight fingers on each hand, and wrote astonishing songs which managed to make a certain amount of sense about a subject which generally doesn't – or, to use the generic term, love songs. It might have been just show business to him, but to me, everything etched onto vinyl possessed the portent of something carved into marble.

*

Apparently unbothered by the Roddy Frame debacle, Margaret assigned me a phone interview with The Sisters of Mercy. I had gleaned from *Melody Maker*, which doted on the Sisters, that singer Andrew Eldritch was an intellectual boulevardier and very plausibly the coolest human being currently above ground. However, at a very late stage of setting the interview up – between fax machines and opposing time zones, this process could take weeks – we were told that Eldritch was 'tired', and had punted the *On the Street* interview to his bass player, Patricia Morrison.

Experience would eventually teach me that 'tired' was a euphemism for 'He's barely heard of your country, never mind your magazine, and simply can't be bothered'; we lowly scribes in the colonies got fobbed off with George or Ringo fairly frequently. But while I wasn't altogether surprised, I felt a palpable disquiet. I had researched, so far as it had been possible, Eldritch. My knowledge of Patricia Morrison consisted of the following: i) she was American, and with the exception of a few US Army exchange officers and their families who'd lived on the same bases as my family, I'd never spoken to an American; ii) she had at one point been in The Gun Club, Jeffrey Lee Pierce's legendary Los Angelean underground blues band, about whom I knew nothing beyond the copy of The Gun Club's *Fire of Love* I'd borrowed from a friend, and pretty much all I'd understood of *Fire of Love* was that Patricia Morrison hadn't played on it, having not yet joined the group; iii) she was, to judge by the video for the Sisters' monstrous Jim Steinman-produced pop opera 'This Corrosion', which I'd seen on *Rage*, a strutting nine-foot-tall – three feet of that in backcombed hair alone – she-devil who breakfasted on the bones of creatures vastly stronger than myself.

She also dressed like she might be a goth, but I didn't expect this to help much. I knew a few goths – the subculture had flourished in Sydney, despite the monumental unsuitability of the local climate, and some streets in Kings Cross all but streamed, of a balmy Saturday night, with the makeup that melted from artificially pale faces. And what I knew from knowing these goths was that all goths, and people who look like they might be goths, react with indignant hostility to being called goths. As I paced the hall carpet, waiting for the phone, I wasn't sure what to say to Patricia Morrison, but I at least knew not to ask her about being a goth.

So, I asked her about being a goth. Happily, this elicited more than a sigh of 'Oh, dear God,' followed by a dial tone. I got a couple of decent quotes about Eldritch's pathological Francophobia – he refused, so the story went, to speak to French magazines or accept royalties for French album sales – and the revelation that he nursed a crush on Daphne from *Neighbours* (this may have been a practical joke on Morrison's part, vengeance for Eldritch's dereliction of his promotional duties). But the piece I wrote, and which *On the Street* ran, utterly sucked, to the extent that, after reading it back in print, I sat down at my typewriter in my bedroom with the interview transcript propped up on the clock radio and wrote it up again, and again, and again. These versions all sucked as well. But they successively sucked less.

*

I kept getting work. I was as incredulous as I was grateful. Didn't anybody else – especially somebody who might have been good at it – want to do this? Free records, free tickets, and just enough money to thwart parental suggestions that instead of spending so much time listening to music and going to gigs you might want to think about getting a job – because I was able to reply, insufferably, that listening to music and going to gigs *was* my job. And I got to meet musicians, and in circumstances which obliged them to at least participate in the delusion that I was remotely qualified to be doing what I was doing, and talk to me.

This was becoming, in some circumstances, less terrifying. Almost certainly unwittingly, I'd divided musicians into two categories in my own near-empty head: musicians *Melody Maker* wrote about, and musicians *Melody Maker* didn't write about. With the former, I was hopeless: I extended to them the craven awe that an ambitious provincial panjandrum would to ambassadors from a more sophisticated civilisation. I would certainly have been the only straight teenage male in Australia circa mid-to-late 1988 whose excitement at meeting Wendy James of Transvision Vamp was principally driven by the fact that she knew Chris Roberts from *Melody Maker*.

With the latter, I was improving. The local artists I interviewed seemed more like fellow citizens of the world I inhabited. Simon Holmes from The Hummingbirds was responsible for the finest opening salvos of singles I'd ever heard from one group – a title I still believe The Humming-birds have a claim on – but he was also the stereotypically world-weary Record Shop Guy at Phantom. Weddings Parties Anything had done for Australian folk what The Pogues had for the Irish equivalent – updating the form for the modern era while demonstrating that it had never been anachronistic in the first place – and released two tremendous albums, but I'd seen them humping their own gear between sticky-carpeted pubs and battered Toyota Taragos more times than I could count. The Johnnys were a veteran cowpunk institution whose singer, Spencer Jones, had worked – as part of supergroup The Beasts of Bourbon – with members of mentioned-in-*Melody Maker* groups The Scientists and Hoodoo Gurus, but I'd seen them drunk (I was drunker, on approximately a tenth of the consumption) and beaten them at poker (though I have been reasonably sure ever since the excruciatingly hungover following morning that Jones, a courteous host, took a dive on the crucial hand).

I'm sure I didn't recognise it at the time, but if I was getting better – a relative term, remember – at talking to artists like these, it was because we had something in common. We were Australians, in Australia, trying and hoping to participate in something whose big leagues were situated at the other end of twenty-four expensive hours on an aeroplane. We all wanted the same thing, which is the thing that anyone who has ever loved rock'n'roll wants: more.

ANDREW MUELLER

5

IN WHICH THE AUTHOR'S MOTHER TAKES MESSAGES FROM RUN-DMC AND DWIGHT YOAKAM

My first cover story very nearly coincided with my first complete balls-up of an interview assignment. The subject was Ed Kuepper. Absurdly, given that we both lived in Sydney, it was a phone interview: at the moment it had been decided that Kuepper's third solo album, *Everybody's Got To*, was worthy of *On the Street*'s front page, Kuepper was on tour in Melbourne. He also had an extremely soft and low speaking voice, rendered even softer and lower by his lethargic disinterest in proceedings. Transcribing the recording of the interview was agonising, an interminable task of turning up the volume, and all the trebles on my stereo's graphic equaliser, clamping headphones tight to my ears, and fossicking for discernible syllables in the tape hiss.

I blamed myself, for not having the gumption to ask him to speak up. I blamed Ed, for his truculence – I'd only asked him to engage in a forty-minute conversation which would enable me to broadcast my belief in the merits of his records to thousands of potential purchasers, not tidy his room.

I was wrong to blame either of us. It would have been an unusual nineteen-year-old rock geek who could have found it in himself to say to a figure of Kuepper's titanic stature, 'Ed, mate, could you whack it up a couple of notches? Can't hear a word you're muttering.' And I didn't understand the frustrations of the commercially marginal artist's life enough to understand that Kuepper's attitude might not have been far from, 'Christ. I'm thirty-two years old and I'm one of the most influential guitarists and songwriters of my generation. I pretty much invented punk rock by bashing out "(I'm) Stranded" for The Saints, the work I did with The Laughing Clowns was better than anything by Can, I lead one of the finest live acts in explored space, I'm about to release my third stone classic solo album on the bounce, and I still can't get played on the fucking radio. Like one more interview with one more stammering dweeb from one more half-arsed free sheet is going to make any bloody difference.'

In short, I was overawed, he was underawed. It is not a dynamic which makes for great interviews, and indeed it didn't, though it did add one small swipe to the already impressive – and continuing – rally of bitchiness between Kuepper and his former compadre in The Saints, Chris Bailey. Having recently seen The Saints play the last night of venerable Sydney venue the Tivoli, I reported to Kuepper that Bailey seemed intent on turning the band into a self-parodying cabaret act, complete with smoke bombs, streamers and balloons descending from the rafters, a deadpan grotesque of a pop group, a subversive send-up of . . .

'I think you'll find,' smirked Kuepper, cutting me short, 'he's actually quite serious.'

Still, it was a cover story, even if the interview had been dreadful, even if my name had been misspelled in one of its two appearances on the page bearing the piece, and even if the cover itself had been defiled by a misplaced apostrophe – advertising an interview with moderately hopeless Sydney pop group 'The Venetian's' (I was already an incorrigible and humourless punctuation fascist, to the extent that I refused to shop at a local grocery store that advertised 'tomatoe's').

More covers followed. The next was an interview with INXS guitarist Tim Farriss, on the phone from Los Angeles during the world-conquering *Kick* tour. I didn't much care for INXS's music, partly because I really didn't much care for it, mostly because I was a pompous snob who thought that enjoying popular music was an indicator of fatuous gullibility or – depending on the self-righteousness of my mood – outright moral depravity (I have grown out of this sufficiently to concede that 'Burn For You', 'Mystify' and 'Never Tear Us Apart' are fine pop songs). Seized with the blundering zealotry of the evangelist, I even once played Nick Cave's 'The Mercy Seat' to one of my grandmothers, as if there was really much chance that someone whose only known utterance on the subject of popular culture had been an approving reference to Olivia Newton-John would take a liking to a forbidding seven-minute dirge narrated from the perspective of a condemned murderer.

But even if INXS were high on my list of cultural malefactors with whom there would surely be a ruthless reckoning when the revolution came, I had never spoken to a proper rock star before. Tim Farriss was unquestionably qualified on that front. He was checked into his hotel under a pseudonym (Neil Downe, a gag which wouldn't have inflamed jealousy in Dorothy Parker, but I would learn that touring reduces the most sensitive of individuals to infantile sniggering at dismal punsmithery). The night before the interview, Farriss and his band had headlined before a crowd that Farriss estimated at not less than fifty thousand. I asked what this was like. 'It's like,' laughed Farriss, 'playing fifty Manly Vale Hotels at once.'

I did not yet appreciate the rarity of Farriss's straight-forwardly cheerful attitude to being showered with money and bathed in applause for doing something you started out doing for nothing and nobody. I eventually met Farriss seventeen years later, in London, when I was writing a story for the *Guardian* about INXS's talent-show quest to find a permanent replacement for the late Michael Hutchence. I was distracted: I was due to travel to Iraq on assignment for the *Independent on Sunday* later that week, and mentioned this to Farriss, altogether unnecessarily. At the expense of the limited interview time I had, he was curious and solic-itous about this, which made me feel every bit as bad as it should have, given that I was probably just trying to prove to myself how far I'd come from the lackwitted hack he'd spoken to seventeen years before, not that he'd have recalled this if I'd brought it up.

It's amazing that more successful musicians don't go completely loopy. They are heroes, villains, cameos and clowns in the internal dramas of millions, with no oppor-tunity to rewrite their lines or resign from the production. Most of us only matter that much to people to whom we can try to justify ourselves.

*

The more frequent the interviews got, and the bigger the names became, the more pleasingly surreal life grew. Pre-email and pre-text message communications were slow and imprecise, so it often took several attempts before journalist and artist were on the same line at the same time. I came home one night to a note by the phone from Mum listing the day's callers: Steve, Kirstin, Jam Master Jay from Run-DMC ('says he'll call back tomorrow'), Adam. Thanks to a farcically long sequence of misunderstandings and missed connections,

Mum struck up enough of a rapport with Dwight Yoakam that once the interview was finally enacted, and he had no further need to call the house, she quite missed him. This, as I understood it, was principally because he addressed her as 'ma'am'.

It would be risible to claim that it gave me any useful understanding of the lives of my illustrious interviewees, but at around this period I became very slightly famous myself. ABC-TV's Saturday morning kids' magazine, *The Factory*, interviewed me outside *On the Street*'s new offices on Bellevue Street in Surry Hills for a short piece they were doing about rock journalists. A few weeks after that, the producer called, explained that the reporter who'd interviewed me was leaving the show, and offered me the job. This delighted me for more than the obvious reasons: it also meant that I could frame my confession to my parents that I was dropping out of university for the second time as a bad-news-good-news scenario.

Working for *The Factory* consisted, in practice, of reporting to the ABC's studios once a week, convening around the pool table in the canteen with the affable crew, trying to think of something that might fill five minutes of television, and charging off to make it. *The Factory* was based in Melbourne, and I was nominally its Sydney correspondent, so we had the city to ourselves. We were hamstrung by a dearth of resources, lacking even the wherewithal to acquire sufficient makeup to occlude my volcanic acne, and it is little surprise – though a considerable relief – that our output continues to languish behind theremin-playing cats and trampolining foxes in the priorities of YouTube uploaders. But we interviewed local musicians and fashion designers and actors and singers (and Jason Donovan) and even – when all else failed – the general public. Possibly because I had no particular desire to work in television, I was able to regard the experience as a liberating and unexpected hoot. Possibly because of this, the ABC didn't call to offer me my own series when *The Factory* got canned a few months later.

The blitheness I felt about the television gig was a contrast to my writing for *On the Street*, which was still nervous, hesitant, trying too hard and burdened by my dreams of working for *Melody Maker*. I'd had my first experience of getting chased around the letters page by readers, a few of whom had taken umbrage with my review of Public Enemy's *It Takes a Nation of Millions to Hold Us Back*, in which I'd expressed reservations about some of Public Enemy's views in perhaps shriller tones than were proper for a middle-class white kid from Sydney mediating the rage of inner-city black America. Though I maintain that Public Enemy's preferred preacher Louis Farrakhan is a dunce and a loon, and I remain pleased that my reply to the choleric correspondence called out the reader who excused Public Enemy as only 'mildly sexist', I was hurt.

'You're a bit stunned, aren't you?' said Margaret, as I leafed through the seething letters, and she was right. Like anyone who puts their name on some projectile which gets launched into the public sphere, I wanted to be liked, and admired, and the recipient of imaginative sexual propositions. The people who'd sent me these letters not only didn't like my writing, they'd decided that they didn't like me. I did not have in my life someone who would tell me what I counsel the whelps now, especially those who fear the modern-day blight of instant feedback from the online comments section. This advice is that the critic's or columnist's job is in many important respects analogous to that of a zookeeper. Once you have tipped the succulent mangoes of your prose into the chimpanzee enclosure of the readership, your work is done:

unless it amuses you to watch the subsequent screeching, brawling and faeces-flinging, walk on.

In the 1988 *On the Street* readers' poll, I was voted journalist of the year. In the context of the Australian rock press, it was a triumph not incomparable with being elected the least chocolate teapot.

*

In *On the Street*'s Christmas issue at the end of 1988, my selections of the year's best records were as follows.

The Sugarcubes, *Life's Too Good*

The world's first acquaintance with Bjork's whimsical shrieking. I did like this record. I still like this record. But I decided at the time I loved it largely because *Melody Maker* had told me I should. My relationship to *Melody Maker*'s recommendations was akin to that of a recent recruit to a cult trying desperately to catch up by carrying out Brother Number One's orders with especial zeal. I bought something by almost every artist *Melody Maker* featured on the cover, even when the records were ruinously expensive imports, and listened to them repeatedly, even when they were patently unlistenable. I have not yet tired of reminding certain *Melody Maker* veterans, when the waiter brings the bill, that they still owe me the price of Skinny Puppy's atrocious *VIVIsectVI*, plus accumulated interest.

Weddings Parties Anything, *Roaring Days*

I actually did love this record. It took a lot of nerve for any band to root their music so explicitly in Australian references, risking sounding corny and provincial – or, worse, like John Williamson. When I interviewed WPA for *On the Street*, I asked principal songwriter Mick Thomas about this.

He replied, rightly, that he'd never been to Galveston, but this didn't stop him feeling Jimmy Webb's song of the same name.

Iggy Pop, *Instinct*
Still furiously plugging the manifold gaps in my knowledge of rock'n'roll history, I had Iggy Pop erroneously pigeonholed as a desiccated novelty act, a cousin to Billy Idol. I bought *Instinct* only because Chris Roberts had written in *Melody Maker* that it was 'Just another masterpiece from the man Jesus Christ calls "Sir".' He was right.

The Go-Betweens, *16 Lovers Lane*
Roughly the ninth-best album ever made by anybody, ever.

The Pogues, *If I Should Fall From Grace With God*
Roughly the eighth-best album ever made by anybody, ever. (*Melody Maker*'s 1988 Christmas issue, incidentally, would declare 1988 the best year for music of all time; I believe that my calculations confirm this.)

Thin White Rope, *In the Spanish Cave*
Colossal country metal, another purchase made at *Melody Maker*'s insistence, cost nearly a day's pay on import, and felt like a bargain.

Cocteau Twins, *Blue Bell Knoll*
I am unable to reflect on what I thought of this fine album at the time due to the always unpredictable editing of *On the Street*, which contrived to paste my enthusing for Luxuria's equally terrific *Unanswerable Lust* beneath this heading (*Unanswerable Lust* was the first of two albums made by Luxuria, a collaboration by Howard Devoto, late of

Buzzcocks and Magazine, and a Japanese musician known as Noko: it's one of the great lost albums of the 1980s).

The Mexican Spitfires, *Lupe Velez*
Bhagavad Guitars, *Foreverglades*
The Tripps, *Never the Twain*
Local groups. All of whom, it was my contention, deserved better than to be regarded as such. I haven't owned copies of any of these for years, but I can still hear at least one track off each in my head. My memory isn't brilliant, so at least some of each of these records were.

Aztec Camera, 'Somewhere in My Heart'
House of Love, 'Christine'
Nick Cave and the Bad Seeds, 'The Mercy Seat'
The Hummingbirds, 'Get on Down'
They Might Be Giants, 'Don't Let's Start'
My candidates for single of the year. Four of these were astute and righteous choices. One can only be understood, if not actually excused, by remembering that I had until quite recently been a student.

ANDREW MUELLER

6

IN WHICH THE AUTHOR GETS A GUITAR LESSON FROM BILLY BRAGG

I moved out of home late in 1988. I had no particular urge to do so – nobody with that view of Sydney Harbour would have – but Dad had been posted to Canberra, a place people only go when issued with orders by uniformed superiors. With my friends Clancy and Sally, I signed a lease on a dilapidated four-bedroom terrace in Stanmore, within window-rattling distance of a railway bridge, equipped with what looked like one of the first kitchens ever installed in New South Wales and an antique gas-fired shower which had to be carefully lit before use, endowing each morning's ablutions with the itchy thrill of life in a bomb-disposal squad.

The fourth bedroom was taken by a respondent to an advertisement we'd placed in some Sydney University publication. He was a tall and fearfully handsome sort with billowing hair and a general air of Byronic dash, which may have been why Clancy and Sally outvoted my preference for any of the procession of stereotypically prim Chinese, Vietnamese and Korean students who also applied for the space, all of whom reflexively washed our coffee mugs straight after using them, which struck me, at least, as a

81

good sign. It was only minor consolation that my reservations about our new housemate were rapidly confirmed: he barricaded himself into the tiny box room at the rear of the house, where he constructed bulwarks of rarefied literature we were pretty sure he never read, wrote self-pitying poetry on the walls, little of which even rhymed, and left his dishes on the floor, where microbiotic civilisations flourished in the leftovers despite the predations of grateful mice.

Sally, seized by a sudden desire to cohabit with her boyfriend, moved out. Her room was subsequently occupied by a parade of unreliables before eventually being taken, for a pleasant few months, by a pair of cheerful Welsh backpackers – though if they're still wondering where their much-beloved, much-played copy of The Alarm's *Declaration* got to, they should return to 57 Liberty Street, head about fifteen paces north and four west from the back door, and dig maybe two feet – and finally by an unnecessarily bohemian woman who played violin in an assortment of terrible local groups. Perhaps in part due to a desire for shelter from our haphazard domestic arrangements, Clancy and I became a couple during this period.

This made me happy, as did the fact that, as a resident of Sydney's indisputably cool inner west, I felt slightly less like a try-hard blow-in from the middle-class arcadia of the lower North Shore as I furthered my trade as a rock journalist. It was also, I felt, a boon to my credibility that mistimed incoming interview calls from international rock stars would no longer be fielded by my parents. My plan was to return full time to work in the record shop in Crows Nest by day, and carry on writing for *On the Street* by night and at weekends. This, I figured, would amount to a perfectly decent living for a twenty-year-old with zero material ambitions beyond the acquisition of records, most of which I was now getting for nothing anyway. This combination worked brilliantly for about a month, up until the point at which I had some entirely trifling argument with the record shop's manager, an excellent fellow with whom I liked working enormously, and who was certainly correct to have pulled me up on whatever it was, and stormed out.

It was a stupid thing to do: the pointless burning of bridges is. Altogether unfairly, it paid off: Margaret created a full-time position at *On the Street* for me. I was endowed with the title of editorial assistant, awarded the kind of salary generally offered to clueless youths who can't believe their luck, and installed at a desk on the upstairs floor of *On the Street*'s headquarters. My job, it swiftly became clear, was to sit at my typewriter from ten in the morning until six in the evening, and write, and write, and write: features, reviews, news stories, picture captions and the entire sprawling rear section of the paper, called Street Talk.

It was an absurd workload to drop on one writer, however keen – regularly, I guess, nudging ten thousand published words every Wednesday. And it was a ridiculous imposition on the readership – nobody wants to read that much of anybody (possibly in recognition of this fact, a lot of what I wrote appeared in print minus my by-line.) But it was a regime for which I've been grateful ever since. It meant that I never got into the habit of writing slowly. It meant that I learnt that the first idea you have, especially if you have it in the state of twitching panic engendered by a descending deadline, is usually the one that reads best later. And it also meant that, even if only to keep myself amused as yard upon yard of copy spooled from my typewriter, I had to find something like a voice. I had no choice but to get better.

I also had no choice but to interact with *On the Street*'s staff and the paper's other contributors. Given the peripatetic nature of the freelancer's life, I hadn't done much of this, and

I wasn't unhappy about this fact. This wasn't because I didn't want to be friends with them, but because I worried that they wouldn't wish to be friends with me. I was making the elementary error of assuming that I was the only awkward, unqualified and uncool person working in the rock press, having not yet understood that almost everyone who works in the rock press is awkward, unqualified and uncool, which is why they work in the rock press.

Across the room from me sat the assistant editor, Michael Smith, an Englishman whose hair betrayed a past playing bass in glam bands who had never quite cracked it (best known of these were Scandal, who'd had a minor hit in 1978 with a version of Ace's 'How Long'). Reception was manned by Karen Baranenko, whose exclusively black dress code was at sharp odds with a sunny disposition, and whose composure in the face of visiting Sydney rock royalty was exquisitely judged just this side of rudeness (to the lead singer of The Church, announcing himself with serene majesty from behind gratuitous sunglasses as 'Steve', Karen replied, 'Steve who?' Having elicited the crestfallen response 'Er . . . Kilbey,' she persisted: 'From?').

The production office out the back, where pages were pasted together and last-minute edits were still performed with razor blades – although occasionally, when gripped by prima donna grievance at an especially abrupt cut, I'd suspect the employment of a halberd and a blindfold – was dominated by Jack Marx, a gravely laconic figure who would, many years later, become the author of one of the wisest and most truthful books ever written about rock'n'roll (*Sorry: The Wretched Tale of Little Stevie Wright*) and one of the wisest and most truthful books ever written about Australia (*Australian Tragic*). Jack's company was a continual lesson in the value of questioning lazy writing and cliché. Vexed by the number of musicians-wanted classified advertisements *OTS* received that contained the meaningless qualification 'No time-wasters', Jack took to calling the numbers, solemnly expressing interest in joining whichever group it was and then hesitantly confessing, 'I do waste quite a lot of time, though. Is that really a deal-breaker?'

I had many ideas about modifications that could make *On the Street* a better paper, which is to say that I had many ideas I'd lifted from *Melody Maker* which I thought would make *On the Street* more like *Melody Maker*. Though nobody at OTS ever said, 'Nobody is interested in your creative input, copy-monkey, get back to work,' nobody was interested in my creative input. Every so often, I'd manage to get a band I liked half a page, but mostly I just did what I was told. I would never acquire the faintest understanding of *On the Street*'s editorial direction, or learn to predict its apparently random tacks and tics. When Margaret announced that we were putting Sonic Youth on the cover, in honour of their colossal and influential *Daydream Nation* opus, and that I was to get on the phone to Kim Gordon in New York, I thought, and said, 'Okay, cool.' When Margaret announced that we were putting useless, irrelevant – and deservedly unremembered – Australian metal-lite group Candy Harlots on the cover, and that I was to call them in Melbourne, I thought 'Huh? They suck, and they're a total laughing stock,' but did not say it.

I had reasons for muting my insistence that *On the Street* become more like *Melody Maker*. One was a still-nagging awareness that a magazine more like *Melody Maker* would be less likely to let me write half of it every week. Another was that such ambitions were being partially sated by getting to interview more of the sort of artists who appeared in *Melody Maker*. Elvis Costello, in Sydney promoting his album *Spike*, discerned quite rapidly that he was in the presence of someone almost too terrified to speak, and was far more patient and solicitous than he is generally reputed to be: he gave me more time than I had tape. Billy Bragg, at the end of an interview crammed by travel logistics into a car ride to the airport, unpacked his guitar on the departures concourse to teach me a couple of his riffs that I mentioned I'd been having difficulty with. Both men were excellent interview subjects – smart, funny, thoughtful. I was still a dreadful interviewer – dim, clumsy, far too keen to impress both subject and readership, still some way from understanding that you're more likely to do both the less you labour to do either.

*

On Fridays, I wrote Street Talk. This was the wilderness at the rear of the paper, where herds of paragraph-long items roamed the veldt between *On The Street's* cheaper advertisements. Street Talk would often run to more than sixty items, of between twenty and a hundred words, every week. It was assembled from the letters and press releases which had accumulated in my in-tray since the previous issue had gone to press, rumours and gossip collected in my general gig-going, jokes that I thought might at least raise a laugh from Michael or Jack, whatever else seemed like a good idea at the time, and the very occasional outright invention to see if anyone was paying attention.[1]

---

1   A few years later, I would, for a while, write a similar, if briefer, column for *Time Out* in London. Once, when told that I'd come up too short, I bashed out an item about a new lizard, recently discovered in South Africa, and named – by altogether fictional Britpop-obsessed herpetologist Dr Charlemagne Nkobo – Codling's Gecko, in honour of Suede's keyboardist. With due professional diligence, I called the press office at Regent's Park Zoo to get a quote confirming they had 'no plans as yet' to exhibit the creature, and sent the paragraph to my editor. The existence of Codling's Gecko was later reported as fact in the Guinness 'Rockopedia'.

Street Talk was pretty much what I chose to make it. Most readers, I assumed, were musicians scanning to see if a plug they'd submitted for a gig or tour or record had got in. I gradually made it clearer that they'd be more likely to be granted this indulgence if they worked for it, with the result that I started getting fewer bulk-photocopied press releases, and more handwritten letters and assorted promotional tat, some of which brightened the day immeasurably. We received much enthusiastic correspondence, from closely clustered postcodes, and in not dissimilar handwriting, praising a hapless western suburbs metal group called Stoker – happily, this only grew more voluminous and indignant the more we questioned its veracity.

Occasionally, we created a monster. We joshingly repeated a rumour that spandex-swaddled poodle-rockers Poison, who were due to tour, maintained a computer database of volunteer groupies, and invited submissions: depressingly, we received dozens.

The value of such in-jokes and running gags is something that most of today's print publications, desperate as they are not to scare potential new readers, have forgotten: if you can make people feel like they're members of a club, entrusted with knowledge of its codes and rituals, they won't want to leave. Even after a year or so of regular readership, I still didn't understand a lot of what went on in *Melody Maker*, but – and this is the important part – I wanted to.

I'd discovered that it wasn't necessary to wait three months for the British music weeklies that arrived in Australia by sea freight. A few record stores in the city got small consignments of *Melody Maker* and *NME* sent by express airmail – published in London on Tuesdays, I was usually able to pick them up after work in Sydney on Thursdays. They were shockingly expensive, at least as a percentage of what

I earned – four dollars a week for each magazine, out of a pay packet that came in at under three hundred. The *NME* was usually tossed away after being read twice or thrice. *Melody Maker* was kept, in a stack, by the rusty, obsolescent gas stove on the enclosed balcony adjoining my bedroom, and read over and over.

One of the things I had understood from my obsessive consumption of *Melody Maker* was that it and the *NME* were rivals (although, and you may bet that I knew this long before it was my work address, their offices were only a floor apart in the same building – King's Reach Tower in London, headquarters of IPC Publishing, which owned both titles). This antipathy wasn't overstated – while *Melody Maker* would take the occasional swipe at *NME* in print, the much bigger-selling *NME* rarely retaliated, in the lofty manner of a football team refusing to get drawn into a brawl when six goals in front. But you only had to look at them to realise that you had to pick a side. *NME* was printed on nasty, fingertip-blackening newsprint, and its appearance was wilfully ragged and brash, like a tabloid newspaper laid out by students. *Melody Maker* had bigger, beautifully designed pages, and appeared on gleaming glossy stock which lent maximum illumination to its photography and greater gravitas to its words.

Magazine style and magazine content have a relationship as symbiotic and circular as that of the chicken and the egg. *NME* had an air of cheerful cheapness, regarding everything as a bit of a lark, propounding a jovial, inclusive view that pretty much all music was pretty good if you liked that kind of thing. *Melody Maker* was serious, assiduous and reverent, discussing music and matters arising as if they were scarcely less important than the air one breathed – except when *Melody Maker* was being funny, in which case it was ruthless and hilarious. The difference boiled down to a divergent interpretation of the job of the music critic. *NME* writers, though there were exceptions to the rule, saw themselves as cheerleaders, there to orchestrate the adulation of the crowd so as to encourage the players. *Melody Maker* writers saw themselves as bouncers – the rare artists who met the *Maker*'s standards were solemnly admitted to the sanctum, while everybody else was bundled unceremoniously back down the stairs, seat of trousers indented with boot print. Snarling little egotist that I was, the latter role appealed to me enormously.

ANDREW MUELLER

7

IN WHICH THE HOODOO GURUS TAKE UMBRAGE

I was getting away with far too much at *On the Street*. I fumbled a phone interview with fleetingly fashionable chanteuse Tanita Tikaram, distracted by that morning's disconnection of the gas supply to the house in Stanmore. Not only did I spend far too much of the allotted time outlining my rage at this injustice to Tikaram – who was sympathetic, if bemused – but I was so consumed that I neglected to depress the red button on my tape recorder. All of which was bad enough, but I then spent the first three paragraphs of the story I subsequently wrote attempting to laugh off this dereliction. Margaret really should have applied her blue pencil liberally to my entire introduction, then poked me in the eye with it.

I was, however, discovering what would remain a ceaselessly replenishing joy of the job of being a music journalist – that of being entranced by something you'd never heard before, and being in the position to talk to the people responsible for it, and maybe to encourage other people to listen to it. I don't recall who first steered me in the direction of Flying Nun, the New Zealand independent label, but they did me

91

a resounding favour. At around this time, Flying Nun were on a roll comparable with the golden eras of any independent label you care to name, having discovered that the small southern college town of Dunedin was apparently entirely populated by people who were in the best rock'n'roll bands in the world.

These groups visited Sydney regularly, which presented me with the excuse to nag Margaret on their behalf. I duly undertook the exacting trial of a phone interview with the fabulously baleful Shayne Carter of the mighty Straitjacket Fits, a supremely gifted songwriter and guitarist cursed with a maddeningly acute understanding of his band's brilliance, and of the awesome unlikelihood of this ever being widely recognised. I sat down in a Sydney pub with the wry, professorial figure of Graeme Downes from The Verlaines – who, when he wasn't singing in the band, was working towards a PhD on Mahler. And I spoke to the monarch of Dunedin's unlikely hive, David Kilgour of early 1980s Flying Nun pathfinders The Clean, who offered an explanation for his decision to re-form that seminal band which was a study in the terse matter-of-factness that characterises his people. 'It's because,' he said, 'everybody overseas has caught on to The Clean four bloody years after we broke up.'

My interviews were still hit-and-miss affairs, partly because I was still trying to figure out how to do them, mostly because all interviews are hit-and-miss affairs, akin to a blind date with an even smaller chance that anyone's going to get laid at the end of it. I learnt, also, that a certain amount of tension can help, even if I hadn't generated it deliberately. I was thrilled sideways to be interviewing Hoodoo Gurus on the occasion of their fourth album, *Magnum Cum Louder.* I had hardly been to a party at which at least one of their first two albums (1984's glorious *Stoneage Romeos*, 1985's brilliant, despite dreadfully pallid production, *Mars Needs Guitars*) was not played.

I arrived at Hoodoo Gurus' manager's house in Coogee, the sleeve of *Stoneage Romeos* and a marker pen wedged into my bag along with my tape recorder, and applied a sweaty, trembling fist to the door. I was ushered into a room where I sat alone for a while. A couple of times I was certain I perceived the iguana-like visage of Hoodoo Gurus singer Dave Faulkner regarding me through an interior window before disappearing. Eventually, I was joined by guitarist Brad Shepherd and bass player Rick Grossman.

'Now,' began Shepherd, 'about that shitty fucking review . . .'

I was nonplussed. I loved Hoodoo Gurus. I was pretty certain I'd said so, often, in print, with my by-line attached. I'd no more give Hoodoo Gurus a shitty fucking review than I'd punch my cat. I squinted quizzically at Shepherd.

'Of "Come Anytime",' he elaborated.

A few weeks previously, I'd included 'Come Anytime', the first single from *Magnum Cum Louder*, in a column rounding up new releases. I'd opined that, while better than most of its competition, it fell perhaps somewhat short of Hoodoo Gurus' transcendentally lofty standards.

'It's a great fucking melody,' persisted Shepherd. 'It's just amazing, and I don't understand why you don't think it's amazing.'

I rallied slightly, muttering that Hoodoo Gurus' thankyou notes for everything else I'd written about them seemed to have got lost in the post. Faulkner appeared at the window again, and vanished once more.

'That's why we hate rock journalists,' continued Shepherd. 'You guys don't print retractions. "Oh, I'm sorry, I was wrong." That never happens.'

Shepherd, in fairness, was less diva-ish than the above might make him sound. His complaints were enumerated in the drawling deadpan of a man who believes proceedings to be a mile beneath him, and the rest of the interview went pretty well. Though Faulkner never deigned to join us, and I left with my album unsigned – I didn't ask – the hostility gave both the interview and the finished piece an edge: it felt like something more than an advertisement for a record. And, at a distance of half a lifetime, upon noting that 'Come Anytime' is the most-played Hoodoo Gurus song in my iTunes library, I'm prepared to offer Shepherd the following: I was wrong, and I'm sorry.

On other occasions, I was gifted the kind of inter-view subjects who do most of the work themselves. Andy Partridge of XTC, phoning from his inexplicable home town of Swindon to discuss the album *Oranges & Lemons*, was an expansive spirit whose refusal to take anything seri-ously verged on the heroic, even/especially when asked for his views on the case of an American school student who had compelled his principal's secretary, at knifepoint, to play XTC's 'Dear God' over the school's public address system. 'He should,' said Partridge, 'have taken some hand grenades in with the entire album. Or, you know, "Play the whole catalogue, I've got a tank outside."'

John Lydon of Public Image Ltd, on the phone from Los Angeles, reacted to my stammered introduction of myself and my paper with a long, phlegmy sigh, followed by a singsong jeer of, 'Ooh, yippee. My favourite publication.' He spent much of the interview trying to start a fight, before reacting to a question about what he'd been like at school – an attempt on my part to head off another of his defen-sive declamations about his own ironclad integrity, which I wouldn't have had the nerve to question even if I wanted to, which I didn't – with a quiet vulnerability.

'I was dreadful at school,' he said. 'I started out incredibly shy, and very, very quiet. I wouldn't even answer a question if the teacher asked because I'd be so embarrassed. As the years progressed, I steadily got really sick of myself, and decided to do something about it. I learnt to grow up, I learnt not to feel so inadequate. So finally, they eventually threw me out for talking too much, for asking too many questions.' This confession of shame and embarrassment was delivered in the same snotty snarl that scoured The Sex Pistols' 'Pretty Vacant', and PiL's 'Public Image'. It was like hearing Nana Mouskouri tell you that she used to sell crack.

There was a reason why a free street paper was getting access to this calibre of artist: lack of competition. Australia had never had an especially vigorous tradition of a rock press, even when it did boast – as it did, in the late 1980s – a rock scene of singular vibrancy by any standards, never mind the standards of small islands in the middle of nowhere. In Sydney, *On the Street*'s only rivals were a local franchise of *Rolling Stone*, which appeared monthly, and *Rock Australia Magazine* – known as *RAM* – which appeared weekly.

RAM was a better publication than *OTS* – it looked nicer, and was better written, and had something resembling a coherent editorial aesthetic. But *RAM* required of its readers that they paid money for it, which rather circumscribed its circulation, which meant *On the Street* had the advertisers, and the pages, and the numbers. We were the *NME* to *RAM*'s *Melody Maker*: not as good, but more popular. This is often the way of things, but more so in rock'n'roll than in most.

ANDREW MUELLER

8

IN WHICH THE AUTHOR QUESTIONS JOHNNY ROTTEN'S SARTORIAL CHOICES

Early in 1989, I decided that I needed to step up where *Melody Maker* was concerned. Having noticed that *Melody Maker* had granted some coverage to the bands on Flying Nun, I wrote a review of a show by The Chills at the Tivoli and posted it, along with an introductory letter, to the reviews editor, Paul Mathur. On Thursday evenings in ensuing weeks, after collecting my air-freighted copies of *Melody Maker* and *NME* from Metropolis, the Pitt Street record store which reserved them for me, I leafed through the *Maker*'s live review pages on the bus back to Stanmore in neither hope nor expectation, and arrived home in the state of weary sulkitude one feels when not even disappointed at the failure to occur of something you knew wasn't going to happen anyway.

A few months later, having noticed that *Melody Maker* was still writing occasionally about Flying Nun's bands, and that Paul Mathur had been replaced as reviews editor by someone called Everett True, I tried again. I wrote an account of a gig by Straitjacket Fits at the Lansdowne Hotel. The show was fantastic. The review I wrote was absolute fucking rubbish. It was a wretchedly inept appropriation

97

of the defining tropes of my favourite *Maker* writers – the belligerent fervour of the Stud Brothers, the wry poesy of Chris Roberts. I posted it, and another introductory letter, to this Everett True character. I included a self-deprecating plea to Mr True not to condemn me to the fearful indignity of touting myself to the *NME*.

Among the many, many things I didn't know at this point were the following: i) Everett True had until very recently been employed by the *NME*, for whom he had contributed as The Legend!, under which name he had also made some formidably atrocious music (when Creation records became globally famous as the home of Oasis in the mid-90s, an official line held that the label's first ever release had been 'Upside Down' by The Jesus & Mary Chain. This was a wilful – if understandable – Stalinist lie, attempting to erase from history the real CRE001, a calamitously terrible track called '73 In 83', by The Legend!); ii) Everett True had an immense passion for the obscure, and had recently become a zealous fan of the output of Flying Nun – which, from where he was sitting in London, was about as obscure as it got.

On collecting my copy of *Melody Maker* from Metropolis one Thursday after posting my review, I noticed that Everett, taking his turn to review the singles, had accorded Single of the Week honours to Straitjacket Fits' four-track EP, *Life in One Chord*. Everett described it as 'one psychotic strait-laced feline mutha of a record'. Well, I thought. I wonder if. The following week, I undertook my usual saunter down Pitt Street, leafing through an issue featuring The Cure's Robert Smith glowering from the cover for what felt like the dozenth time in the last few months (another thing I didn't know was that Smith didn't much care for the *NME*, and would usually only speak to *Melody Maker*, and as The Cure were enormous at around this point, *Melody Maker* rather made the most of it). I noticed that among the live reviews, in roughly the middle of page 19, which also carried write-ups of The Wedding Present, Miles Davis and The Godfathers, was one of Straitjacket Fits. Bugger, I thought. And at the Lansdowne Hotel in Sydney, as well. What were the chances of that? Still less the odds of there being another writer based here called Andrew M . . . hang on.

It was another dose of the feeling I'd had on first seeing my name in *On the Street*, but much more severely disorienting, the overwhelming rush of joy and excitement faintly tainted, on this occasion, by the suspicion that this must be some species of practical joke. I looked at the cover again. Yes, it was definitely *Melody Maker* – and not even, so far as I could tell, a special edition dedicated to the most laughable recent submissions from incompetent wannabes. I leafed back through the paper to the live reviews. And that, in the stentorian capitals favoured by *Melody Maker*, was definitely my by-line.

*

The pattern of my early experience with *On the Street* was repeated, inasmuch that nobody from *Melody Maker* had told me they were going to run my review, and nobody called me asking for more – but, I chose to believe significantly, nobody asked me to stop. I sent more live reviews, either of touring groups who I imagined might register on *Melody Maker*'s consciousness, or of shows by Flying Nun bands that I knew Everett cared about even if nobody else did – The Proclaimers at the Enmore Theatre, The Verlaines at the Graphic Arts Club, Poison at the Sydney Entertainment Centre, The Bats at Paddington RSL. My Thursday evening bus rides home from town became more gratifying, especially when I found a couple of my submissions – The Triffids at the

Enmore Theatre, Transvision Vamp at the Hordern Pavilion – elevated to the lead review on the page, ennobled with a thick black border, a photograph of the artist in question, and a headline in a chunky bold font.

One morning, the phone rang at the house in Stanmore. 'Is Andrew there?' enquired a voice which sounded like someone doing an impression of a weedy Englishman with a nerdishly obsessive interest in unpopular indie rock music. 'It's Everett from *Melody Maker*.' Better people have nurtured greater dreams – freeing their people, curing disease, bellowing their national anthem from the top step of the podium, and so on – but this was mine, and it appeared to be coming true. Everett suggested bringing order to bear on our working relationship, asking that I fax details of upcoming shows in advance, rather than randomly posting him stuff, and promising to enact the bureaucracy that would ensure I got paid. Exercising superhuman restraint, I did not begin approaching random strangers and announcing, 'Hello, I now appear to be working for *Melody Maker*. That's right – the music magazine in London.'

Well, not that often.

*

As *On the Street* had a near monopoly on print interviews with international musicians, so I had a near monopoly of *On the Street*. This was not because I was better than their other writers – certainly, had I been editor, there was hardly a commission of mine I wouldn't have punted to Barry Divola, who was funnier, knew more, and was unburdened by my own irrepressible compulsion to persuade the readers how terribly clever I was. My domination of the paper happened because I was on a regular – if meagre – wage anyway, and everything I did was something for which the expense of a freelance was avoided.

So I interviewed John Lydon again barely two months after I'd interviewed him the first time. This encounter was face to face, as Lydon had arrived in Australia for a tour with PiL. I met him in the conference room of a Sydney hotel. Lydon had installed himself at the far end, below a whiteboard on which he had inscribed the words 'Go away'. He was dressed in a luridly striped trousers-and-jumper combination, which looked like a Third World television test pattern, over a multicoloured polka dot shirt. He resembled a jack-in-the-box which had escaped from Toy Corner and seized control of the classroom. I approached him and offered my hand. He declined to stand; his arms remained folded. Perhaps feeling I had little to lose, more likely motivated by genuine curiosity, I offered an unorthodox opening question: What the fuck was he wearing?

He glared. It was an odd feeling. Lydon's glare was well known to me from Sex Pistols and PiL videos, and any number of magazine photos. Its power was not in doubt: John Lydon's glare had been punk's equivalent of Joshua's trumpet, an instrument of vengeance which had laid waste to everything that displeased it. For a nervous few seconds, I felt included amid this horizonless vista of the unsatisfactory.

'Ridiculous, isn't it?' he eventually appeared to agree. 'Of course, only an Australian could have designed it.'

I knew I was the last interview of the day. I got the impression he was glad of the opportunity to use this line, and that previous journalists had been too nervous or too tactful to supply him with the set-up. For whatever reason, Lydon seemed to decide that I wasn't quite the most tedious thing that could possibly befall him right at this moment. He was, for the rest of the hour, wise, funny and acutely – almost painfully – self-aware.

'Most people,' he said, 'seem very scared of their own personality, and they cover it up in illusions and delusions. Very foolish. If I live for anything, it's individuality, thank you. I follow no trend. The tragedy is that I create quite a few in my wake.'

In retrospect, it's a poignant observation. PiL had just released what would turn out to be their last useful album, 9. Lydon would surely have been mortified to know that he was on the verge of a long wander through a wilderness of nostalgia and self-parody which would include a regrettable Sex Pistols reunion, a cameo in a celebrity game show, a stint as a spokesmodel for butter, and ultimate elevation to the role of universally beloved, harmlessly eccentric British national treasure. It's perhaps indicative of punk's ultimate victory that the former Johnny Rotten is unhesitatingly accepted as a family entertainer and saleable brand image. But it's also the irony that eventually crushes most mavericks: they change the world, only to be co-opted by the new reality they helped create.

Johnny Marr came to town with The The, on the antipodean leg of their pompously titled 'The The vs The World' tour, in support of their pompously titled album *Mind Bomb*, which had spawned a minor Australian hit in the pompously titled single, 'The Beat(en) Generation'. This would scarcely have been Marr's first experience of service as a sideman to a vainglorious figure given to inane pronouncements upon matters about which he knew little, and it was instantly apparent how Marr stood it: with a regime of absolutely ruthless self-effacement. He was modest, humble, as unlike a lead guitarist as any lead guitarist could be. He also had extraordinarily small hands: it seemed improbable that all those impossible riffs could have been wrung from a fretboard by fingers so tiny.

The interview with Marr, beside some hotel's rooftop pool, was an introduction to negotiating the complex dynamic which often governs such encounters – that is, the one thing the interviewer (and his readers) want to know about most is the one thing that the subject wants to discuss least. It was just two years since Marr had quit The Smiths – time in which he'd busied himself doing a great deal other than talking about quitting The Smiths, including working with The Pretenders, Talking Heads, Bryan Ferry and Kirsty MacColl, among others, before joining The The. Blame for the split had been largely laid, by The Smiths' morbidly possessive fans, at Marr's feet. It had occurred to me that if I could get Marr to talk about any of this, it might mean a debut as a feature writer for *Melody Maker*.

In the event, I didn't have to feign interest in the portentous twaddle of *Mind Bomb* for long (Marr had only co-written one track). Marr, like most people with a story to tell, wanted to tell it, and was as susceptible to a sympathetic ear as anyone. I asked him if he'd been bothered by being cast as the villain of the piece where The Smiths were concerned.

'I got incredibly bothered about it,' he replied. 'To me, it was a very personal thing, where I felt that I did the right thing. Personally, I think I saved everybody's butt. I would never point the finger at anyone, but I think we were egos out of control towards the end. And a lot of people painted me as this upstart, who wanted to be a guitar hero, and that was the last thing on my mind . . . I think it would have been more of a sell-out to just stick with it, rake in the bucks, and con people.'

It seems incredible to a twenty-year-old – certainly it did to this twenty-year-old – that anybody would walk away from a job playing lead guitar in an adored and brilliant rock group. It might well have seemed incredible to Johnny Marr when he'd been twenty, as he had been just five years previously. If dreams can come true, though, so can nightmares.

'There comes a time in everybody's life,' he said, 'when you're just as miserable as sin, and you've got to get out and save your sanity.'

Melody Maker ran my interview over two full pages, and also bought the photos of Marr taken by Tony Mott, *On the Street*'s house photographer, an amiable English expatriate impossible to describe without acknowledging an eerie resemblance to Ronnie Wood. I thrilled to the delectable half-truth someone inserted in the standfirst – 'Andrew Mueller joined the tour in Australia', as if my involvement had been more extensive and intimate than a forty-five-minute chat in the middle of a weekday afternoon.

*

It became known around the traps that I was now writing reasonably regularly for *Melody Maker*, mostly because I usually contrived an excuse within the first fifteen seconds of any conversation to remark that I was now writing reasonably regularly for *Melody Maker*. While it is unlikely that this impressed anyone half as much as it impressed me, it did make me more confident – gusting overconfident – as a writer and interviewer. I had what felt like reasonably grown-up conversations with such local luminaries as Mick Harvey of the Bad Seeds (about life on tour with Nick Cave), Weddings Parties Anything's former guitarist Dave Steel (about his fine solo album) and No's Ollie Olsen (about Max Q, his much underrated collaboration with INXS's Michael Hutchence). I finally met Ed Kuepper in the flesh, and found him no less essentially mordant, but radiating genuine passion for his work and a lightly confrontational wit that hadn't translated at all over the telephone. 'I like a certain degree of mystery about music,' he said, 'something intangible. I don't need to have my favourite records explained to me by the people that created them. But then, I'm not a journalist.'

But it was, shamefully if understandably, the contacts with what I perceived as *Melody Maker*'s realm which excited me far more. To my continual and mounting vexation, these were made mostly by telephone, a means of communication which perpetually thwarted, betrayed and infuriated me: if I'd been paying any attention at all when the Greek myths had come up during my brief attendance at university, I'd have identified closely with Tantalus, and regarded these encounters as equivalent to his hapless, hopeless swipes for the fruit hanging just beyond his reach. As it was, I just swore a lot. An interview with Happy Mondays' Shaun Ryder was hastily shorthanded on the back of a takeaway menu when he called the house erroneously at some ghastly hour of the morning (Ryder, having read something about the immense all-night dance parties which were big in Sydney at the time, greeted me with, 'Just got in, have you?'). A playback of an interview with The Pogues' Phil Chevron yielded only the snatches that had been caught by a wrinkled tape. An interview with Pete Shelley of Buzzcocks had to be done all over again when the playback didn't even yield that.

The absolute worst was Dinosaur Jr's proverbially torpid J Mascis, whose answer to almost everything was a half-yawned: 'Uhh.' His longest response to any question came to sixty-one consecutive syllables, amounting to forty-four entirely un-illuminating words about Dinosaur Jr's decision to cover The Cure's 'Just Like Heaven'. After ten minutes of Mascis's somnambulant grunting, I hung up on him. It was only the second time I'd ever done this, the other victim being disgraced Miss America turned soul belter Vanessa Williams, who had been perfectly pleasant but dull beyond endurance, which was why I'd cut the call off halfway through one of my own questions, leaving technology to take the blame. With Mascis, I just told him that if he couldn't be bothered, neither could I. 'Uhh,' he replied.

There is nothing wrong with an artist not wishing to do press. But if they really don't want to do it, they really shouldn't do it. The artist who complains about doing press while doing press, and/or is gratuitously belligerent about the process, is both a bore and a boor. Though it was a view I developed early on, it was reinforced by my first meeting with someone who really had no need to do press at all: B.B. King, visiting Australia as U2's support act. The fabled bluesman happily signed the bagful of albums – and one guitar neck – that friends had given me to take along for his autograph, taught me some riffs on his famous Gibson 335, 'Lucille', and talked for ages in that unaffected manner some Americans have that makes you believe the pleasure is indeed all theirs.

It is often the case that the most dysfunctional egos are possessed by those who've never quite made it, and who fear – or, more corrosively still, know – that they never quite will. The genuinely legendary musicians are (almost) invariably humble, talking of themselves as servants of their muse rather than its master: this may be, of course, how they came to be legendary in the first place. 'You learn at an early age,' said King, when I asked whether such accolades as 'King of the Blues' were an honour or a burden, 'not to believe everything people tell you. But if people do believe that, and treat you as such, you work hard to try to earn their respect, to earn that title that they gave you.'

My fervent belief that King's touring companions had earned no such deference was expounded in a screechingly self-righteous indictment of U2's show at cheerless concrete barn the Sydney Entertainment Centre, which *Melody Maker* ran over half a page. It was basically an attempt to impress the people I desperately wanted to think of as my colleagues, by affixing my by-line to a tract of the sort of vituperative iconoclasm for which the British music press used to be famous and feared – and U2 presented, at this point, a hefty and slow-moving target, mired as they were in the viscous hubris of their *Rattle and Hum* period, essentially an exercise in hanging their own portraits in the rock'n'roll hall of fame.

The review wasn't a bad piece of writing. I was at least developing an ear for *Melody Maker*'s tenor of sneering abuse, writing U2 off as a shambles who were 'led by someone who looks like Worzel Gummidge and have precisely two songs', further observing of Worzel that 'he's not a rock star, he's a shepherd', and characterising his relationship with his vacantly adoring flock as 'the bland leading the bland'. It was pious and pleased with itself, but young people are. I'm not sure how I'd have reacted had someone emerged from a time machine at around this point and said, 'Hey, I've been to 2013. That band you just reviewed like they'd been caught pitching kittens into a burning orphanage have carted you around the world several times, and paid you on time and really quite generously for program notes for one of their tours, and sleeve notes for the twentieth-anniversary reissue of this fantastic album they'll release three years from now.'

The U2 review prompted the first angry correspondence about my work on *Melody Maker*'s letters page, Backlash. Clare Sweeney of Maidenhead called me 'jealous, low-paid, useless', an assessment which probably scored about two and a half out of three, and 'with, may I add, no taste in music.' (I loved the 'may I add') Hannah Lane of Bath offered the unarguable if irrelevant retort that 'U2 can play to packed out audiences at Wembley, while the hip, trendy indie groups which your paper likes only play to half-filled pubs.' I was pathetically thrilled that I'd inspired outrage in people I'd never met on the other side of the world. It's one of the enduring joys of writing for a living – the opportunity to disrupt or direct, however trivially and fleetingly, the internal monologues of strangers.

Having acquired a taste for sacred cow, I set about demolishing The Ramones' drowsy performance at the Enmore Theatre ('Joey wears the weary demeanour of a career factory worker, Johnny plays his guitar like he's gutting fish for hungry tourists, and Marky, under an obscenely obvious wig, might as well be asleep'). *Melody Maker*'s subeditors rose majestically to this diatribe with the headline HEY HO, LET'S STOP.

*

In *On the Street*'s 1989 Christmas issue, I declared the following to be the year's best records.

Elvis Costello, *Spike*
The Pogues, *Peace and Love*

These two had nothing to do with each other, save the coincidence that Costello had produced one of The Pogues' earlier albums. I bracketed them together by way of acknowledgement that both artists made my list every year. They both still sound fine to me. *Spike* is the Costello album on which his eternally itching desire to impress is reined in shortest of oppressive overreach – it's feverishly smart, and often very funny, containing some of his most beautifully arranged songs ('Harpies Bizarre', 'Any King's Shilling'). *Peace and Love* necessitated a lot of compensating by the rest of The Pogues for the infirmities of Shane MacGowan, but they were equal to the task, most notably on Phil Chevron's 'Lorelei', which Roy Orbison should have lived long enough to record.

The Darling Buds, *Pop Said*
Transvision Vamp, *Velveteen*

It's conceivable that I enjoyed neither of these records as much as I enjoyed what Chris Roberts wrote about these groups in *Melody Maker* – certainly, it strikes me as retrospectively miraculous that my efforts to write like Chris during this period did not get *On the Street*'s offices burnt to the ground, and the smouldering ruins danced on by cheering crowds. However, both albums retain a certain charm. The Darling Buds' sparky punky Motown alchemised into a couple of great singles ('Burst', 'Hit the Ground') and Transvision Vamp's wilful preposterousness on this, their somewhat conceptual second album, almost occluded the fact that it was in no respect as good as their first.

The Hummingbirds, *LoveBuzz*

The Hummingbirds were one of a batch of promising local bands swept up by a new Australian label by the name of rooArt – an exercise in branding unforgivable for both its parochialism and its stupid kooky capitalisation, for which somebody should have been buried neck-deep in an anthill and smeared in honey. And then hit with a shovel. *LoveBuzz*, The Hummingbirds' debut album, was nevertheless perfect. The fizzing promise of their indie singles was redeemed by the wisest choice of producer imaginable – Mitch Easter, whose fiercely requited love for the rock guitar can be appreciated on earlier recordings by R.E.M., among others. I'd still be abundantly prepared to argue that 'Blush', the lead single, has the best ending to any song, ever.

The Jesus and Mary Chain, *Automatic*

Not the Jesus and Mary Chain album you're supposed to like, but I fail to see how anybody could be unamused by Jim and William Reid impersonating Billy Idol.

Cindy Lee Berryhill, *Naked Movie Star*

Another act championed by *Melody Maker*'s Chris Roberts. Measured against the works of the phalanxes of female singer–songwriters who would be herded over the top by desperate record companies to near certain ignominious doom in no-man's-land in subsequent decades, *Naked Movie Star* stacks up okay – Berryhill is sharp and sarcastic and blessed with a winning drawl.

The Stone Roses, *The Stone Roses*
Happy Mondays, *Bummed*

Not audacious choices at the time, but not wrong, either. *The Stone Roses* is a resounding expression of the headlong arrogance of youth, untarnished by The Stone Roses' subsequent follies – and I speak as someone who was part of the aghast throng present at The Stone Roses' comeback at the 1996 Reading Festival, the rock'n'roll equivalent of witnessing the *Hindenburg*'s 1937 arrival in Lakehurst, New Jersey. *Bummed* is just awesome – sleazy, lazy, altogether disreputable, like early 1970s Rolling Stones rewritten by the uncle everyone warned you about.

Dutiful Daughters, *A Superfluity of Nuns*
Falling Joys, *Omega*
No, *Once We Were Scum Now We Are God*
Plug Uglies, *Knock Me Your Lobes*
Snapper, *Snapper*
Chad's Tree, *Kerosene*

My picks of the year's local indie offerings (the concept of 'local' being extended, in the instance of Flying Nun signing Snapper, across the Tasman). None of these bands amounted to much in the grand scheme of things. All of them, however, made records I'm still glad I heard – and glad now that I heard them when I heard them. There are certainly artists much like these in existence now – interesting and worthwhile acts, just beneath the radar – but I'll never know. I barely have time left to listen again to everything I already know I like.

ANDREW MUELLER

9

IN WHICH THE AUTHOR MAKES UP THINGS FOR A SCURRILOUS SCANDAL SHEET

There are few creatures in the world so tiresome and risible as a journalist who has become convinced of his own omniscience. By the turn of the decade, if I hadn't turned into an irredeemable grandstander, I was exhibiting tendencies in that direction, slapping around records by local groups and sneering at local interview subjects in the style of someone who thinks his work beneath him. There's nothing wrong with a journalist being confrontational or abrasive – even, when the occasion and/or hapless indie rock album demands it, abusive – but carrying that act off requires (obviously) genuine wit and (counter-intuitively) leavening humility, and I possessed neither. It is hopefully some consolation to the musicians of Sydney who regarded me as a prematurely advanced, self-important dickhead that, cringing through the scrapbooks two decades later, I could scarcely agree more.

I began 1990 with a rash of *On the Street* cover stories, some of which weren't disastrous. Shane MacGowan called from the Perth stop of The Pogues' Australian tour, and once I'd talked him out of playing with a toy synthesiser with which he seemed preoccupied, he was excruciatingly uninhibited, in the way that the very drunk often are. 'I'm a selfish person,' he slurred down the line to a total stranger. 'I'm not a responsible person, I'm a late person. I'm a person who can be incredibly bad on stage on certain nights and incredibly good on other nights. I'm a person who can feel there's absolutely no reason for living whatsoever, get absolutely fed up, get absolutely suicidal, and then the next day think, you know, everything's alright.'

Steve Kilbey of The Church was cagey about revealing anything at all, but unexpectedly funny about his reasons for it. 'I'm interested in William Shakespeare. I wonder what he was like. But I'm kind of glad I don't play golf with him.'

Another conversation with Pete Shelley of Buzzcocks imparted the lesson that some insights can be gleaned from phone interviews after all, by making the simple enquiry about what your subject had been doing just now. Shelley, it turned out, was watching the Super Bowl, a detail I treasured because whatever it was I imagined punk rock's Smokey Robinson did with his Sunday evenings, it wasn't shouting at American football (he'd bet on Joe Montana's 49ers to beat John Elway's hapless Broncos, which further suggested that he knew his stuff).

A frequently and frustratingly postponed interview with Deborah Harry went as well as might be expected, given that the brief amounted to Margaret putting her head round the door and saying, 'Debbie Harry. It's on. Ten minutes' – and replying, when I asked if she meant it was happening in ten minutes or I had ten minutes for the interview, 'Both.' The sole triumph of this hopelessly forced encounter was reducing Harry to apparently genuine hysterics by asking if she felt herself underrated as a lyricist (it was a serious question: I refer the sceptical to Blondie's 'Dreaming', which contains not only the greatest drumming on any track ever, but a contender for one of the best dozen opening couplets of all time).

But I didn't want to be in Sydney, interviewing these people for *On the Street*. I wanted to be in London, interviewing them for *Melody Maker* (I'm wretchedly certain that I spent at least some of a phone interview with Mudhoney asking them what Everett True was like, and similarly pressed The Sundays about Chris Roberts). The agony was exacerbated by the fact that I now knew it was only the small matter of 17,000 kilometres, give or take, that was stopping me. I'd sold *Melody Maker* my interview with Steve Kilbey, and another with Belinda Carlisle (she'd been as blandly pleasant as her solo recordings if perplexed by my attempts to argue the merits of her previous group as post-punk stormtroopers; my copy of The Go-Gos' *Beauty and the Beat* is the only autographed album I ever owned that I couldn't quite bring myself to donate to some charity auction or other in the mid-1990s). Better still, *Melody Maker* had actually commissioned me to do a couple of interviews, one with The Hummingbirds and one with Peter Garrett of Midnight Oil, whose management office was conveniently situated on the same Glebe street to which Clancy and I had relocated.

Garrett in conversation exhibited exactly the same tics as Garrett on stage, illuminating his passions with a jerky semaphore of arm movements that resembled the tics of a gangling marionette being operated by a chronic hiccuper. This was endearing, yet kind of alarming in the confines of the small booths of Badde Manors cafe at the end of Glebe Point Road. His appreciation of Australia's contradictions was as affectionate as it was astute. 'A vast contrast,' he said, with an illustrative sweep of forearm that threatened to upend our coffees, 'between philistinism and creativity, easy-going openness and narrow-minded parochialness.'

*

Aside from the inconvenient fact of my corporeal presence in Sydney, I was elsewhere. Reconciling this dissonance proved so stress-free that, were I that way inclined, I'd have suspected some benign cosmic force at work. Clancy also wanted to go to Europe, to study Italian and to travel, so no traumatic domestic sundering would be called for: we'd go together. Everett assured me that I wasn't just getting space in *Melody Maker* because they didn't know anybody else in Sydney. Clancy and I picked a date in May, and booked tickets. All I needed now was some money, and I wasn't going to save much in a hurry on what *On the Street* paid.

I had heard via Jack Marx that there was decent cash to be made in the wilder reaches of Australia's tabloid market. A couple of friends of his worked for the *Picture*, a new and entirely appalling periodical published weekly by Australian Consolidated Press. The *Picture*'s contents were split between photographs of not overclothed women, and pages of not overtrue news stories. I took a day off from *On the Street* and presented myself for a try-out. There was much for me to absorb. Not only had I never had any editorial discipline applied to my writing, let alone the unforgiving rigours of tabloid subediting, I'd never operated a computer. Astonishingly, they let me stay longer than it took me to ask, 'Er, how do I switch this on?' I left my job at *On the Street* that week, and stayed at the *Picture* for three months. I still believe that I have never since laughed and learnt so much in such a compressed period.

Though the *Picture* was mildly pornographic and thoroughly irresponsible, it was beautifully written. The commanding presences on the features desk were former *RAM* editor and future Walkley winner Paul Toohey, and former *RAM* contributor and future *Australian Weekend Magazine* editor David Brearley (*RAM* had gone down with all hands in 1989). Between them, the pair had cultivated a house style which tacked away from the shrieking sensationalism of, say, the UK's *Daily Sport* or America's *National Enquirer* towards a dry, self-parodying vernacular closer to an Australian answer to *Viz*. Their brilliance as word-wranglers can be gleaned from just one subheading, to a story they'd crafted about American travellers being taken by a tiresome tour guide to Australia's dullest pub: 'Bush blowhard dishes out the verbal valium and bores the doodles off Yankee dandies'.

In the *Picture*'s brash, lurid pages, tabloid conventions were religiously observed while being ruthlessly subverted: where other periodicals of the sort occasionally capitalised key words or phrases for emphasis, the *Picture*'s writers would engage their Caps Lock button for words or phrases which were either utterly irrelevant, briskly offensive or entrancingly rococo. Though the entreaties from readers which appeared on the letters page were expressed in the basic lexicon of tabloid emotion – sentimentality, outrage, hang-'em-high vindictiveness – they often contained surprisingly, even suspiciously, detailed praise for recent shows and records by the bands in which various members of the *Picture*'s staff played.

By dispensing with such time-consuming irritants as research and facts, the *Picture* was able to operate a breezily streamlined editorial process. The features editor bought interesting, disgusting or outrageous photographs from news agencies. These would be dumped on the desk of a feature writer with a word count and a memo suggesting possible storylines, usually footnoted by a reminder that you were welcome to proceed on your own initiative if you had any better ideas. Once a feature writer had come up with a draft he liked, it would be punted round the desk so that the others could make suggestions. It was an unusual day that did not, at least once, see the entire office incapacitated by laughter or engaged in impassioned debate about the correct spelling of 'bazoombas'.

A typical story was the heart-rending yarn of Ima. Quite early in my employ by the *Picture*, I arrived at my desk to find a bundle of slides of a girl, probably in her early teens, who'd been born with no legs. The *Picture* did a lot of weepy human interest stories, as all tabloids do – this was the provenance of these photographs in the first place. The memo from the features editor sighed something along the lines of 'uplifting, inspiring, struggle against the odds, you know the drill, 400 words'.

I had no idea who the girl was, or where she was from, or when the pictures had been taken (we almost never knew anything about our subjects – while it's tempting to believe that this was a deliberate policy of the *Picture*'s high command to prevent human empathy from impeding the onslaught of their underlings, it strikes me as more likely that they just couldn't be bothered finding anything out). I decided to set the story in South Africa. The country had been in the news a lot recently, what with the end of apartheid and release of Nelson Mandela (almost all the *Picture*'s stories were datelined in remote locations, due to a belief that this reduced the chances of us getting called on, or sued for, something we'd written). I named the girl Ima, for reasons I no longer recall. I then decided, in light of the International Olympic Committee's decision to admit the reforming South Africa to the 1992 Games, to cast her as an athlete, preparing to run the marathon in Barcelona on her hands – or, as the *Picture* would report it, ON

HER HANDS. I filled in some touching background colour about her recent birthday party – or, as I should have been more ashamed to have called it, KNEES-UP. I then sent it to Brearley and Toohey, and nervously awaited the response of the sages.

'Not bad,' was Brearley's assessment, 'but you're missing a key word.' The word in question, Brearley noted, was 'plucky'. All stories of this sort, he explained, refer to the doughty infant in question as 'plucky'. Brearley dashed through my copy, shoehorning in increasingly demented variations on the term: she spoke 'pluckily', was 'pluckier' than somebody else, was the 'pluckiest' of all the athletes training for the Games, 'pluckified' other people by her mere presence, and so on.

I learnt a lot about journalism from my brief stint at the *Picture*, even if 'journalism' was never quite the word to describe what the *Picture* did. Writing for a tabloid taught me how to structure stories – how to tell my beginning and my middle from my end, and how to make jokes serve the copy, rather than the other way around. And the – to put it charitably – pure-hearted credulousness of the readership inculcated some overdue respect for the power of the written word. To my befuddlement, people often reacted to the stories we'd written as if they were other than honking bullshit dreamt up by guffawing rock writers.

The tale of plucky Ima prompted letters asking how one might go about sponsoring her training. We received serious and quite distraught offers to adopt another child I wrote about – in real life, a two-headed baby about to undergo surgery to remove its half-formed Siamese twin. I called the child Aziz and set the yarn in Turkey, larding it with some nonsense about how superstitious local peasants, believing the infant cursed, were proposing to chop off one of its heads

(sample paragraph, burnished with the archaic demotic to which *Picture* writers were prone: 'The only person who hasn't been consulted in this WOEFUL BUSINESS is Aziz. No one wants to know him. Even the lawyer going to defend him in court is only doing it FOR A LARK.')

None of which compared to the uproar that greeted a piece I wrote about the execution of an elephant. It was, in fairness to those who phoned, faxed and posted their outrage, the closest to the truth of anything the *Picture* ran during my tenure, which is to say that the photo of an elephant being hanged with chains from a railway derrick was genuine (or, at least, was a possibly modified image of an event that had actually happened). It had been taken or forged, however, in 1916, when employees of the Sparks Brothers circus, travelling through Tennessee, strung the animal up for fatally trampling one of their colleagues.

As the features editor noted, the lynching of an elephant seventy-four years earlier wasn't news – but the travails of Australians who had recently been executed or sentenced to death for smuggling drugs in South-East Asia were. I took the cue, set my report in present-day Thailand, and included some bellicose quotes from Thai authorities, including the judge who sentenced the hapless pachyderm – or, I suppose, HAPLESS PACHYDERM – ('This country will take no prisoners in its war on drugs, especially not smelly grey ones that cost a fortune to feed') – and a Bangkok narcotics detective named Sok Hung Dong ('You don't want to buy an UMBRELLA STAND, do you?') The story, which ran beneath the headline DRUG-RUNNING DUMBO COPS THE DROP, moved several readers to announce that they were cancelling planned holidays in Thailand, and prompted a minor trickle of furious phone calls. With next week's issue to plan, we gave these people the number of the Thai embassy in Canberra and left them to get on with it.

One *Picture* reader's letter in particular remains a valued memory, which I draw upon still at those moments during which some sappy fondness for humanity at large fleetingly descends, and I find myself momentarily lulled by the delusion that there really is much hope for western civilisation. It was a response to a lengthy investigative feature I'd written, inspired by some photos we'd dredged up of a Las Vegas drag queen preparing for his turn as Marilyn Monroe. My story asserted that these pictures were from declassified CIA files revealing the shocking news that Marilyn Monroe was really a man – or, as the headline summarised this extraordinary scandal, MARILYN WAS A BLOKE, SO SHE KILLED HIMSELF!

The *Picture*'s senior editors thought this amazing scoop worthy of further illustration. They hired a model to wear a white gown and stand above a grate, while a photographer took what we captioned as the hitherto unrevealed 'below' shot of the famous scene from *The Seven Year Itch*, in which a gust of air rises from the subway on the corner of Lexington and 52nd in New York City, billowing Marilyn's dress to iconic effect. The *Picture*'s photo clearly showed a protuberance in the undergarments above the grate – which, we chose to report, was something other than a strategically placed cucumber. At least one reader was not fooled. My brilliant correspondent thought it was in no way a waste of his time and money to write in pointing out that in the grate in our photo, the mesh ran vertically, while in the original movie scene, the mesh ran horizontally. 'That,' I replied, 'is what they want you to think.'

I loved working for the *Picture*. It was hard to leave a magazine that would concoct a story about the Soviet propaganda rag *Pravda* adjusting to Mikhail Gorbachev's program of liberalisation by introducing page-three girls, just so it could bless posterity with the headline WHAT A PAIR O'STROIKAS!

10

FOR WHICH THE AUTHOR FAILS TO THINK OF A LESS CLICHÉD SUBTITLE THE 'LONDON CALLING'

Like every new arrival in London, I had a list of things I wanted to see: the peerless repository of stolen goods that is the British Museum, the ghosts and ravens of the Tower, the lights of Piccadilly Circus. Like possibly no other visitor in the city's history, my list was topped by a drab brown office block on the south bank of the Thames. I didn't even wait for the jetlag to subside.

Few journeys I've undertaken since have inspired such anxiety and excitement, without involving armed checkpoints. None have been so minutely mentally rehearsed. From the flat in which we were staying, a walk to Mile End tube. From Mile End, three stops on the Central Line to Bank. At Bank, change to the Waterloo & City Line, one stop to Waterloo. From Waterloo, a stroll along Stamford Street to the lobby of King's Reach Tower. From the lobby of King's Reach Tower, a lift to the twenty-sixth floor.

The *Melody Maker* office was in every respect a nondescript beige cubicle battery, aside from the colourful characters it accommodated. Through a combination of the magazine's editorial creed of rampant first-person

self-indulgence and in-crowd in-jokery, and my own obsessive consumption of same, I felt like I knew most of the
staff before we exchanged handshakes. Everett True really
did appear to be a study in shambling gormlessness who
really was wearing what could very easily be mistaken for
pyjamas. The Stud Brothers, Ben and Dom, really did give
every impression of having just returned from some remote
frontier of depravity, along which they had witnessed
things of which they should not speak. Tom Sheehan,
veteran staff photographer, whose fondness for rhyming
slang was a staple of the *Maker*'s self-referential mythology, really did upbraid me in the pub for jostling a table
and 'spilling Germaine on me hinge'.[1] David Stubbs really
was an apparition of diffident gentility entirely incongruous
in such surrounds, suggesting John Le Mesurier dreadfully
miscast as Lester Bangs; everyone called him 'Wingco'.
Chris Roberts really was wearing a Primitives T-shirt
(actually, almost everybody, bar the sartorially punctilious
Stubbs, wore a band T-shirt of some sort, not to display any
particular allegiance, but because they used to come free in
the post from record companies).

What mattered most was that nobody informed me that
my association with *Melody Maker* up until this point had
been the result of some *My Fair Lady*-style wager, in which
they'd bet the *NME* twenty quid and a Cocteau Twins box
set that they could pass a random antipodean hayseed off

---

1 Germaine Greer = beer, Hinge & Bracket = jacket. It took me a while, as
well. Other favourite Sheehanisms down the years include the declining of
an offer to join colleagues for a midday meal as he was trying to lose weight
('No, I'm gonna skip Brady – I'm on a Brixton') and an announcement that
he intended to apply some adhesive powder to a snooker implement ('I want
to Peter my Regent's'). Brady Bunch = lunch, Brixton riot = diet, Peter Falk
= chalk, Regent's Park Zoo = cue.

as a rock journalist. They even gave me some work to do, downpage live and album reviews and minor interviews, each of which I considered a significantly bigger deal than, say, being set a dozen exacting labours by Eurystheus in return for immortality.

I quickly learnt that the stakes had been raised. *On the Street* was only read in Sydney, and – it seems fair to assume – was taken seriously only by the small minority of the people who paused in the features section en route to the gig listings. *Melody Maker* had a global reach, a readership that cared enough about what it wrote to pay for it, and the clout that came with being the world's second-biggest music weekly. When you wrote things in *Melody Maker*, people noticed. An early instruction in this fact of my new life was the reaction to my review of *Deicide*, the self-titled debut album by execrable Satanist speed metal shredders Deicide.

'Whoever it was,' nudged my opening, 'who said that the Devil had all the best tunes never heard Deicide.' The review grew less complimentary from there. On publication, I was called by the press officer at Deicide's label, Roadrunner, who imparted the grim tidings that Deicide's major domo, Glen Benton, had cast a hex on me. Undaunted, a year or two later I would review Deicide's next album, as well, concluding with the challenge: 'Come and have a go if you think you're hard enough, you great fairy.' To date, I have suffered no ill effects as a consequence of my impertinence. Perhaps Benton is biding his time.[2]

---

2 Deicide were not the only Beelzebub-botherers to attempt to turn the Hounds of Hell loose in *Melody Maker*'s offices. One or other member of dreadful Bostonian Lucifer-lovers Upsidedown Cross often called the news desk, muttering imprecations and/or incantations, which would be put on speaker-phone for the enjoyment of all present. On one great occasion, he announced that he was going to cause the ghost of King Arthur to appear in the editor's

I was also acquiring – or, rather, was trying to figure out how one acquired – a taste for travelling on assignment. This had been one of the grand romantic thrills of reading *Melody Maker*, inflamed further when I started writing for *Melody Maker* – the stories filed from around the world, whether gonzo dispatch from the road or sit-down interview in some glamorous locale. Aside from the regular upheavals consequent of being the child of a soldier, I'd never really been anywhere. The people who were now my colleagues seemed to have been everywhere, several times over. I assumed that *Melody Maker* had an enormous travel budget which enabled this epic swanning. I was wrong. Almost all the travel of *Melody Maker* writers, it was explained to me, was underwritten by the record companies of the artists they were covering. I was mildly shocked by this, although not sufficiently that I made any binding statements of refusal to participate.

The beginnings of my own record-company-sponsored gallivanting offered but the faintest taste of the giddy thrill of travel paid for by someone else. I was flown to Glasgow for the day to interview never-quite-to-happen soul outfit Horse, and thought Glasgow gloomy, damp and handsome. I went by train to Manchester to review Aztec Camera, and thought Manchester gloomy, damp and ugly, though this mattered less than the fact that I got to stay in an actual hotel, with a television and a minibar and everything. Glasgow again to

---

office. After a few mumbled verses, our caller declared his abracadabra complete, and asserted that the royal phantom should now be swishing Excalibur in the vicinity of Allan Jones' desk. 'Wait a second,' said Mat Smith. 'I'll go and check.' Mat crossed the office, knocked on Allan's door, and asked if he'd bumped into King Arthur. 'Not today, old boy,' replied our chieftain. Mat returned to the news desk phone. 'Jonesy hasn't seen him,' he reported. There was a long pause, before the reply, 'That's strange . . .'

see The Wonder Stuff at Barrowlands, Manchester again for Pixies at the Apollo (still, probably, the greatest rock'n'roll show I've ever seen), Newcastle for the flour-dusted pomp of ludicrous goth-prog cowboys Fields of the Nephilim at the Mayfair, Milton Keynes for the exuberant camp nonsense of Erasure at the Bowl, Glasgow again for The Pogues at Barrowlands.

Going to concerts at the whims of Everett True was a random way to see a country, but an enjoyable one. Rail travel had not yet been ruined by the advent of mobile phones and other electronic moron distraction gadgets, and watching England from a train window is hypnotically agreeable, mile after mile of green pleasantness, rarely interrupted by anything offensively grotesque or divertingly marvellous.

By the summer of 1990, Clancy had left for Italy to spend some time studying in Perugia, and I'd relocated to a vast shared house in Streatham Hill, where £28 a week rented me the upstairs kitchen, into which I could just about fit my rucksack and myself, if I laid my sleeping bag diagonally across the floor with my feet underneath the sink. It was all I needed: I was rarely there. I went to gigs most evenings, and spent my days at *Melody Maker*. Sometimes I had a reason to go in, borrowing a spare desk to write my reviews. A lot of the time, I just went to hang out. So did the other writers and photographers. This was, like so much other human behaviour, dictated by the limits of technology – there was no other way to deliver copy, keep up with what was going on, pitch for work, kick ideas around and do all that other day-to-day stuff of journalism which can now be accomplished without leaving the house, enabling you to maintain long-term professional relationships with people you wouldn't recognise if they moved in upstairs. The convenience of all this is, well, convenient, but it has come at the cost of the camaraderie that used to make great publications great: it's hard for any title to cultivate a distinctive and coherent identity if the people who write it never meet each other.

Melody Maker's elder statesmen were more or less genial, despite appearances and/or reputation. The editor, Allan Jones, was a revered figure who had been with the paper since the mid-1970s, and was the subject of many anecdotes swapped in whispers among the rest of the paper's writers, all barely believable, many involving fistfights with rock stars, and most turning out to be true. The assistant editor, Steve Sutherland, was the paper's enforcer, his furiously riffed declamations against whatever had drifted into his sights a recurring refrain of the office soundtrack. Steve occupied the desk next to Everett, a set-up which offered passing writers a handy choice of passive and aggressive.

One afternoon, Everett was talking me painstakingly through something I'd written, outlining in his awkward, patient and kind way where I'd gone wrong – which was, in this case, just about everywhere. He gently critiqued and suggested and encouraged until Steve rose from his seat, leant over the partition into Everett's cubicle, and without acknowledging my presence said, 'Everett, for fuck's sake – just tell him it's bollocks and he has to write it again.'

A silence descended as Steve returned to his seat.

'Andrew,' said Everett evenly, 'this is bollocks. You have to write it again.'

Across the office from Steve and Everett, the news desk was manned by Carol Clerk and Mat Smith. The cupboards above them were plastered in cutout tabloid headlines featuring variations on the word 'scuppered'. Many journalists have a special fondness for certain words or phrases, and Carol and Mat treasured 'scuppered' above all others: a considerable proportion of their working week was spent attempting to lever it into the headlines on their pages.

Carol, usually addressed as Wee Clerkie, was a tiny Northern Irishwoman with violently dyed hair, a monstrous, gleeful cackle and a connoisseur's joyful love of all forms of profanity. She had been at *Melody Maker* since 1980, and was the incarnated spirit of the paper. Where many a lesser hack had found themselves ejected and/or disbarred from individual hostelries, Carol had once – in the company of Hanoi Rocks – been instructed to never again darken the doorstep of an entire country (Israel, which doesn't scare easily). She conducted journalism and hedonism with a no-nonsense purposefulness, equally regarding reporting and carousing as work to be done well and thoroughly, and displaying considerable enterprise and charm in both arenas. An assignment to New Jersey to interview Bon Jovi resulted in a permanent standing invitation to be a holiday houseguest of Jon Bon Jovi's mother. More than once, when seeking a taxi in London and finding none available, she simply planted herself in the rear seat of the next car that drew up, brandished a tenner and instructed the bewildered motorist as to her destination.[3]

Mat, Carol's deputy, was affectionately known as Black Mat Smith, due to a certain fondness for the dark side: several giant inflatable bats hung above his desk, which was also overlooked by a sign warning 'There will be no fire escape in Hell.' Mat was also known for his somewhat brisk manner with members of the public unfortunate enough to be put through to his extension. Once, I overheard one of Mat's interactions with our readers. It ran, in full, 'Hello?

---

3   Carol died of breast cancer in 2010, aged 55, which was far too short a time for her to be here, but there was no doubt that she made the most of it.

What? No, I'm afraid I don't have Phil Collins' tour dates to hand. And if you ever call this number again, I will destroy you.'

The policy of being rude to anyone who had the temerity to speak to us was observed until the glorious dawn upon which someone figured out that it was possible to patch incoming calls through to the telephones in the King's Reach Tower lifts.

*

Gradually, I chalked off the milestones of acceptance into the *Melody Maker* fold. I was asked to review some big London shows – Prince at Wembley Arena, The Cure at Crystal Palace Bowl. The former inculcated a horror of the freeform instrumental solo which endures to this day, Prince apparently motivated that evening primarily by a fear that anyone might have arrived unaware of his competence as a guitarist. The latter featured one of the most daringly jarring acts of stagecraft I've ever witnessed, a floral-shirted Robert Smith introducing the poignant, yearning 'Just Like Heaven' with the joke about the cheese and tomato sandwich that goes into a pub.

After much ostentatious hinting, I was permitted to review the singles. This was done over a page, and usually overnight – the assigned hack would occupy the room in the office which contained a stereo, and whittle the pile of singles sent in that week down to twenty or so which were excitingly good, entertainingly bad and/or by artists too big to ignore. It was the page on which *Melody Maker*'s best writers shone brightest, there being no end of room for digressions, jokes, manifestos and tangents. I played my first one pretty straight, awarding Single of the Week honours to The Pogues' slurred postcard 'Summer in Siam' and Cocteau

Twins' glistening 'Iceblink Luck'. I extended further hospitality to Janet Jackson's 'Black Cat' and The Jesus & Mary Chain's *Rollercoaster* EP, passed more-in-sorrow-than-anger judgement against That Petrol Emotion's 'Hey Venus' and The Fall's version of 'White Lightning', and gently clobbered bloated FM rockers Dan Reed Network and lager-sodden pub-rockers Quireboys.

I was also allowed to edit Backlash, *Melody Maker*'s letters page, for the first time. Backlash was, as a rock paper's letters page should be, a cross between a forum in which the clever and thoughtful could have their ideas discussed and debated, and a bear pit in which the daft and unhinged could be teased and taunted. Unlike the letters pages of most publications, rock magazines gave themselves the liberty of the last word, replying to readers in authoritative bold type. Editing Backlash involved selecting the most intelligent, amusing and idiotic dispatches that had arrived that week, typing them out, and adding replies. Among the contributors to my first Backlash were a concerned Christian aggrieved that we had recently featured Deicide, someone convinced that *Melody Maker* kept being rude about The Soup Dragons because The Soup Dragons were Scottish (that there might be a more prosaic explanation, i.e. that The Soup Dragons were really very bad, seemed not to have occurred to them), a couple of people wishing to insult *Melody Maker* writers who'd insulted artists of whom they were fond, and the sniffy Smiths fan without whom no music press letters page of the period was complete.

Even more excitingly, I was asked to be part of *Melody Maker*'s team covering the 1990 Reading Festival. I'd never been to a rock festival before, and I hadn't been a journalist on a British rock paper very long, so I wasn't aware that the likely reason I'd been asked was that nobody else would go unless chloroformed, bundled into a sack, driven to Berkshire and tethered to a stake in front of the main stage for the duration. Rock journalists hate covering rock festivals, especially once they've been to enough of them to realise that you can recreate the experience at home by turning a fire hose on your garden, neglecting to clean your bathroom for twenty years, inviting over loads of people you can't stand, ingesting terrible food, and listening for hours and bloody hours to music you hate.

I was assigned to review the festival's main stage on the Friday, opening day. It had everything that the opening day of a festival usually has. There were the unobjectionable, upbeat curtain-raisers (dreadlocked garage-poppers Mega City 4). The blustery stadium wannabes who've been signed by some major label that thinks they are going to be the next U2, and who are shortly going to be dropped because everyone else thinks they suck (Irish windsocks An Emotional Fish). The band you've really been looking forward to who've cancelled at the last minute because the singer has been stricken by 'laryngitis' (Jane's Addiction), a useful illness, almost as beloved of rock publicists as 'a stomach complaint'. The alterna-rock cult heroes (Seattle grunge godfathers Mudhoney, who bounded on stage with a merry cry of 'Hello, Glasgow'). The superstar DJ, inexplicably declared an attraction in his own right, rather than the space-filler between acts (Gary Clail, an early beneficiary of the bizarre extension of celebrity to people who inflict their record collections on others). The genuinely titanic, totemic artist, whose appearance at a festival feels somehow wrong and undignified, akin to seeing the Queen carrying shopping (Nick Cave and the Bad Seeds, as ever predictably awesome, like a geyser that regularly erupts mahogany furniture). The proper stadium band (Faith No More, who demonstrated the futility of seeing bands at festivals by looking fantastic but sounding like they were being listened to on next door's stereo by a thoughtful neighbour who was trying not to interrupt your nap). The living-legend headliners (The Cramps, whose T-shirts had been widely favoured by my peer group back at school, but who were fucking dreadful and actually kind of embarrassing, like bumping into your parents at a fetish ball).

Back in London, my working week continued to consist of days lounging around the office and nights attending gigs at the sort of venues, and by the sort of bands, where the representative from *Melody Maker* constituted a noticeable percentage of the audience (*Melody Maker*'s reviews sections were vast, and we therefore reviewed almost anybody who owned an amplifier). Most of these shows were terrible, as most bands are. The defanging of the British music press in recent years is mostly to be regretted – its once uncompromising asperity promoted some fierce and funny writing, and encouraged a fluid and fecund music scene by maintaining artists in a state of invigorating disquietude. But some of my critiques were disproportionately violent, in much the way that you'd think, on witnessing your neighbour weeding his lawn with a flamethrower, that he was overdoing it a little.

The Ogdens (at the Plough, Stockwell) were essentially well-meaning sorts, and at worst were doing nothing worse than inflicting dreary indie rock on a few dozen nodding students. They didn't deserve to read of their grim Wedding Present pastiches that 'We may well have to develop an entirely new regime of derision to deal with this.' Helter Skelter (the Falcon, Camden Town) were from the name down obviously cold-eyed chancers desperate to look and sound like the sort of thing that some thick major label A&R

type might mistake for edgy alternative rock, but everyone's allowed to dream. It wasn't fair to shake them – and any potential record company interest – awake with an opening paragraph reading 'Helter Skelter will have a major deal within a year, and a flop debut album within two. They will be vaguely famous for six or eight months and will be able to laugh witheringly at the dim dark days of yore when they were the first band ever to be compared to An Emotional Fish. And then they'll vanish.'

As it turned out, I rather overestimated their chances.

*

At the end of October 1990, I set off to meet Clancy in Italy so that we could serve our tours of a young Australian's duty, spending a few months annoying European rail commuters with our phrasebook direction-seeking and overstuffed rucksacks.

Melody Maker did not solicit my list of favourite albums of 1990, as by the time production deadlines for the Christmas issue loomed, I was somewhere in Hungary, Romania or what was then Czechoslovakia or what was then Yugoslavia, and therefore unreachable – a now barely imaginable state of being. If I had been asked, however, I'd have sent a postcard from Belgrade declaring myself for the following.

The Fatima Mansions, *Viva Dead Ponies*

This earth-scorching barrage was a survey of Cork-born Cathal Coughlan's adopted London as a Hobbesian dystopia, a filthy and heartless kleptopolis, a 'victim farm', its avaricious citizens bafflingly unperturbed by 'the queues, the burning trains, the squalid, mute despair,' and unheeding of a returned Jesus Christ – who, as the title track explained, was now operating, for reasons known only to his father, a newsagent's in Crouch End. At the heart of it fumed Coughlan as a sandwich-board Jeremiah balefully wandering the gold-paved streets, largely failing to interest passers-by in their impending doom. 'I could have been important,' he roared, 'if I'd been somebody else.'

Pixies, *Bossanova*

Bossanova suffered from comparisons to its predecessors, *Surfer Rosa* and *Doolittle* – two albums which demanded compulsive repeat playing if only to confirm that you really had just heard that. By the time *Bossanova* was released, Pixies had forfeited the element of surprise, and had been so mercilessly championed by the music press that their third album would have seemed disappointing even if it had proved capable of ridding the world of cancer, and Sting. Taken on its own merits, though, it's a brilliant and deranged synthesis of sixties psychedelia and seventies surf-rock: Dick Dale goes to the moon.

The Replacements, *All Shook Down*

The 'Mats sign-off: a careworn, downbeat farewell to a career-long saga of chronic self-sabotage about which Paul Westerberg sounded all at once apologetic, defiant and wistful. A decade or so on, I'd travel to Westerberg's native Minneapolis to interview him about his solo album, *Suicaine Gratifaction*, one of the more sensational entries in his lengthy catalogue of disregarded classics. Talking him through The Replacements' career, I noted that when the group released, in 1989, the album that was clearly supposed to be their tilt at mainstream success, they called it *Don't Tell a Soul*. 'Yeah,' he grinned. 'I never understood why some people got so angry that we weren't bigger, because it seems like they were also the people who wanted to keep us an underground cult, and not want anyone else to love us because we were their own precious little thing. Those who really know what we were, and what we were capable of, realise that that kind of success would have destroyed us all the faster.' Wise man.

The Sundays, *Reading, Writing and Arithmetic*

An album I listened to obsessively as I prepared to move to London. It was good practice for living among the British, as it turned out, for this was a record whose unmistakable subtext was 'Everything has already happened, we are dwarfish in the shadows of history, it's never going to stop fucking raining, and we must therefore wring what delight we might from small pleasures, however fleeting and inane they may be when set against the certainty of lonely death.'

The Chills, *Submarine Bells*

My personal history as a music fan has been characterised by a penchant for underappreciated genius, for the ill-rewarded caster of pearls before swine. A ruthless diagnosis might identify this as symptomatic of rampant snobbery. A more charitable one might acknowledge it as indicative of rarefied taste. The truth, I think, is that the greatest pop has beneath its surface froth an undertow of melancholy, and that few figures are so poignant as the artist who takes miracles to market only to see his stall ignored while assorted pedlars of mediocrity are trampled in the rush. Martin Phillipps of The Chills is just such a creature, conjuror of any amount of opulent majesty, rewarded by little more than respectable chart placings in his native New Zealand – something which could be organised by anybody with a large family. *Submarine Bells* essayed the magnificent audacity of opening with the aptly titled 'Heavenly Pop Hit', a song which recognised all at once its own brilliance and the total certainty that absolutely no bastard was going to buy it.

The Blue Aeroplanes, *Swagger*
All albums should start with the line 'Pick a card, any card. Wrong.'

Jane's Addiction, *Ritual de lo Habitual*
If you moved in alternative rock circles in 1990, proclaiming yourself in favour of *Ritual de lo Habitual* was an act of reckless individuality comparable with breathing air. However, there are occasions on which everybody else is right, and this was one of them, a dizzy glam romp which sounded like Marc Bolan being chased around the yard by The Stooges, both the Pop/Asheton/Williamson and Larry/Moe/Curly variations.

Happy Mondays, *Pills 'n' Thrills and Bellyaches*
Loved this at the time, as did everybody. Can't imagine that I've listened to it since. The curse of defining a moment is that you are doomed to live it forever, and this was the album that condemned Happy Mondays to an existence as their own tribute band. It didn't help that the follow-up, 1992's *Yes Please!*, was a record that accomplished little beyond demonstrating that crack-addled hubris can be incredibly boring; I was unable to resist the temptation to adorn Simon Reynolds' meticulously dismissive review with the headline NO THANKS.

Prefab Sprout, *Jordan: The Comeback*
Every note of these nineteen sumptuous ballads sounds like it was plucked or plinked with exquisite care by someone who might well have been wearing a cape. I eventually

interviewed Paddy McAloon in his native Newcastle in 1997, circa the release of Prefab Sprout's space-age country record *The Gunman and Other Stories.* I arrived at the appointed restaurant and saw a Panama-hatted figure dressed entirely in white, sipping lime and soda, and stroking his splendid eagle's nest of a beard as he read a second-hand biography of some early twentieth-century classical composer through the lens of an immense, ornate magnifying glass. I did not require the waiter's assistance to identify my table.

Midnight Oil, *Blue Sky Mining*

Their last great album: Midnight Oil's discography beyond this point represents a slow capitulation in their career-long struggle with their own earnestness. Not that their records up to and including this one had been short on zeal, but this had always been leavened by a sense of mischief, which in turn animated what was, lest anyone forget, a truly great rock'n'roll band. Beyond this, though, their hearts weren't audibly in it. Peter Garrett, as subsequent events would confirm, was unusual among rock'n'roll activists in being willing to attempt the difficult and compromising work of actually getting things done, as opposed to assuming the easy and gratifying pose of demanding that things be done.

11

IN WHICH THE AUTHOR
MANS THE HOME FRONT

When I returned to London in late January 1991, I discerned a minor but telling change in *Melody Maker*'s office decor. The wall behind the perennially unstaffed reception desk was adorned with a copy of E.V. Kealey's World War I recruitment poster, depicting a stricken wife, caught between grief and resolve, farewelling a platoon of khaki-clad riflemen, above the plaintive caption, 'Women of Britain say . . . Go!' In the Persian Gulf, Britain and thirty-odd other countries had gathered beneath the banner of Operation Desert Storm to chase Iraq out of Kuwait, and some wag had blu-tacked up this relic by way of ironic commentary. It jarred with me a bit, partly because I came from a forces family myself – albeit one thankfully untroubled by the demands of active service – but mostly because I couldn't figure out why it was there.

It may have been a subtle agitation in favour of peace, but I doubted it: while the individual politics of most *Melody Maker* writers tended towards *Guardian*-reading wishy-washy liberalism, their views on this war tended, like mine, towards the view that it wasn't like Saddam Hussein hadn't been asked nicely to knock it off. The poster may, alternatively, have been a humble acknowledgement that several thousand young Britons, of an age similar to that of many *Melody Maker* contributors, were about to be put to a stiffer professional test than filing a 700-word review of a Happy Mondays concert from a malfunctioning hotel fax machine in Sheffield while drunk, but I doubted that, as well: *Melody Maker* wasn't really in the business of humble acknowledgements.

It was, most likely, another instance of a fact of British – specifically, English – life to which I still hadn't attuned: an overarching carapace of irony which cannot be cracked even by the spectacle of their army carrying their flag into battle (or, in this case, into an exemplary arse-kicking of a hopelessly overmatched opponent). The English tendency to regard almost everything with wry amusement isn't necessarily a bad thing – especially when they bring that whimsical resignation to bear on personal or national misfortune. And it's certainly a less generally destructive thing than self-righteous passion. But it is a thing – and the reason why, in the main, the English make better pop stars than rock stars, and Americans make better rock stars than pop stars.

The lead news story of my first issue back – 2 February 1991 – rounded up the effects that Desert Storm was having on the world as *Melody Maker* covered it. Bomb the Bass and Massive Attack had changed their names for the duration (so had the Stud Brothers, now by-lined The Scud Brothers). Queen had hastily edited a new video to remove images of World War II bombardments, and The KLF had excised gunfire from the opening of '3 A.M. Eternal'. The BBC had distributed to local radio outlets a list of sixty-seven potentially inflammatory or insensitive records that DJs might think twice about playing, including The Bangles' 'Walk Like an Egyptian', Bruce Springsteen's 'I'm on Fire' and Maria Muldaur's 'Midnight at the Oasis' – but not, as *Melody Maker*'s report triumphantly noted, The Clash's 'Rock the Casbah' or The Cure's 'Killing an Arab'. Donny Osmond and MC Hammer cancelled UK dates, citing unwillingness to fly – twin blows which *Melody Maker*'s readers, to judge from the lack of outraged correspondence, appeared to absorb with laudable equanimity, almost as if they didn't care at all.

*

Clancy and I moved into the attic of a Muswell Hill terrace which had been subdivided into a teetering warren of bedsits. The teenage ska fan of just a few years earlier was tragically excited to have an address mentioned in a Madness song (Suggs announces his habit of driving to N10 in the last verse of 'Driving in My Car'.)

The first issue of *Melody Maker* I worked on after my return, cover date 2 February 1991, was – even by *Melody Maker*'s standards – a riotously eclectic farrago. There were feature interviews with dance acts Orbital and the artist shortly to be formerly known as Bomb The Bass, a profile of hip hop stars A Tribe Called Quest, and a lengthy update on the ongoing feud that had riven Spacemen 3. Elsewhere, the Stud Brothers interviewed a pimply, frantic Manic Street Preachers, which Tom Sheehan brilliantly illustrated by photographing the band's custom-stencilled shirts hanging on a bare wall. This was also the interview in which the Manics solemnly promised to record one thirty-song double album and then split, a death-or-glory declaration more properly rock'n'roll than any of the overgenerous catalogue of ballsachingly tedious albums they would go on to issue.

The issue's cover stars were Dream Warriors, a briefly stellar Canadian hip hop duo. Though the early part of the year was traditionally a period in which music weeklies would take the odd punt – the marquee names generally having made the rounds in the build-up to Christmas – Dream Warriors were a noteworthy gamble for an unworthy reason: King Lou and Capital Q, as the pair styled themselves, were black, and conventional wisdom had it that black artists didn't sell weekly music papers.

I never saw documentary evidence to support this, but I don't have much difficulty believing it. *Melody Maker*'s readership, like *Melody Maker*'s writers, were overwhelmingly middle-class white males, and largely preoccupied with music played on guitars (which, speaking as a middle-class white male largely preoccupied with music played on guitars, was one of the reasons I'd started reading the paper). The *Maker* had done some exemplary coverage of hip hop, but it was never a realm in which the paper seemed entirely comfortable: the only other black face to appear on the cover in 1991 was that of Seal, and that was a front page shared, as if in demonstration of irresolve, with grim Mancunian twonks Inspiral Carpets, and appalling prog hippies Levitation.

My own anguish at the Dream Warriors cover was, shamefully, less to do with the fact that black artists were underrepresented on *Melody Maker*'s cover than the fact that I was underrepresented in the paper's flying circus of globetrotting hacks. Everett had written the Dream Warriors piece from a wintertime Toronto. (It was a sign of my unworldliness that I was actually jealous, yet to learn that Toronto is essentially the set of a science-fiction horror movie in which the population of Canberra has been abducted and replaced with Canadians.) The cover of the 23 February edition was Steve Sutherland interviewing Perry Farrell of Jane's Addiction by a hotel pool in Hollywood. Two weeks after that, it was Ted Mico crawling Sunset Strip with The Charlatans. I was still stuck riding the rails for the live review section, schlepping to Leeds for Jesus Jones, Manchester for Ride, and to other even less glamorous locales for much less distinguished artists.

My luck finally turned – or, rather, my whining, wheedling and scheming was finally rewarded – with an overnight trip to Paris to interview Vini Reilly, the Durutti Column guitarist who had, a couple of years previously, broken from his usual avant-garde obscurity to provide accompaniment on Morrissey's solo debut *Viva Hate* (issued in Australia as *Education in Reverse*), which would be the last unatrocious album with which Morrissey would be associated.

Paris is one of those cities which radiates a collective municipal determination to live up to every clichéd expectation a newcomer may be nurturing, and the Durutti Column show I attended was gratifyingly athrong with beret-clad poseurs emitting drifts of putrid Gitanes smoke. But the pleasures of the location were merely a bonus – in the circumstances, I'd have been beside myself in hell, or even Geneva. I was abroad, on a feature assignment, even if only a quarter-page 300-worder, for *Melody Maker*.

Reilly was quiet, small and thin. It was suddenly impossible to believe persistent stories that he'd once been a good enough footballer that Manchester City had taken an interest – he looked like the least purposeful of tackles would snap him. He was also quite movingly fretful. Beneath the watchful gaze of his long-time manager and drummer, Bruce Mitchell – who wore a waistcoat, pillbox hat and monocle – Reilly worried aloud that his career-defining disdain for traditional musical form was an attempt to legitimise his own inadequacies as a communicator.

'I really envy people like Morrissey,' he whispered, 'because he can express things using words, which I don't seem to be able to do. I regard his art as superior to my thing.'

There would be, I observed, any number of articulate people who'd submit to some docking of their facility to be able to play guitar half as well as he could.

'I'd swap them any day,' Reilly replied, sounding sad.

*

Melody Maker's editorial process was a little more organised than *On the Street*'s. Every Tuesday, when the latest edition arrived in the office, there would be an editorial meeting, helmed by senior staff and attended by as many regular contributors as had managed to haul themselves out of bed (or, in the odd case, at least one of them distressingly long-term, out from their improvised accommodation beneath one of the desks). The new issue would be critiqued – largely, and in briskly expressive terms, by Steve Sutherland – and ideas for future editions would be submitted by writers, in tones ranging from blithe confidence to timorous terror according to length of service and certainty of tenure. The news editors, Mat and Carol, would announce their likely lead stories (it was in this context that I would have heard, for the first of many times, the standard music press euphemism for a slow week on this front: 'Glen Miller's still missing.') Gossip would be swapped. The pub, in due course, would be descended upon, and rarely deserted before closing time eleven or twelve hours later.

The cover of the 23 March issue was split three ways between Ocean Colour Scene, Chapterhouse and Moose. It seemed to have been decided somewhere, by someone, that a scene of some sort was afoot, constituted of fey, floppy-fringed waifs setting fragile, adenoidal melodies to churning squalls of effects-laden guitar, while observing an onstage and in-interview regime of withdrawn, apologetic self-effacement. The genre would eventually be shorthanded, with affectionate derision, as 'shoegazing'. Other pillars of this largely London-based movement, such as it was, included Lush, Curve, Slowdive, Swervedriver, *Melody Maker* favourites Ride and, at this early stage in their development, Blur. It wasn't hard to see where these groups were coming from – specifically, they were coming from The Jesus & Mary Chain's *Psychocandy* via My Bloody Valentine's *Isn't Anything* – but it was difficult to perceive them as heralds of a blinding new dawn, however good some of the records were (Lush's Robin Guthrie-produced *Mad Love* and Moose's Mitch Easter-produced *XYZ* have aged especially well).

Melody Maker tried, however. Steve Sutherland's breathless feature on Chapterhouse sought to cast them as a cadre of barricade-straddling shock troops poised to evict the entire rock'n'roll pantheon predating the Mary Chain's feedback-laced Year Zero. This was a stretch, given that Tom Sheehan's accompanying photographs depicted a bunch of heroically winsome young chaps in chunky, grandmother-knitted jumpers who looked as if they would have difficulty dislodging a cherry from a fairy cake (in due course, *Melody Maker*'s funny page, TTT, established the running joke of a Shoegazers' Beard-Growing Contest and ran the same clean-shaven portraits week after week). Ted Mico's Ocean Colour Scene piece attributed singer Simon Fowler's ardent embrace of his muse to a desperate desire to escape the suburban mundanity of Solihull, and compared it – one hopes deliberately archly, though it was sometimes difficult to tell with Ted – with Max Ernst's plunge into surrealism to occlude hideous memories of the Western Front.

It was all over the top by a sensational margin, but it was also *Melody Maker* – indeed, the music press of the time in general – at its frolicsome best. There was no way you could read this stuff and not want to hear Chapterhouse's

145

'Pearl' – and when you did track it down, you'd already be half persuaded that what was merely a decent alternative rock record was indeed a fanfare for a gilded epoch – and/or, probably more usefully, at least go and look up this Max Ernst character (*Melody Maker*'s forays into non-musical cultural references were an especial boon for someone who should have learnt this stuff at university, instead of dropping out of university to try to write for the music press). *Melody Maker* chose to believe that if our write-ups of certain artists were a street more exciting than their actual music, it was hardly our fault.

Now that I no longer had Australia to myself, my outings as an interviewer were initially confined to Sidelines, the section at the front of the magazine filled with short interviews with the up-and-coming, the nearly-but-not-quite-happening, the been-and-gone, and the odd act from outside the *Maker*'s usual indie rock remit to which one or other writer had taken a perverse or wilful liking. Sidelines' board of fare in the Ocean Colour Scene/Chapterhouse/Moose issue was pretty much representative.

The lead item, which consumed a full page, featured fervently touted (by me) and immediately ignored (by everyone else) Liverpool combination Fishmonkeyman. Elsewhere in the section, other writers made passionate – but, in posterity's judgement, misguided – arguments for the Magik Roundabout, Vicious Circle, Bourbonese Qualk, Dreamgrinder, Small Town Parade, Josi Without Colours, Cavedog, The Cuckoos and Love's Young Nightmare. Revisited, this section of *Melody Maker* has something of the poignance of war memorials: screeds of names of young people who set off on a great adventure with ambitions of changing the world for the better and perhaps accruing personal renown, only to be engulfed by oblivion (with the not inconsiderable difference that those who perish on the battlefield are deprived of the option of a subsequent career regaling taxi passengers with the anecdote about that time they opened for Mega City 4 at the Pink Toothbrush in Rayleigh).

Only two names from that issue's Sidelines have any resonance now (or, really, had any resonance then). One is that of Chicago-based noiseniks The Jesus Lizard, spotted early by the Maker's Jon Selzer, who would eventually appear on the Maker's cover, late in 1993. The other is that of Susanna Hoffs, recently ex of The Bangles, who was in London spruiking her debut solo single, 'My Side Of The Bed'. I volunteered to meet Hoffs in her Piccadilly hotel suite, partly out of an honest conviction that The Bangles had made some fine records – their 1984 debut, 'All Over The Place', in particular – and partly in the vague hope that, one day, an account of our unlikely introduction, fondly burnished over time, would delight our grandchildren.

In the event, the interview was unremarkable aside from what still ranks as the most shameless act of media manipulation to which I've ever been subjected, or to which I've submitted so gratefully. Barely had we shaken hands than Hoffs remarked admiringly upon the suede jacket I'd bought on my travels in Italy, and asked if she might borrow it to wear in the photos. The trouble with this tactic, of course – and, now that I re-examine the moment, the best argument that she might actually have been paying the only honest compliment on my dress sense I've received in my life – is that it probably only works if you look like or indeed are Susanna Hoffs, in which case you probably don't need to try that hard in the first place.

And while it was nothing to do with me, that same issue was also noteworthy for what was probably the cruellest

– and, not coincidentally, possibly the funniest – review of anything I ever saw *Melody Maker* run. Everett, in an act of fabulous malice, had not only asked the Stud Brothers to write up the new solo album by Martin Degville, former singer with annoying-in-the-80s scamsters Sigue Sigue Sputnik, but had permitted the Studs a quarter of a page over which to unload, space vastly disproportionate to Degville's standing in the cultural firmament of the time, which would have been more accurately represented by a misspelt photo caption in the third item down in the 'Where Are They Now?' column, if *Melody Maker* ran such a thing, which we didn't. The Studs began by noting that even the sorriest and least continent of the dishevelled denizens of the cardboard settlement which huddled near Waterloo Station could avail themselves of the consolation that 'Well, I haven't got a job, I live in a box, I'm a drunk, my wife and kids hate me and I haven't had a bath since October. But at least I'm not Martin Degville.' They ended by chiselling the epitaph 'Degville should forget it. He is small, undignified and ridiculous. A bat staring into the noonday sun.'

No music magazine would print a review like that anymore, still less the obvious and inferior imitation I dashed off a couple of weeks later when assigned Simple Minds' blood-freezingly banal *Real Life* (I hung the whole thing on a metaphor about a balloon which, overinflated with Jim Kerr's hot air, had not exploded dramatically, but instead had collapsed to 'one of those sad, shrivelled, scrotal husks left behind when the party is long over'). The reason that no music magazine would do that now is easily understood – they're fearful of alienating the readers and advertisers they still have, whereas music magazines of the pre-internet age could alienate their readers and advertisers all they liked, secure in the knowledge that there was nowhere else for their readers and advertisers to go. But it's a logic that denies a fundamental truth of the relationship that the sort of people who buy music magazines have with music: they love hating the music they hate nearly as much as they love loving the music they love.

This seething, superior rage at bad music ebbs with age, largely because you realise there are more important matters upon which you could be expending your energies. In this specific case, it ebbs even further when you find yourself, years later, alongside Jim Kerr on some radio panel, and he's charming and humble and even kind enough to laugh as if he hasn't heard it before when you interrupt his announcement that he's planning to open a sushi restaurant with a terrible joke about 'I Promised You a Mackerel'. But it never dies entirely, and it's one of the things that divides the music press reader – and certainly the music press writer – from the obviously better-adjusted majority. Most people simply ignore music they don't like. Only a few regard it as an insult.

*

I was beginning to feel, to my undimming disbelief and delight, like a nearly-fledged member of the flock. I had my own pigeonhole, which was gratifyingly stuffed with demo tapes, records, press releases and letters from readers, not all of them calling me a wanker. I'd begun venturing a tentative negative, on occasion, when Everett asked me to review especially dull-sounding gigs at the Venue or the Mean Fiddler – neither disagreeable rooms in and of themselves, but situated in parts of London, respectively New Cross and Harlesden, which I would later regard as having been useful background when I forayed into war correspondence.

And more weeks than not, I was now compiling the *Maker*'s gossip column.

This contained – as does every variety of showbiz coverage – two kinds of gossip. There was the prosaic but accurate, and the entertaining but invented. You can apply this sliding scale to the vast, absurd celebrity coverage of today with almost unswerving accuracy – the more lurid or scandalous a story is, the greater the likelihood that it is barely adulterated bollocks.

The stories I printed which were adjacent to reality tended to be wrap-ups of which musicians had been spotted at the after-show parties of which other musicians, freighted with the unsubtle implication that we had been there, and you, dear but pitiable reader, had not. Such gatherings, while sometimes entertaining in the way any party can be, were mostly an existentially terrifying psychological hall of mirrors, in which most of the attendees spent most of their time thinking 'Who the fuck are all these ghastly people?', the intensity of the enquiry and the emptiness of the answer building in proportion to the security of their own ego, which is why actually famous or powerful people almost never attended them, even when convened in their honour.

The rest was mostly stories which were, to invoke the escape clause beloved of generations of journalists, too good to check. If the press officer for one particular bunch of attention-seeking chancers told me that Basque separatist terrorists had hijacked a truck containing the entire Spanish print run of a New Fast Automatic Daffodils album, I couldn't be blamed if directory enquiries didn't have a number for the elusive guerillas of Euskadi Ta Askatasuna. This, at least, was what I told Allan Jones, for this was one of the rare occasions on which he was moved to emerge from his office with a printout of the copy and ask, 'Are you sure about this?' It is the measure of the man that when informed of the extent of my investigation, he replied with a benign beam, 'Ah, well. You tried.'

12

IN WHICH THE AUTHOR ATTEMPTS ROCK JOURNALISM IN THE LEAST ROCK'N'ROLL CITY IN AMERICA

If you're trying to understand a new country, there are few better ways to do it than by imbibing the works of, and the critical writing about, its artists – especially the successful ones, as they clearly speak for some constituency of their compatriots. I found myself in the privileged position of interviewing a few of these people, and by so doing was able to find out something about the people among whom I was now living.

For all that an Australian is conditioned to regard an Englishman as chinless, effete and duplicitous, a snaggle-toothed wearer of socks with sandals who probably has a collection of something, I found myself liking most Poms. They were funny but not oppressively zany, smart and self-deprecating, decent without making a show of it, heart-breakingly poleaxed by a desire not to offend. There were, however, exceptions to this latter characteristic.

I found The Wonder Stuff in the sort of ebullient form you'd expect in a young band who've just been told that their new single – in this instance, the terrific 'Size of a Cow' – was likely to enter that week's charts at number three. Possibly as a consequence of this, The Wonder Stuff were also minded to be unusually forthright about the aspects of their job they didn't like. Top of this list were their record company, of whom the band spoke in affectionately abusive tones, noting that their paymasters had thought the chart-busting 'Size of a Cow' an injudicious choice for a single. ('And right now,' sighed guitarist Malcolm Treece, 'they're probably getting well pissed and having a great knees-up at our expense, I imagine.')

The relationship between artists and their record companies, back when artists had record companies, was almost always a dysfunctional chemistry of mutual resentment. Artists generally regarded their record companies as a contemptible coven of venal halfwits, and record companies tended to view their artists as spoilt, snivelling prima donnas and/or clueless rubes who'd signed away their futures for a fistful of magic beans.

What I hadn't heard before arriving for this interview in a West London studio was the specifically English dismissal of all who dwell over the Channel or across the Atlantic: Johnny Foreigner. Monsieur/Herr/Senor/Signor Foreigner was, it seemed, a creature for whom The Wonder Stuff did not care overmuch.

'I am,' conceded fiddle player Martin Bell guiltily, 'slightly xenophobic.'

'There's this myth about touring,' explained drummer Martin Gilks, 'that it's like you're seeing the world, but you're not. You're stuck on a bus. I mean, I like going away, but I choose the places I want to go. So if you're on tour in Germany and you're bored and you can't get anything to eat, it's going to piss you off. Because you're not there to see Germany, you're there to play to some krauts. Whoops-a-daisy.'

While backpacking in Italy and Eastern Europe the year before, Clancy and I had run across the occasional outbreak of Englishness Abroad: the descendants of a people who'd once conquered and co-opted the world fussing about the tea in Naples, or complaining that they couldn't get a pint of flat, tepid ale in Prague.

'That's me!' announced singer Miles Hunt breezily. 'Like, Martin went off for two or three weeks to Thailand and all these other places. I can't fucking understand it. I mean, what the hell do you want to go there for? Why spend perfectly good money to go there? No, I'm quite happy here. If I want to see the world, I'll watch it on telly. I just feel uncomfortable anywhere else. I like my record collection, I like my telly, I like my cups of tea and my bacon sandwiches the way I cook them.'

Hunt's Wolverhampton whine lent the rant a melancholy pathos.

'You said all that,' reminded someone, 'about French food before we found that restaurant in Lyon.'

'One restaurant,' shot back Hunt, 'in a country ten times bigger than ours is no real recommendation.'

I asked if he'd ever attempted to put his feelings for J. Foreigner into song.

'Yeah, I have,' grinned Miles. 'This lot wouldn't play it, though.'

Hunt was regularly wigged by more right-on commentators of the time for these attitudes. I was perhaps mildly scandalised, but mostly uncomprehending – I wanted nothing more than to see the world, to go where I wasn't comfortable, to see and do stuff I had not seen or done. I'm not an Englishman, though, and so don't have the view of the world, and Europe in particular, that many of the English still do, even if they won't admit as much in public or to themselves: that it's a haphazardly stitched patchwork of Ruritanian fiefdoms teeming with silly and querulous folk who, every so often, cook up some grandiose and idiotic idea that will ultimately compel you, when it all goes tits up, to set aside your village cricket and model railways and spend the best years of your life waist-deep in Belgian mud eating rats in between artillery barrages.

The essentially genial Wonder Stuff were a convenient but insufficient warm-up for the next English curmudgeon I met. Whether or not it was someone's idea of a prank to pack me off to meet The Fall's Mark E. Smith I never discovered. If this was the case, whoever it was could only have been more pleased with the jape if Smith had actually chinned me – which, at a couple of points during our meeting, seemed a proximate possibility. Smith wasn't present when I reported to the designated rendezvous in the lobby of the Kensington Hilton. Instead, waiting for me was a pleasant enough chap called Simon, who introduced himself as The Fall's drummer. I was prepared to extend Simon the benefit of any doubt about this – he was over twenty-five and had a Mancunian accent, so even by April 1991, the chances that he had not at some point been in The Fall were statistically remote.

Simon explained that his boss would be along directly. My fervent hope that this was indeed the case was no reflection on Simon, who was entirely agreeable company. I was worried enough about meeting the legendarily cantankerous Smith. The prospect of returning to *Melody Maker*'s office with a tapeful of the insights of his drummer did little to settle my nerves.

Smith eventually sauntered into view, and dismissed Simon with a nod. Even before I switched on my recorder, I realised that I'd made two mistakes. One was to have shown up wearing shorts, only excusable in retrospect by noting that it was a warmish spring day, and that in 1991

I still had the legs for it. The other was to address Smith with an obviously antipodean accent. It was instantly clear that Smith was caught between amused disdain for his interlocutor, and disgust that *Melody Maker* had apparently dispatched some exchange program intern to interview him. He observed, in the tone of someone describing recent hernia surgery, that he had recently visited Australia. I asked if he'd had a good time.

'As good a time as you can have, yeah,' he spat.

Perhaps, I offered, his view of my homeland was somewhat clouded by the internecine squabbling which had led him to fire two more members of The Fall while he was out there.

'It's just such a wonderful place,' he sneered, maintaining a baleful monotone. 'The sun, the beaches. And I know so many people who want to go there, too. Poor kids. A year's savings, just to get on a plane. Bloody hell.'

The reason for our meeting was *Shiftwork*, The Fall's umpty-eighth album, and one of their very finest: a chrestomathy of vicious vignettes, incongruously leavened by the most straightforwardly pretty song in The Fall's canon ('Edinburgh Man') and one of the oddest cover versions ever recorded by anybody (a bleary boogie through the Big Bopper-penned country standard 'White Lightning'). My interview plan, already in an advanced state of unravel, had been to work backwards from *Shiftwork* in order to identify the place occupied by The Fall in the lineage of specifically, definitively English rock artists – alongside The Kinks, The Smiths, The Sex Pistols and others (such as The Wonder Stuff, say) for whom dissatisfaction was the ends as well as the means. Certainly, I suggested, perhaps impudently, it was impossible to imagine The Fall hailing from any other country but England. Smith responded to this tack with an expression of reptilian ennui.

'I don't really see any point in this line you're taking, Andrew,' he sighed. 'What are you trying to get at?'

I repeated my potted thesis, suggesting that The Fall, whether Smith liked it or not, were as English as abandoned Test matches. A lengthy silence ensued, during which Smith's sickly, greenish visage arranged itself slowly into the expression of someone wondering whether he can really be bothered thumping the person opposite. Though already starting to think that I might be better off presenting myself to my editors with a black eye than with the interview as it stood, I pushed on, remarking on comparisons made elsewhere between Smith and Ray Davies. To my surprise and inexpressible relief, Smith brightened somewhat.

'I find that a big compliment, yeah,' he enthused. 'The thing with The Kinks was that they didn't really appeal to the English, though. The English don't like being told things like that. But a lot of my stuff is pretty obscure. I'm not as disciplined as Ray Davies.'

I seized gratefully on this outbreak of humility, and tossed Smith the stock question of what he perceived as his own strengths as a writer.

'Well,' he replied, 'what do you think they are? This is a pretty one-sided interview, this, isn't it? So why, so where, so what? Let's have some opinions, man.'

I struggled to banish all thought of John Wayne's 'You want that gun? Pick it up' moment from *Rio Bravo*. I told Smith that my favourite Fall songs were the ones that made me laugh. 'Lucifer Over Lancashire', 'Shoulder Pads #1', 'Australians in Europe' (of course) and, on *Shiftwork*, Smith's gleeful *j'accuse* of television, 'A Lot of Wind'.

'Ah.' Smith brightened unexpectedly. 'That's good, that you like that one. It wouldn't be any good, see, if it wasn't delivered right. It's got to be done like that.'

Asked to elaborate, Smith chuntered cheerful contumely about the programs that inspired it – chiefly the daytime burlesques in which aggrieved peasants were goaded by a sanctimonious host and a studio audience of screeching imbeciles in tracksuits into inflicting unnecessary intimacies upon the viewer, an American invention which had recently washed up on British shores. Almost as if concerned at appearing untowardly affable, Smith caught himself, narrowed his eyes, and declared, 'Australian telly's worse.'

I disputed this, as far as I dared. And then asked Smith what he made of the then-popular David Lynch serial, *Twin Peaks*. Smith said nothing. Filling the silence, concerned that he was about to fall asleep or start hurling furniture, I opined that it was rubbish.

'It is!' whooped Smith, absolutely banging a fist on the table. 'It's crap! And no one will own up to it, will they? It's not as a good as *Dallas*, is it? Do you want a drink?'

This was more like it. Smith was off, a sudden gust of anecdote culminating in the verbatim recitation of a recent, ill-advised appearance by Jason Donovan on Dame Edna Everage's chat show. He confessed to the habit of videotaping the hapless *Neighbours* star's television appearances: clearly, there was at least one Australian who amused him.

It took me years to figure it out, but the crucial attribute of the English is their anger. Their great modern artists, especially their great songwriters, are all disappointed misanthropes – it is impossible to imagine English people even attempting to make music approximating the optimistic joy of Bruce Springsteen or the guileless passion of U2, and even harder to imagine how ridiculous they'd appear if they tried. The English may try to sublimate this intense and animating rage in layers of irony and wit, and sometimes they may even succeed, but the truth is that at twitching heart they're furious – with each other, themselves and almost everybody else.

There was a curious postscript to my encounter with Smith. Eight months later, *Melody Maker* sent its annual end-of-year questionnaire to assorted luminaries from the world of alternative rock. Among the queries on this census was 'What was your highlight of 1991?' In a possible bid for inclusion in the *Guinness Book of World Records*, establishing a new category for Most Sarcastic Retort, Smith answered 'Meeting that Australian journalist from *Melody Maker*.' Back at you, Mark. Right back at you.

*

While there was no doubt, at least not in my mind, that London was the centre of the strange little ecosystem that was the rock press, I was equally and frustratedly certain that you were not really a proper rock journalist until you'd been one in America. The *Maker*'s senior writers continued to shuttle back and forth across the Atlantic with enraging frequency, returning with tales from places which were mentioned in rock songs (while there are also many British places mentioned in rock songs, this usually happens only when they are indicted as the place the singer wishes to leave, while Americans tend to sing about where they wish they were – and, as a consequence, where we wish we were).

I was, at least, getting to interview some American rock singers as they passed through London. Grant Hart, formerly of Hüsker Dü, now of Nova Mob, was as tiresome as he was tired, a man at the end of both a lengthy promotional schedule and his reserves of will to live. I thought him a petulant pain in the knackers, and I probably wasn't entirely mistaken, but it can't be much fun promoting a record nobody is really interested in to the fifteenth spotty herbert that day alone who only wants to ask about 'Don't Want To Know If You Are Lonely'. Bongwater – a collaboration between Shimmy Disc impresario Mark Kramer and actor Ann Magnuson, who had made an inspired album-cum-manifesto entitled *The Power of Pussy* – turned out, disappointingly, to be subscribers to the addle-pated dogmas of conspiracy theory (JFK, AIDS and so on), and as over-keen to explain their views in relentless detail as such people always are. The interview was useful only for Kramer's excellent credo, 'I want, and I think I'm speaking for Ann here too, I just want to ride my machine and not get hassled by the man.'

Michael Gira of Swans was less forbidding than his records, drawing on a cigar and drawling quips of impeccably turned wryness. Swans' records had recently evolved from putrid, piledriving noise, evocative of a bulldozer ploughing up a cemetery, to baleful acoustic folk, the sort of thing that might have been written by court jesters of yore to commemorate an especially bad month on the Black Death front. My favourite song on Swans' new album, *White Light From the Mouth of Infinity*, knelled 'Na na na na, why are we alive?'

'Yeah, I thought that was pretty funny,' said Gira, whose resolutely sombre demeanour and aristocratic visage rather put me in mind of Sam, the perpetually unamused eagle from *The Muppet Show*. 'But no one ever asks that, do they?'

Least of all twenty-two-year-olds such as my then-self, desperate to wring all they can from their good fortune before someone realises there's been some sort of mistake. There have been actual members of actual poor, huddled masses less keen to get to the United States than I was. The difficulty, as I was beginning to discern, was that the plum American trips tended to be for stories about big-name artists, which meant they usually got snapped up by the editorial grandees who had long-standing relationships with the record companies and independent press offices who laid these junkets on. What I needed was an act who met the following criteria: album or tour imminent; either American or going to be in America; well-known enough that they'd have a record company with a promotional budget; not so well-known that they'd have been pushed at the paper already; yet big enough, or potentially big enough, that the *Maker* would agree to at least a page. (Though the paper's folklore did contain tantalising tales of desperate or gullible or foolishly magnanimous record companies flying writers to New York to write a 300-word gig review, they usually wanted reasonable space guaranteed before they'd cough up the airfare.)

I noticed, leafing through *Melody Maker*'s news pages one Tuesday morning, that a new Violent Femmes album – their fifth, *Why Do Birds Sing?* – was imminent. The Femmes, I thought, might fit the bill. They were cultishly adored and critically admired without being especially famous or fashionable. The *Maker* might part with a page near the back, and their record company might play along for that amount of space. My fondness for this idea was not exclusively cold calculation. I adored Violent Femmes. In another of those inexplicable long-range cultural exchanges of the pre-internet era, Violent Femmes' self-titled 1983 debut had been a massive hit among the teenage bohemians of Sydney's lower North Shore: it would have been an unusual party I attended during fifth and sixth form at which the windows did not rattle to Gordon Gano's lust-wracked whining of 'Add it Up' and 'Gone Daddy Gone'. 'Blister in the Sun' was the first thing I'd learnt to play on my first guitar (it was a significant element of that album's charm that it sounded like the same was true for Gordon Gano).

I called Violent Femmes' UK record company and airily enquired as to whether the group might be coming to the

UK to promote the album, or if, uh, maybeIcouldgotoAmericaandinterviewthemthere. The record company asked how big a piece I was thinking of. I could only answer this by getting the idea past Ted Mico, *Melody Maker*'s features editor. I approached his desk and delivered a passionate pitch for Violent Femmes, suggesting that they retained a keen following (they might have), that *Why Do Birds Sing?*, a throwback to the acoustic angst of their first and best-loved album might well add to said keen following (not absolutely impossible), and that the single from it, the sarcastic sing-along 'American Music', was getting radio play (probably the case, though on precisely which station I would not have wished to be pressed). Furthermore, I elaborated, Gordon Gano was a massively underrated songwriter, a key link in a chain connecting the guilt-ridden, God-plagued, sin-tempted torment of Jerry Lee Lewis, the art-school Americana of Jonathan Richman, the beat absurdity of current *Maker* favourites like Pixies, and . . .

'Huh?' interrupted Ted, squinting at something on his computer. 'Uh. Yeah. Cool. Whatever. Keep it to a page.'

Trying not to sound like a man claiming a lottery win, I called the Femmes' record company again. There was good news, they said, and bad news. The bad news was that Violent Femmes weren't playing right now, so there would be no opportunity for the proper on-the-road story I'd been hoping for, having imagined, in the few steps from Ted's desk to a spare telephone, my immediate future as, essentially, Grand Funk Railroad's *We're an American Band*, a vista of the United States smeared across a tour bus window, in a haze in Little Rock, etc. The good news, however, was that Gano would be doing interviews. In New York.

The game was now afoot. The trick with American trips, as I had enviously gleaned from my superiors, was to prolong them. Once the relatively expensive trans-Atlantic flights were secured, the next move was to ring round every other record company, finding out which artists were available stateside – I may well, I fear, actually have used the word 'stateside' – at that moment, and seeing if you could leverage internal flights and hotels in return for coverage. The logistics were complex, and the resultant schedules could be murderous – as dazed hacks found themselves deposited in, say, Chicago, Albuquerque, Calgary and Miami on different tours on consecutive days – but the office's black-belt scammers, like Everett, Steve and Ted, could exile themselves for weeks at a stretch.

Lacking contacts and confidence, all I elicited was a nibble from the handlers of Soho, Londoners who'd recently enjoyed a hit with 'Hippy Chick', a slinky tune built atop a sample of Johnny Marr's shuddering introduction to The Smiths' 'How Soon is Now?' I'd met Soho earlier in the year, when they'd opened the Jesus Jones show I reviewed in Leeds. They were now in the US as the support act of Jesus Jones' tour there, and for a lead live review in *Melody Maker*, necessary arrangements could be made. After I was done in New York, I could catch their show in Salt Lake City.

One reaps diminishing returns from most things one does repeatedly, but even though I've taken the ride dozens more times since, the yellow taxi from JFK to Manhattan has paled not one shade. Something about America encourages a certain shedding of one's psychological armour, and attendant pre-ironic behaviour. In the iPod age, if making this trip alone, I'll set the view to an appropriate playlist of songs about New York, or by New Yorkers, or both (Blondie's 'Union City Blue', Steve Earle's 'NYC', Ramones' 'Rockaway Beach', Tom Waits' 'Downtown Train', Simon & Garfunkel's 'Only Living Boy in New York', Leonard

Cohen's 'First We Take Manhattan', The Magnetic Fields' 'Luckiest Guy on the Lower East Side', both the Ryan Adams and Frank Sinatra variations of 'New York, New York'). It says much about the effect of travelling to the United States that I don't feel self-conscious doing this, nor about announcing to the vast readership of this bestselling memoir that I've done it.

Listening to anything on my Walkman on that first ride in would have been an immense discourtesy to my travelling companion, *Melody Maker* photographer Stephen Sweet, a burly, shambling Geordie accompanying me on what would be the first of many foreign escapades together, and an especially treasurable boon companion on this one. Though Sweet had been to America often, he allowed me to enjoy my first time properly, i.e. in a state of naive near-hysteria. He did not, in response to my many breathless observations at New York's overwhelming New Yorkness, make a single patronising remark to the effect that the place wasn't what it once had been.

We stayed at the Gramercy Park Hotel. The Gramercy Park was a rock'n'roll hotel, like Hollywood's Hyatt on Sunset, or London's Columbia – an establishment which, for reasons nobody seems too clear on, has become the city's crashpad of choice for generations of touring artists. You never know it to look at them – the Gramercy Park was by all appearances just another moth-eaten three-star sort of place. You just have to know. Knowing it about the Gramercy Park permitted the illusion that one might have been occupying a room once dreamt in by Bob Dylan, David Bowie or Joe Strummer – it was certainly imaginable that their very fists had once rained similar encouraging blows upon the same antique, malfunctioning television sets. As if that wasn't exciting enough, the Gramercy Park is on Lexington Avenue, which is mentioned in a Velvet Underground song. My pleasure at this was diluted not even slightly by the fact that Lexington Avenue is a long street, and that the precise address of Lou Reed's rendezvous with his dealer in 'I'm Waiting For the Man' was 104 blocks away.

All of which, it turned out, was more rock'n'roll than the actual act of rock'n'roll journalism we'd gone there to do. The interview with Gordon Gano occurred in his record company's offices in the gleaming high-rise corporate labyrinth of the Rockefeller Centre. (Sweet, initially despondent at the lack of interesting backdrop for the accompanying portrait, eventually found a decorative jukebox in the reception area, which echoed the theme of 'American Music' nicely). Gano himself was as unlike a rock star as Ozzy Osbourne is unlike driven snow. 'The last time I saw anyone quite like Gordon Gano,' my introduction would eventually assert, 'he was beating a swift and undignified retreat across the front yard, pursued by the cat and assorted well-aimed vegetables and leaving a trail of hastily jettisoned pocket bibles in his wake. Today, everything about [Gano] seems polished and buffed to a high sheen, his smile, his shoes, his glasses, his manners.'

This was poetic exaggeration as regards my own behaviour – I've never really thrown groceries at an evangelising doorknocker, though I've asked a couple for their home address and the time they expect to be relaxing in the bath next Saturday – but it was an accurate rendering of Gano. I knew that Gano had some sort of a thing about God – much though I'd loved that first Violent Femmes album, I harboured a minor preference for its successor, 1984's *Hallowed Ground*, which sounded like a punk group from Milwaukee trying to teach itself to play country gospel, because that's exactly what it was. I just didn't know how to broach the subject, quite. I'd been raised by unbelieving parents in a country where religion is generally regarded as an eccentric hobby, engendering a lifelong blind spot where interviewing the devout is concerned. Part of me always wants to say, 'But seriously, off the record – you don't really buy this colossal crock of cowfeathers about flying horses/talking snakes/six-armed elephants, right?' So I asked Gano about what I referred to as his 'infatuation' with gospel music.

'Well,' he replied, 'you say infatuation, I would just call it love. To me, that's a very significant point. As much as I love the music, as a style or whatever, the driving motivation for me is really the spiritual content of the lyrics. I grew up going to church every Sunday – my father's a minister – and for me in my life, words that to certain people may sound clichéd, for me really are symbolic of the most positive experiences in my life. They really are a source of strength.'

It was a good answer, the gentlest of rebukes to my implicit assumption that a fondness for gospel, like a reverence for God, must be essentially ironic, or even fraudulent – and a reminder, to me anyway, that people often made the same assumption about my own increasingly nagging affection for country music (though I'm still sure jazz fans are only pretending). It was also a useful caution about our next port of call.

*

We flew to Salt Lake City via Cincinnati, an experience unremarkable in every respect, except that I found every respect of it remarkable. For the geekish aficionado of popular song, any such workaday yomp across the United States is powerfully evocative. You may be tired, hungover and drinking the bad coffee in which America specialises in a nondescript regional airport, but you're tired, hungover and drinking the bad coffee in which American specialises in the nondescript regional airport which services the city about which The Walker Brothers sang 'Lights Of Cincinnati', Dwight Yoakam sang 'South Of Cincinnati' and Ray Charles sang 'Cincinnati Kid'. And said city is, of course, in the state about which Neil Young sang 'Ohio', Phil Ochs sang 'A Boy in Ohio' and almost everybody has sung 'Banks of the Ohio'. Although the airport actually lies over the border in Kentucky, so that's The Louvin Brothers' 'Kentucky', Stephen Foster's 'My Old Kentucky Home' (via Randy Newman's waspish rewrite) and Bill Monroe's 'Blue Moon of Kentucky'.

For these reasons and many others, and although my travel ambitions were indiscriminate and limitless – we only get to inhabit this planet once; it seems sensible to try to see as much of the place as possible – the United States was always likely to debut at the top of my list of favourite places to visit, and to stay there ever after. Such sealing of the deal as was still necessary was accomplished by the nature of my introduction to it. A planet that can accommodate New York City and Salt Lake City is remarkable enough. A country that can do it is . . . well, it's America.

Prior to arriving in Salt Lake City, I'd only spoken to Mormons in somewhat tense circumstances, often grasping a bath towel about my sodden form and occasion- ally thinking, 'Bloody hell, it's Gordon Gano of Violent Femmes.' I thought vaguely that it might be fun, now that I was in their neighbourhood, to knock on a few doors and ask whoever answered if they'd considered the possibility that all faiths were a cross between a pyramid scheme and a protection racket, and that God has been created by man as an authority for tyranny and excuse for irresponsibility. But everybody was – as everybody in America almost always is – disarmingly nice. You don't go around telling the truth to

Americans in the same way that, however Scrooge-like your own proclivities, you don't acknowledge the festive season by hanging an effigy of Santa Claus outside the gates of the local primary school.

I didn't get much chance to expand my circle of Mormon acquaintances. Salt Lake City was my introduction to rock'n'roll tourism, a frustrating pastime which involves absorbing the essence of a place between touchdown and soundcheck, or soundcheck and show, or – though this is obviously a desperate measure – in the morning, before everybody else gets up. So I fleetingly admired the wide streets, which reminded me of those in country towns back in Australia. I caught a sufficient glimpse of the surrounding mountains to perceive that they were pretty. I took a photograph of the home of Brigham Young, the fulminating dingbat who had led the Mormons to Utah in the 1840s and founded the city. I briefly visited the Latter-Day Disneyland of Temple Square. I learnt very little about the people who'd built this place, or why they'd come here, or what they believed – about as little, indeed, as they'd ever learnt about evolution, science, reason, that kind of thing.

Mormon theology was not, at any rate, my priority. I had grander ambitions than reviewing Soho – indeed, grander ambitions, according to my narrow sense of priorities, than leading my persecuted brethren on an epic trek across hostile wilderness in search of a place where we might practise our faith unmolested. *Melody Maker* had recently been trying to land an interview with Jesus Jones, who had grown suddenly enormous – 'Right Here, Right Now', the single which had got Jesus Jones a black and white page near the back of the paper when I'd interviewed them in London upon its release a few months before, had become a colossal global hit, capturing something of the optimism of the immediate post-Cold

War period (in America, it reached number two). We had been knocked back, however, probably because some sort of exclusive had been stitched up with another publication. My hope was that I could capitalise on our earlier acquaintance by approaching the band directly – artists were generally unaware of, or indifferent to, the politicking that attended their press. My giddy fantasy was that this might earn me, for the first time, *Melody Maker*'s cover.

My plan consisted, I explained to Sweet, of waiting in the hotel lobby until Mike Edwards appeared. We did. He did. We asked if he fancied being interviewed for *Melody Maker* again, and possibly appearing on the cover thereof. He did.

Being a rock star appeared to be agreeing with him.

'This is all brilliant,' he declared. 'This is as much fun as you could ever possibly have.'

It is, indeed, fun being in – or being with – a rock group at this point in their career, as they adjust to the idea that the vehicle they have assembled from ambition, ego, talent and sweat actually flies. The bills that hobbled their early endeavours are being paid without them noticing the bills were ever there. The girls whose rejections inspired their songs in the first place are queueing outside the dressing room. The lyrics that were written in the forlorn hope that someone, somewhere, might somehow understand are being dutifully chorused by choirs of the devoted.

'That's what it's all about,' confirmed Mike. 'I've been obsessed with fame, with rock bands and with fame, since I was five years old.'

Mike had toiled doggedly to haul Jesus Jones from their first London pub gig to a sold-out headline spot at Salt Lake City's Fairgrounds Coliseum in a little over two years. Mike, unlike most people in his line of work, was unabashed about admitting this – even on tour, he was awake early, planning, writing or exercising. A decade and a half later, I'd be a beneficiary of Mike's dauntless determination – it would be his drive that turned my midlife crisis and half-considered whim into a functioning, recording country group. (Feel free to purchase The Blazing Zoos' critically acknowledged debut album, *I'll Leave Quietly*, to which Mike contributed exemplary lead guitar, and on which Jesus Jones' drummer of this period, Gen Matthews, played drums. A few copies remain available. Quite a few, in fact.) Mike's post-rock star career, to which he is entirely suited, is fitness instruction.

Back in the UK, Jesus Jones had endured a critical backlash which seemed far more personal than artistic. The same journalists – especially the more anxiously middle-class ones at the *NME* – who'd championed Mike when they thought he was a snarling skate punk from the mean streets of Finsbury Park had cavilled on discovering that he was, in fact, a courteous, civilised and well-spoken chap in the regular habit of reading unillustrated books. In America, nobody seemed to object to this.

'It's when you come out here,' said Mike, gesturing out the window at the proverbial mountain majesty, 'you can understand that "Joshua Tree" thing, you can understand why people do that. It looks so crap, back in England, when people do that and this Americana overcomes them, but the thing with America is that there's so much enthusiasm, so much exuberance. And it's such an incredible place, such a momentous place. The scale of it, the physicality. Everything about it is designed to impress you. No wonder the pioneers all went God-crazy.'

Nowhere more so than around here. In Utah and in some similarly inclined parts of the US, Mike's band were billed on posters as 'J. Jones'.

I got my cover. A week's worth of visits to London newsagents to commit surreptitious rack-shuffling and pile-stacking to ensure maximum visibility for *Melody Maker*, and to occlude the *NME*'s Ice-T exclusive, ensued.

13

IN WHICH THE MONKEY BECOMES THE ZOOKEEPER

The issue of *Melody Maker* which featured Mike Edwards gurning triumphantly from the cover, above the headline JESUS SWEPT! JESUS JONES CLEAN UP IN AMERICA was also the first in which my name appeared on *Melody Maker*'s masthead as reviews editor. This promotion occurred more or less by osmosis. My early patron, Everett, had been asking me to oversee the reviews pages during his increasingly heroic sponsored absences writing about cacophonous American hairies to whom I couldn't imagine anyone was ever going to pay attention (Nirvana? Hole? Mudhoney? Soundgarden? Surely he was making some of these up). So when Everett persuaded Allan to designate him staff writer so he could spend even more time in the United States drinking other people's expense accounts, I happened to be sitting in his chair, so there I stayed.

The fates, as the fates will, attached a hefty caveat. While ever greater quantities of everything I'd ever wanted were being delivered, Clancy was working in a sandwich shop. Making sandwiches is a respectable occupation – sandwiches won't make themselves, and anybody who provides sustenance and nourishment is certainly doing a more useful day's work than, for example, someone who makes fun of Elvis Costello's beard for a living – but Clancy felt, correctly, that it was not the optimum use of a considerable mind. She was bored, frustrated and homesick, and living with someone who was having far too good a time to notice. Sometime during the summer, we made the sensible and mature decision that she'd return to Sydney while I milked my good fortune in London. I'd spend quite a lot of the imminent future believing sense and maturity were overrated components of decision-making.

Though describing any aspect of rock journalism as work is inviting a clamour of derision, serving as reviews editor came perilously close. My job was to commission and edit everything in the live and album review sections – assigning writers and photographers, choosing pictures, writing headlines, chasing tardy copy, supervising layouts. In that 13 July 1991 issue which featured Mike on the cover, this amounted to twenty-nine individual reviews, and that was a relatively thin issue. The technology of the time also meant that every conversation about every one of those pieces had to happen on the phone, a device whose drain on my time I quickly grew to resent. It wasn't just that I had to call a lot of people – it was that lots of people called me. Lots and lots. Phone-ringing-again-the-second-you-put-it-down quantities of them.

They were within their rights to do this – they were mostly press officers trying to scare up space for their artists. But I was really very busy, and the ring of any telephone translates essentially as an aggressive demand of 'Stop whatever you're doing, and pay attention to me!' (Really, when you think it through, it's incredibly rude to ever call anyone, unless you're trapped beneath a fallen wardrobe.)

It was never a deliberate decision, but I developed a habit of being what a tactful obituarist might describe as 'brisk'. A representative conversation of the period went thus:

Probably Quite Nice Press Officer Calling on Deadline: 'Hello, I was wondering if *Melody Maker* will be sending a reviewer to see Paris Angels this week?'

Me: 'No.'

PQNPOCOD: 'Ah, that's a shame. May I ask why not?'

Me: 'They're crap, and we hate them.'

(They were, and we did, but good manners cost nothing.)

Inevitably, I earned a name for being a graceless berk who confirmed every stereotype that Barry McKenzie had suggested of my people. I found this more amusing than I should have. I also acquired a reputation for undue lordliness towards certain of the paper's roster of freelancers. This was doubtless due largely to the fact that I was insufferably pleased with myself, but it may have been amplified by my habit of keeping my directory of writers arranged within an oval on my computer screen in the formation of an Australian Rules team. Writers are frail and nervous enough without having to wonder whether being a half-back flanker is a good thing or not.

There was no shortage of people wanting a guernsey. The other species of enquiry I received regularly was from people who wanted to write for *Melody Maker* – I was now occupying the same position that Everett had when I'd first written to him. Everett, a creature of prodigious and barely discriminate enthusiasm, had operated something of an open house policy, granting column inches to almost any half-competent, barely qualified blockhead who fancied their chances – he had, for example, hired me. Possibly hypocritically, I was determined to impose more exacting – i.e. any – standards.

The first order of business was cashiering some of ET's more outré recruits. Most took the hint after a couple of weeks of solid negative response to everything they suggested. Only one proved tougher to shake, a transvestite weirdo (this reference is purely descriptive, there being no reason why cross-dressing should impede literary prowess, to say nothing of the vast acres of empty space that would have been left on *Melody Maker*'s pages following the institution of a no-weirdos regime). He just couldn't write. He continued to phone in ideas for reviews, with the heartbreaking diligence of a dog howling on the grave of its master, for months past the point at which I'd run out of synonyms for 'when Beelzebub buys mittens'.

I was also more ruthless about responding to the babbling stream of letters from hopefuls. Most of them were just boring – earnest, predictable, unable (and, on the available evidence, unlikely) to conjure the phrase or observation that lodged in the head or heart. Their efforts went into the bin (and later, in a couple of cases, to my smug delight, into the *NME*, clearly their second choice). A few submissions, however, were distinguished by such sensational ineptitude and/or insanity that it seemed folly to throw them away, on the grounds that they might provide the office with merriment on slow afternoons for years to come. These went into a khaki binder labelled – I report this with no pride whatsoever – The Mong File. (Many editors of my acquaintance retain such an archive, often – though this excuses nothing – nearly as crassly named: I have heard, in my time, of a Fuckwit Folder, a Dickhead Drawer and a Twatheap.)

The leading cause for inclusion in the File was pretension. This was almost invariably the consequence of trying to write like Simon Reynolds, which is difficult if you're not as smart as Simon Reynolds, and almost nobody is. The all-time, all-comers champion in this field was a review of indie gloomsters Cranes at the Coventry Tic Toc, which commenced with the following beguiling sentence:

> When the trajectory of Manchester's phantasmic effervescence is so strategically semiological, the vacuous product of pied-piper [Tony] Wilson's strutting marketeering of simulated perspectival space through a stroboscopic hyper-radiation of the Symbolic, Cranes are the necessary by-products of the excremental culture, the clammy arhythmic racket of the death-throes of referential finalities, the Lynchian underside of the terroristic valuelessness of the floating signifier.

This, at least, was the order the words happened to be typed in: it made precisely as much sense whichever way you jumbled them.

Dullness could earn a place in the File, but it had to be the truly rarefied stuff, the sort of plodding drear that challenged the stamina of your eyes, as they struggled to remain open to the end of the paragraph. The guiltiest were usually those who rather overdid the backstory, like the would-be reviewer of a show by Ala-Tex (me neither) at the Albany:

> I met my friends at Great Portland Street tube and we were deciding where to go when over the noise of passing traffic came something very pleasing. We decided to investigate.

Or, better yet, from a review of The Velvet Underground on their reunion tour:

> When I was just a kid, in 1967, I was in New York for two hours. My Dad took us in a yellow cab from JFK to La Guardia to catch a connecting flight to Atlanta. I had not heard of The Velvet Underground, and I doubt whether my folks had.

This continued in a similar vein for some considerable yardage, before bowing out with the splendid closing lines:

> Everything we had but couldn't keep. Not that it was anything to do with me, but a year after we moved to the States, Martin Luther King and Robert Kennedy were dead. So there you go.

On the occasions on which readings from the File were conducted, this was one of the most often requested.

I also had a soft spot for hopefuls whose preparations for making their pitch had clearly not involved reading *Melody Maker* in the last thirty years or so. These tended to be peppered with jocular outbursts, inane hyperbole and passe hipster-speak, and always put me in mind of those pop pages in regional newspapers, atop which some semi-suicidal middle-aged hack in a straining leather jacket leans resignedly against his own by-line. Examples included: 'The end of the first song set the scene for what was going to be a great night of R'n'B. The crowd went wild!' (Ruthless Blues, apparently, at the Oxford Brewhouse); 'Ned's Atomic Dustbin get down to what they're good at – entertainment' (disputable opening to review of said group at NightTown, Rotterdam); 'This four-piece set-up hailing from another planet descended on

SW6 and took prisoners, so open your mind and prepare to be challenged' (introduction, implausible at a number of levels, to Kastravelva at the Kings Head in Fulham).

The swiftest route into the File, though, was the maladroit simile or metaphor. When regular contributors perpetrated such an infelicity, I'd call and ask them to draw the image they'd conjured, then fax it to me. Tempting though it was, I inflicted no such cruelty upon the author of an unsolicited review of Bivouac at the Warehouse in Derby, who kicked off with:

Watching Bivouac perform is kind of like panning for gold. You know that amongst all this dirt and gravel is some of that elusive shiny stuff that is oh so rare. It's just a matter of separating the 'wheat' from the 'chaff'.

He received a bonus gold star for spelling the name of the venue 'Wherehouse', and for the gratuitous inverted commas he arranged around 'wheat' and 'chaff', as if wheat and chaff were modish inventions of which folk remained slightly suspicious. He was writing from Derby, of course, so this was not impossible.

Just occasionally, I'd sift some gold from the chaff and add a new writer to our line-up. The author of faint but intriguing pencilled postcards who signed themselves KT Blue turned out, when the included number was called, to be a teenage tornado from Wolverhampton called Caitlin Moran, later superstar columnist with *The Times* and mega-selling author. (I'm not bitter; but I made her, and I can break her.) The editor of an extremely amusing fanzine called *Perturbed*, which arrived on my desk from I knew not where, turned out to be a super-naturally affable yet deceptively waspish character called Peter Paphides, later a correctly admired writer and broadcaster, and also Mr Caitlin Moran (him, too). Some submissions from Brighton were the first of many things in several publications above the by-line David Bennun which would make me i) laugh, and ii) jealous of a preternatural ability to be clever and funny without showing off about either.

David's fine second book, *British as a Second Language*, contains his recollections of his service at an extremely thinly disguised music journal called *Harmony Fiddler*, whose reviews section is presided over by an even less convincingly altered irascible Australian interloper named Sandy Miller. David's utterly uproarious first book, *Tick Bite Fever*, a memoir of his upbringing in Kenya and Zambia, is also full-throatedly endorsed. Mostly, however, I recommend an online search for his *Melody Maker* review of a batch of Tangerine Dream reissues, which I think might be my favourite thing the paper ever ran: declining to address the music at all, David composed a diary of a lonely Arctic explorer, which was at once completely irrelevant and profoundly evocative.

However, no correspondence I received during this period was stranger than a handwritten note expressing umbrage with a predictably disdainful review I'd written of a terrible solo album by ex-Genesis keyboardist Tony Banks, in which I'd also taken the opportunity, while I was up that way, to be rude about his best-known former colleague.

Dear Guys,

Many thanks for the recent name check in the review of Tony Banks' album. I haven't, to my knowledge, been in the *Melody Maker* for ages, so it was a real thrill for me. I actually thought your paper didn't exist anymore, still, it's great what you're doing for music.

Cheers,
Phil Collins.

This was superior sarcasm, and certainly brought me greater pleasure than anything else Collins had ever put his name to.

*

Every day was a holiday, every night a party, as *Melody Maker*'s writers proceeded from office to pub to gig to whatever was still open, before returning home to regroup before doing it all again on the morrow. This is probably the point at which a proper rock'n'roll confessional should detour into a rueful homily chronicling the drug-addled, booze-fuelled descent into madness and squalor by at least one of the protagonists, but there wasn't much of that about. While most were definitely drinkers, none were really drunks. Various of my colleagues took various things from time to time, though I never did – I had no moral objection, merely a terror of ever boring anybody so murderously as people under the influence of cocaine, in particular, had bored me.

There are a few possible explanations for this (relative) abstemiousness. One is that nobody could afford much beyond what they could persuade record company people to buy them at after-show parties – a life of Dionysian excess is not readily reconcilable with ten pence a word. Another is that it's tough to write coherently to deadlines with blurred vision, sputtering motor skills, and/or pink elephants performing a conga in your head. Though every young hack will, at some point, experiment with writing something while slugging mouthfuls of Jack Daniel's patent rock'n'roll mouthwash, they will also read it back when they wake sober the next morning, and thank whichever god they pray to that they didn't send it to an editor, who would now be slipping it into a green cardboard folio with vague ideas of making fun of it in some sort of memoir a few years down the track.

Mostly, though, I think there was a general, subliminal recognition that there was simply no point in attempting to compete with the record established by our editor. If rock journalists were awarded campaign medals in the manner of soldiers, Allan would have been barely able to stand for the weight of tin dangling beneath his left lapel. Allan, famously, had landed his job on *Melody Maker* back in the mid-1970s by telling the interview panel that 'Your magazine needs a bullet up the arse. I'll be the gun if you'll pull the trigger.' He would later tell some of the resulting stories – not the Thin Lizzy one, though – in the long-running Stop Me column in *Uncut*, but at this stage they were a whispered mythology of getting arrested with The Sex Pistols, stoned with Lou Reed, beaten up by Black Sabbath, wreaking mayhem with The Clash, having sandwiches thrown at him by Patti Smith, having a heart attack on the doorstep of a rock star whose identity varied with every telling (Allan's autobiography remains the greatest book about rock'n'roll never written, not merely for the quantity of the unfeasibly fabulous yarns, but for the quality of the writing. Anybody trying to learn how to write about music – or, indeed, anything – should acquaint themselves with Allan's oeuvre forthwith.)

By the time I joined *Melody Maker*, Allan had reined it in a bit, but the old magic could still be glimpsed on occasion. During a mob outing to see Thin White Rope at the Marquee, the *Melody Maker* delegation were upbraided by a peevish, ferretish sort for wassailing over-loudly during the support act, a knock-kneed troupe of indie milksops called Life With Patrick, who were as appropriate an introduction to the thunderous gothic country rock of the Rope as fairy bread might be to raw buffalo steak. Allan's initial response was affable enough: 'Fuck off, will you? It's a rock'n'roll gig, not a fucking cathedral.' Our new friend, curiously unmollified, elaborated that he was Life With Patrick's manager, no less, if we didn't mind. Further views were exchanged. The upshot of these deliberations was a rapidly purpling impresario pinned by the neck to the Marquee's wall, while several of *Melody Maker*'s finest hung onto Allan's other arm, to prevent the fist at the end of it from reaching its intended target. I've no idea what became of Life With Patrick. It is possible that the subsequent habit of a certain music magazine of changing their name, whenever it appeared in the gig guide, to Clive With Hatrack or Strife With Catflap, or similar, was unhelpful.

Being reviews editor did not impede my travel ambitions – indeed, it made them easier to realise. I was in more frequent contact with the record companies who paid for the trips and the editors who assigned them – I was now one myself, as we tried to review tours early on, and most tours tended to start in the provinces before reaching London towards the end. And the paper's other editors were always happy to cover during any absences, understanding that they'd need credit with their fellows upon which to draw next time they fancied hitting the road.

So I took myself to Belfast to see The Fatima Mansions, an evening distinguished by the uninvited presence, backstage afterwards, of a platoon of surprisingly friendly – and non-denominational, so far as we could tell – skinheads, wearing T-shirts that proclaimed them The People's Front of Judea. I went to the Isle of Wight, so help me, to interview The Primitives, so help me, a band who'd been regular *Maker* cover stars in the late eighties, but were now well into the deckchair-rearranging phase of their career. A couple of years previously, The Primitives had been selling out multiple nights at biggish theatres with their zestful, punky pop, even becoming a big enough deal to spawn a small legion of imitators (chief among them The Darling Buds, whose

debut album *Pop Said* was a creepily faithful imitation of
The Primitives in every respect, except being – curiously – a
much better record than any The Primitives made).

Now, The Primitives were playing a tiny venue in Ryde,
and they weren't even playing there – the local council
revoked the licence at the last minute, citing concerns about
an 'undesirable audience', provoking mirthless mumbles of
'we should be so lucky' from the band themselves. Proceedings were hastily relocated to a tiny wine bar. The feature
was relegated to half a page near the back opposite a spread
on Gallon Drunk, and most of it was a discourse on zebras,
because one had appeared in The Primitives' most recent
video, and because it was the only thing I could get The Primitives to say anything about, their hearts clearly not being in
it anymore. And what they had to say about zebras was not,
in truth, terrifically interesting.

And I went back to New York, this time to spend the
weekend with EMF, celebrating the chart-topping triumph
of 'Unbelievable'. This trip was as much fun as one might
reasonably expect being in New York with a young British
group having their first hit might be – even the *Melody
Maker* delegation, myself and photographer Steve Gullick,
were assigned our own limousine, idling at our disposal
outside the epically pseudish Philippe Starck-designed Para-
mount hotel. But it was also confirmation of a suspicion
which had been gestating for a while: that *This is Spinal Tap*,
Rob Reiner's immortal music business caricature, was not so
much satire as documentary. The EMI employees present at
the ceremony at which gold records were distributed seemed
not to have regarded Artie Fufkin and Bobbi Flekman as
cautionary grotesques, but embraced them as role models.
It would be an exaggeration to report that I cared. At this
point, as a photograph taken alongside the bowling-alley

length vehicle about to return us to JFK demonstrates, I was still insufficiently refined to have discerned that shorts are never acceptable attire for air travel. Or, unless worn for the purpose of participating in organised sports, anywhere, if you're male and over the age of about fifteen.

ANDREW MUELLER

14

IN WHICH THE AUTHOR RE-EXAMINES, AND PARTIALLY RECANTS, SOME IMPETUOUS YOUTHFUL JUDGEMENTS

Two statements may be made with absolute certainty vis-a-vis young people. One, they think they know everything. Two, they don't. Worse still, in a crucial sub-clause of point two, they don't even know that they don't know everything. A compensating joy of growing older as a music fan is changing your mind about certain artists or records, deriving pleasure from music towards which you once felt indifference or even hostility. Often, this will be because you felt you weren't really supposed to like something because it had strayed beyond the pale of fashion or critical regard. Other times, this will be because you just hadn't been ready for it: the artist had got to a certain place before you did, and was essentially transmitting communiques in a language you didn't yet speak.

The contribution to *Melody Maker*'s coverage of the 1991 Reading Festival by Andrew Mueller, aged twenty-two and a half, illustrates this truth. I passed swingeing judgement upon nine artists who played the main stage on the Saturday. I was right about four of them, wrong about four of them, and the other one is a special case in that while I liked them very much at the time, many years later my personal life would overlap somewhat with that of a member of the group in question, causing me to learn that – whatever the perils of confusing the singer with the song – he was such a massive and preposterous bellend that I could no longer take his works remotely seriously.

The four artists I was wrong about were:

Teenage Fanclub
What I wrote then:

> They're the same dull, derivative pointless outfit they were when I saw them a year ago, and the total of their achievements in the period since has been to get people improbably excited about a single ('Star Sign') that betrays them as a band so utterly clueless that they're pinching tunes ('Like a Daydream') from Ride! Christ throwing wheelstands on a bloody motorscooter, couldn't they at least look to another label for inspiration?

What I think now:

> First, that I need to punch myself in the head for using an exclamation mark outside reported speech. More importantly, that 'Star Sign' is as near perfect as makes no odds, the best Big Star song Big Star never wrote, while I doubt that I've deliberately listened to anything by Ride for twenty years. Teenage Fanclub, as they were about to demonstrate on a run of glorious albums, had an extraordinary depth of understanding of both the lineage of guitar pop they were hoping to join, and of much more besides. Ride were essentially four fringes and four dozen effects pedals.

Blur

What I wrote then:

Bloodless nursery-rhyme vocals mince feebly about against a backdrop of transparent guitars and shapeless tunes. 'There's No Other Way', 'She's So High' and all the other ones sound like each other played at slightly varying speeds. I mean, is there some sort of law, convention or genetic malfunction that precludes these people from having more than one idea, or what?

What I think now:

That this is quite badly written. 'Transparent' was almost certainly not the word I wanted, and the rhetorical question is almost always a quirk of the attention-seeking wannabe populist – right, kids? And as an astute critical assessment, this review may be rock journalism's equivalent of Ernest Rutherford's declaration that the idea of producing energy from the transformation of atoms was 'moonshine'.

The Fall

What I wrote then:

Obstinate, surly and a lovely venomous antidote to the bland complacency of what's gone before. Smith is in spectacularly cranky form, delivering his downbeat rants from behind a lectern and aiming kicks at tarrying roadies.

What I think now:

That there's really not much excuse for treating paying customers with lofty contempt, still less the people who work for you. From the audience, a proper response would have been a mass turning of backs. From the roadies, a vigorous insertion of a microphone stand.

James

What I wrote then:

James are appalling. In less than a year they've managed to progress from being a band possessed of a frequently delightful sense of the askew who looked set for great big things on their own terms to being a Simple Minds/ U2 for trendy undergraduates: smug, pompous, sickeningly and affectedly humble, a lumbering entity quite prepared to rewrite, rerecord and rerelease everything they've got as often as is necessary for success.

What I think now:

I don't care. Not in the sense of not caring about James – 'Laid' and the original 'Sit Down' still raise a smile, and 'Waltzing Along' some hazy but pleasant memories of an inebriated weekend attending the video shoot for same, circa 1997, amid the spaghetti western follies of Andalucía. I mean I don't care in the sense that I acknowledge that it's tough out there, and that nobody sensible thinks there's any nobility in poverty – and James had, at one point in the eighties, kept the group going by volunteering for medical experiments. So I mean that I don't care anymore if an artist sees a chance to make a few quid, and takes it. You're not obliged to listen to them while they're doing it (and there is, I'd have said, a pretty clear moral difference between a hitherto struggling indie group rerecording a single to better please radio programmers and therefore pay their rent, and already-wealthy rock stars trousering further fortunes to play private parties for the children of dictators, as has been done in recent years by Beyoncé, Nelly Furtado and that unmitigated dunderhead Sting, among others).

*

In defence of myself and my kind, being a critic is a little like umpiring sporting events, in that you can only make decisions with the information and experience available to you, and you can't be right all the time. On page 12 of the very issue in which our Reading coverage appeared, by far the smallest live review on a page on which I'd also allotted space to EMF, Fluke, Union Sundown, The Joys and The Lovebirds was of someone or something called PJ Harvey ('This time next year,' announced Ngaire, our correspondent at sweaty laundry box the White Horse in Hampstead, 'you're going to wonder how you lived without PJ Harvey.')

There are those music journalists who possess a radar minutely sensitive to the arrival of a next big thing. And there are those who wouldn't recognise the Next Big Thing if they were a band called Next Big Thing, who'd just released an album called *Next Big Thing* on the Next Big Thing label, and were now selling out halls up and down the country on their sold-out Next Big Thing tour and were deep in production of a documentary called 'How Next Big Thing Became The Next Big Thing'. I am one of the latter. The new band I spent 1991 working hardest to promote were an unwieldy, hyper-literate art school concern from Galway called Toasted

Heretic, for whom, sad to relate, it would never get better than providing me with the opportunity to write, above a review of one of their shows, the headline SYMPATHY FOR THE BREVILLE. (The support act at the show in question, incidentally, were a certain The Divine Comedy; today, the singer of Toasted Heretic is justly acclaimed writer Julian Gough, so I wasn't entirely wrong.)

The journalists with a knack for spotting new talent also had an inexhaustible passion for interviewing new groups. I, on the other hand, had a readily exhaustible passion for it. This wasn't just because interviewing established artists offered much better opportunities for subsequent name-dropping, but because the new bugs rarely had anything interesting to say, on the grounds that very little had ever happened to them, on the grounds that they'd spent much of their brief adult lives cocooned in a cloud of bong smoke, which was itself trapped inside a rehearsal room, which was itself more than likely enclosed by some dismal provincial swamp populated by people who ate hay.

Established artists, however, had been places, met people, accomplished things, led existences of interestingly rootless derangement. I travelled to Berlin to spend a couple of days with Marc Almond, where he'd decided to give his splendidly overblown Trevor Horn-produced *Tenement Symphony* album a test run with a piano-and-vocal-only performance in a church in Kreuzberg. Almond had installed himself in the labyrinthine suite atop the Palast Hotel in what had, until recently, been East Berlin. The Palast had been built in the 1970s as somewhere to stash foreign visitors to the German Democratic Republic for convenient surveillance by the Stasi, and it looked it: a mixture of prison and porn set. It didn't have long to live. The Palast would be closed the following year, having being found to be infused with asbestos, and demolished in 2000.

192

In the meantime, the very presence of someone like Marc Almond somewhere like this represented a trivial but telling victory jig upon the recently dug grave of European totalitarianism. At a more personal level, the encounter occurred in that stratosphere of strangeness in which a pop presence of one's formative youth, during which everybody on *Countdown/Top of the Pops* (delete as applicable) seems an unreachable deity or unfathomable demon, is revealed – and there's no getting round it, there he is, right there – as an actual human being, plagued by vainglory and insecurity, same as the rest of us.

Almond was made much easier to like by the fact that his vainglory and insecurity were no further from his surface than his tattoos. He winced when I recalled Soft Cell's 'Tainted Love' dividing the dance floor at Holder High School's student discos, between delirious, capering girls and scowling, ostentatiously stationary boys, wishing the DJ would can this Pommy poof and put on some more Midnight Oil or Cold Chisel (not, obviously, that we had any plans to dance to that, either). Almond couldn't stand those records, he said, especially 'Say Hello, Wave Goodbye'.

'I know people like that original version, and feel sentimental about it,' he sighed, 'but I just find it excruciating, I really do. And people torment me with it in pubs all the time. The one thing that I hate more than anything else in the world is the CD jukebox.'

It had taken him, he explained, some while to recover from being a pop star.

'I spent six years after the breakup of Soft Cell trying to prove things to people. People said I couldn't sing, so I had to prove that I could. I had to prove that I could write songs, that I could perform. It's always been a battle.'

Almond's current single was a string-spangled souping up of Scott Walker's take on Jacques Brel's 'Jacky', a song which

193

enabled Almond to play the roles of wine bar warbler, disso-
lute showman and bearded Almighty. It was not necessary
to spend long in Almond's company to understand why he
enjoyed singing it. Even his conversation was a performance,
every phrase punctuated with pantomime gesticulation,
clenching his fists, beating his chest, sweeping his arms above
his head in wild exclamatory arcs.

'Lyrically,' he agreed, 'I relate to it all the way through,
to all of the imagery. To me, it's the *Citizen Kane* thing, like
I've got all this success but I've not got it through ways I feel
comfortable with, like the character has been corrupted. He's
yearning for his innocence, for his childhood back, the time
they called him Jacky, you know.'

Was there, I wondered, a halcyon period after which he
hankered, a time they'd called him Marky?

'Ha!' he whooped. 'I think, yeah. I think that's gone through
all the things I've always written about, feeling like this
corrupted person wanting his innocence back. I think that's
something most people can relate to. Somewhere inside, there's
that person you want to be, and you can't get them back.'

*

It would take me a while – until just now, in fact – to properly
appreciate what a wise and sad statement that was. Almond
was thirty-four when we met, therefore nearing that age when
the songs you've grown up with start feeling less like prayers of
aspiration, and more like statements of reproach or measures
of disappointment. It's easy to love, say, Bruce Springsteen's
'Thunder Road' and 'Born to Run' when you are, as Springsteen was when he wrote them, twenty-four or so. Life really
is an open road to a long distant horizon. Your car may be
a jalopy but there's time to save up for a better one. And if
it doesn't work out with Mary or Wendy, well, plenty more

fish in the sea. These are probably harder – though possibly more affecting – songs to hear when you've enough miles on the clock to suspect that you've probably already been as handsome and happy as you're going to get, and Mary or Wendy (or both, if you've been really unlucky) is still hitting you for child support despite having long since run off with her Pilates instructor. When you're young, the songs you love constitute an atlas of fabulous, fantastic places you're going to go. When you're older, those same songs are postcards from places you never went and probably never will, now.

This tilt must be even tougher for those whose politics have been unduly influenced at an early age by a catchy chorus or two. At around the same time as I met Almond, I renewed acquaintance with Billy Bragg, at the offices of his record company in West London. Bragg was staring into a perfect storm of agglomerating uncertainties for any British writer of socialist protest songs. Margaret Thatcher, the colossal nemesis of the British left, had resigned some months previously. Soviet communism, which perplexing numbers of free Europeans were still willing to defend as a good idea in theory, was disintegrating by the hour. And Bragg was a smart man embarking on his mid-thirties. It was little wonder that his current album, *Don't Try This at Home*, was largely devoid of the dogmatic conviction which had characterised, for good and ill, his earlier works.

I wondered how he felt about his future. Thatcher's insipid successor, John Major, was not the sort of man likely to inspire singalong outrage – which was, of course, one of the reasons he'd succeeded Thatcher. And it was becoming less and less possible for those who defined themselves as social-ists to ignore the fact that socialism only seemed feasible as long as you built a fence and watchtowers to stop everybody from leaving.

'The greatest ideology, perhaps the greatest faith, of the twentieth century, Russian communism, has crumbled,' nodded Bragg. 'And I think what's going to happen now is that people like myself, people with left-wing beliefs, are going to have to find new ways of articulating them. And I'm not exactly sure what that's going to be yet.'

I wondered if he felt, artistically or politically, like he'd been left behind.

'Oh, no,' he insisted. 'I mean, although the Soviet Union may not even exist by the time you write this article, the contribution it made is not all bad. I mean, a lot of it is bad, and we shouldn't forget that. You can't ignore what was done by Stalin, and Stalin's heirs. But the USSR has been the only superpower in the last fifty years that's had any kind of anti-imperialist stance . . .'

Aw, come on, I said. Tell that to a Hungarian, a Czech, a Pole, an Estonian, a Georgian . . .

'Well, anti-colonialist, then, in the sense that they've offered an alternative to the emerging colonial nations in Africa and Latin America.'

Which was one way, I supposed, of describing a foreign policy of finding the very worst people available in any given neighbourhood, and supplying them with weapons. I was disappointed to be hearing this crap from Bragg, as I still am on the bizarrely frequent occasions on which otherwise compassionate and apparently reasonable British people go out of their way to make excuses for Cuba – a country which, if its people had been permitted the elementary liberty of free travel, would have been left with a population of about nine by 1960, and all of them named Castro. I've never understood why British people determined to ally themselves to a revolutionary cause don't take more pride in the fact that the one revolution of recent centuries which has been a genuine engine of liberty and social progress – America's – was at least partly inspired, conceived, orchestrated and fought by British people (against other British people, admittedly). But then I've never understood why the British – and the English most of all – dislike themselves so heartily. I asked Bragg if he was at all proud to call himself an Englishman.

'That,' he said, after a rare hesitation, 'is a good question, Andrew.'

This was, I told him, bound to happen sooner or later.

'There are,' he eventually decided, 'aspects of England I'm proud of, certainly, and there are aspects I would be willing to defend. But I'm not the kind of Englishman who thinks everything England ever did is wonderful, or that everything that comes out of England is brilliant – or worse, the kind of patriot who feels that England is justified in whatever it wants to do just because it's England. And we have got away with an awful lot over the years, you know . . .'

Certainly. But so has everybody. And that wasn't what I'd asked.

'First country in the world to have a welfare state,' Bragg began, counting on his fingers. 'That we have a relatively calm political consensus – and I oppose strongly, as you know, the right-wing aspects of that, but this country has never accepted extremism in any form. And, um, the fact that for a relatively small island, we've made quite a large cultural splash in the world.'

Of which Bragg was, by now, a perceptible ripple. But in terms of the causes he held dear, I wondered, did he think he was making any difference?

'No,' he said, with sufficient emphasis to dispel any suggestion of false humility. 'God, no. Pop singers don't make a difference. If, all of a sudden, tomorrow there was no pop music, what would change?'

Both of us, I answered, might have to start working for a living.

'Exactly,' he replied. 'It's a very, very trivial medium.'

*

There is no way I believed that at the time, not least because it was my job to believe that the works and utterances of people like Billy Bragg were worth considering seriously. And I don't believe it now. If a medium which burrows so deep into so many doesn't matter – compare the task of precisely remembering a single painting or a few paragraphs of liter-ature with the reflex of recalling the words and melody of any one of thousands of songs – then what medium does? In the last half century in particular, pop music has become the single most unifying cultural agent ever conceived. Even if more people watch television than listen to music, they watch different television. But everybody listens to the same Beatles. Only a complete idiot would call pop music trivial (Bragg, who is very far from being a complete idiot, was merely indulging his self-deprecating good chap schtick).

It is probably possible to extrapolate from this observa-tion some sort of argument that, therefore, journalism about popular music is important, in the same way that journalism about other important things is also important. But while all journalism is beholden to the great paradox of the craft – which is that while journalism is certainly a serious business, on no account should its practitioners take themselves seri-ously – rock journalism is perhaps uniquely defined by it. Happily, the job comes with any number of inbuilt barriers to pomposity – the money is pitiful, the prospects infinitesi-mal, women think it's a ridiculous way for a grown man to earn his keep and, worse still, they're right.

For an office so full of wilful and eccentric characters as that of *Melody Maker*, there was remarkably little preciousness, and what minor outbreaks there were usually resulted from overenthusiasm. One week, attentive readers might have been baffled to note a new writer called George Caplan making an unusually high-profile debut, undertaking a lead review of Prince's *Diamonds and Pearls* – a commission that would not usually have been bestowed before a lengthy apprenticeship. Over ensuing weeks, the same readers might have wondered why the by-line of this Caplan prodigy, who clearly flaunted a dashing turn of phrase, was never seen in the paper again.

The truth was that the journalist I'd actually asked to review *Diamonds and Pearls*, Simon Price, was so devoted a Prince fan that the responsibility rather gave him the vapours, rendering him so incapacitated by awe that he found himself unable to file anything by deadline. The review we ran was rattled up in an hour by myself and Ted Mico, with the aid of an advance cassette of *Diamond and Pearls* which Ted found buried in the rubble on Steve Sutherland's desk. We had George Caplan – a deliberately misspelled homage to the man who doesn't exist in *North by Northwest* – pronounce *Diamonds and Pearls* an album that 'bristles with the delight of a man who, after a long period of impotence, has rediscovered how to do it'. It's pleasant to think that Ted and I helped entrench the now decades-old, near universal tradition of Prince reviews that pronounce every post-*Lovesexy* album a 'return to form', every one of said plaudits written by people who will never listen to the damn thing again.

I did have some sympathy for Pricey's predicament (although not so much that I didn't impose a terrible, terrible punishment, exiling him to Liverpool on a record company coach trip, full of people with whom I suspected he wouldn't get on, to review a group I knew he'd absolutely detest). It is much, much harder to write entertaining and engaging praise of a record – or anything else – than it is to come up with amusing and invigorating obloquy. Any half-competent rock writer can bang out 1000 words of knockabout abuse of a record he doesn't like in nothing flat, but even the best ones can labour for days over the same quantity of acclamation for a record they love.

Some, like Pricey, didn't know where to start. Others didn't know where to stop. I asked Simon Reynolds to review My Bloody Valentine's *Loveless*, thinking that Simon's combination of intellectual rigour and empathetic imagination would be ideal tools for navigating the Valentines' warped soundscapes. My initial delight at hearing the fax machine ring subsided into bemusement, bewilderment and something approaching despair as sheet after sheet spooled from the device and gathered in drifts about my ankles. I found myself scooping from the floor the rock journalism equivalent of a New York delicatessen sandwich – all good stuff, if possibly somewhat overcooked in parts, but more than a normal human being could digest in a week. I rang Simon to explain as much – not a conversation I was confident about having with someone whose work, carefully cut out of the paper, had featured prominently amid my bedroom decor less than two years earlier.

'You're the editor,' he replied with magnificent equanimity. 'Edit it.'

I did, axing some of the more florid passages – Simon, vastly cleverer than most of the records he wrote about, had a tendency to read more into some music than its composers ever wrote into it – but leaving his unmatchable descriptive riffs: 'Touched' does indeed resemble 'a whale howling Delta blues intermingled with what sounds like Radio Two heard from a wireless at the bottom of a swimming pool'.

I managed to spend some of the winter in places where it wasn't winter.

I made my first trip to Los Angeles to spend a few days with Courtney Love. Courtney wasn't yet terrifically well known. She'd have been recognised probably in about half a dozen bars in Los Angeles and London, and mostly by regular readers of *Melody Maker*, in which Everett True had been ardently championing her band, Hole, with the enthusiasm of someone who'd discovered cocaine and Jesus at the same time. Everett nevertheless offered, the night before I left, what remains the most sage advice I have ever been offered before embarking on an assignment. 'For the love of all that is wonderful,' counselled the great man, 'do not give that woman your home phone number.'

I frequently met people who wanted to be famous. As the occupant of the reviews editor's chair at a music weekly, indeed, I was one of the first ports of call for those that way inclined. Courtney was different, though. Courtney was just going to be famous. She was in no doubt about this, and nor was anyone who knew her. Courtney and Hole were playing at the Palace Theatre in Hollywood, opening for Nirvana, to whom I hadn't been paying much attention. If I'd been paying more, I would probably have milked my backstage introduction to Kurt Cobain for a better quote than 'Tell Everett I said hello.'

And I'd probably have bothered to write a review of a show which – if more so in retrospect than at the time – felt like regime change. This was grunge's Bastille Day, the flag of the north-western punk rock revolt unfurled atop the citadel of poodle-permed, leather-trousered Sunset Strip metal – in Los Angeles, vast emporiums offered 'rock star accessories' for sale, including studded wristbands, stack-heeled boots and pre-teased wigs.

I thought Hole were okay, and that their debut album, *Pretty on the Inside*, was quite good fun, in the way that The Go-Gos playing Black Sabbath tunes would have been quite good fun. But Hole were less compelling than their singer, who radiated the same unnerving, I-am-a-river-to-my-people sense of their own lofty destiny that I'd later perceive, to varying extents, in interview subjects including Benazir Bhutto and Saif Gaddafi. It's a charisma born of an overweening sense of entitlement, an insistence that the universe will bestow acclaim and influence regardless of one's demonstrable willingness to earn them and/or capacity to wield them. It usually works out badly for the person concerned, and those yanked in by their gravitational pull.

'I'm driven,' was the last thing she said to me. 'I really am. I'm driven, for some reason. But I don't know where I'm going.'

At the time, I thought this gothically glamorous, or at least that it would make a good pull quote when the story was laid out. At this distance, it sounds tragic. A better adjusted young mind would regard their future and announce, 'I'm driving, and I'm going over there.' Such people tended not to get interviewed by music magazines, however.

I returned to Sydney late in the year to interview the band who'd kind of got me to London in the first place – Strait-jacket Fits, who'd just been signed to American label Arista, who apparently thought that sending me and photographer Phil Nicholls halfway around the world and installing us in a vast sun-splashed suite in Kings Cross for a week was in no way a senseless and flagrant waste of everyone's money. We and the group had little time on our allotted afternoon together, the day after the Fits had wiped the stage with

My Bloody Valentine, for whom they'd opened at Sydney University's Refectory. Phil, feeling obliged to make the most of our location, photographed the group at Circular Quay, Sydney Harbour Bridge filling the background. 'Aw, fucking hell,' harrumphed Shayne Carter, his Kiwi vowels sounding flatter than ever, 'people will think we're some sort of fucking . . .' He paused, as if trying to summon the worst first impression anyone could conceivably glean. 'Australian band,' he finally spat.

I was back in London in time to work on my first *Melody Maker* Christmas issue. These were monumental undertakings – eighty-eight-page double issues crammed with features revisiting the calendar just endured and observing a long-standing music press tradition of encouraging rock stars to dress like ninnies. Some such subjects were more enthusiastic than others. Our 1991 cover stars were R.E.M. As Allan Jones' dispatch from their hometown of Athens, Georgia, reported, Michael Stipe had done his best to enter into the seasonal spirit, arriving for the photo shoot with props – a bear costume, a Santa outfit, an Uncle Sam hat – which he attempted to force upon his bandmates. Such was their horrified reluctance, however, that we only ended up able to use one in-costume photo – Stipe beaming, the other three sulking fabulously – and that as a secondary portrait inside the paper: on the cover, R.E.M. solemnly clutched candles.

Back in London, my role in the festivities was to cover the photographing, by the great Kevin Westenberg, of a nativity scene in which the roles of the two startled parents and the three wise men were filled by The Wonder Stuff, draped in hired costume in Westenberg's studio near King's Cross. Miles Hunt, I observed on arriving, might have shaved before suiting up as Mary. 'Well,' the singer replied, 'I wanted to look suitably rustic, didn't I?' His bandmates found themselves unable, upon surveying the completed disguise, to rise above ribaldry of the 'no wonder she's a virgin' variety. It was a fitting end to a year which, for me at least, felt like one in which most of my Christmases had come at once.

*

Melody Maker's 1991 album of the year was Primal Scream's *Screamadelica*. This accolade was arrived at by asking all the paper's contributors to rank their ten favourites in order. The album in first place on your list got ten points, the second nine, and so on – it wasn't a rigidly secret ballot, and a degree of vote-swapping and favour-purchasing did go on, all of it in the suspicion/expectation that senior staff would have a final fiddle with the results (much though I loved the record in question, I was unable to believe that Neil Young's live album *Arc–Weld* had arrived in second place without a degree of path-clearing by our editor). *Melody Maker*'s top ten was filled out, in descending order, by R.E.M.'s *Out of Time*, Mercury Rev's *Yerself is Steam*, Nirvana's *Nevermind*, The Wonder Stuff's *Never Loved Elvis*, My Bloody Valentine's *Loveless*, American Music Club's *Everclear*, Throwing Muses' *The Real Ramona* and Guns N' Roses' *Use Your Illusion II*. My own list was six-tenths in agreement.

Neil Young & Crazy Horse, *Arc–Weld*

Young would have been barely older than I am now when he recorded this rampage through his peerless back catalogue – which meant, needless to elaborate, that I wrote about him as some craggy, cranky Methuselah, an inexplicably undead relic of a bygone age, all but wringing feedback from a life-support machine. We would meet fifteen years later in San Francisco, and while the interview was interesting, it was impossible to get past the actually hilarious degree to which Neil Young looks and sounds exactly like Neil Young: if you've been a rock'n'roll fan at all any time in the last forty years or so, it's like witnessing the Lincoln Memorial come to life.

R.E.M., *Out of Time*

The run of eight studio albums released by R.E.M. between 1983's *Murmur* and 1992's *Automatic for the People* amounts to one of the most extraordinary decades in the life of any artist, in any medium, in any period (I've also an unfashionable soft spot for 1994's widely derided demented glam frenzy *Monster*, but I'm about to say something about the fallibility of critical consensus). In retrospect, *Out of Time* is the weakest of that bunch. It contains two of the worst things R.E.M. ever recorded – blundering hip hop crossover 'Radio Song', the excruciatingly wacky 'Shiny Happy People' – and a few other tracks ('Near Wild Heaven', 'Endgame') which sound like the many bands of the period who were trying to sound like R.E.M. without quite succeeding. However, R.E.M. had attained Can Do No Wrong status, a point at which criticism becomes heretical, and just about impossible. If there's one thing wrong with what remains of the music press, it's that CDNW status is now awarded to just about any bunch of clowns who know which side of a guitar the strings are on. The effect on music has been congruent with the effect on educational standards of more forgiving exam marking – if anybody who can spell their own name is guaranteed at least a B–, there's not much incentive to excel.

The Wonder Stuff, *Never Loved Elvis*

A pleasant but flawed album, whose presence on my list was probably principally due to its irresistible lead single, 'Size of a Cow', which sounded like the re-enactment of a cheese-fuelled dream of Slade reinventing themselves as an XTC tribute band.

My Bloody Valentine, *Loveless*
Because parts of it resembled a whale howling Delta blues, intermingled with what sounds like Radio Two heard from a wireless at the bottom of a swimming pool.

Throwing Muses, *The Real Ramona*
It is a cliché of rock journalists and far-gone snobs in general that they prefer a band's earlier works. I almost never do – genuine greatness often doesn't emerge until any given group has learnt to play properly and got over the inane thrill of making a racket for the sake of it. Not that Throwing Muses were ever guilty of this, and are therefore a lousy and undeserving example of the point I'm trying to make, but *The Real Ramona* was both their most technically accomplished album to date, and their best.

Pixies, *Trompe le Monde*
The arrival of this album was one of the few moments at which I recall *Melody Maker*'s staff doing as I'd once assumed they did with every significant new release – crowding around a stereo, waiting to hear what would be unleashed by someone pressing 'play' on the freshly couriered pre-release cassette. In this case, it was a sequence of short, sharp shrieks of feral Dadaist exclamations that sounded like punk rock played by angry Martians.

American Music Club, *Everclear*
Mark Eitzel's American Music Club vied consistently with The Go-Betweens for the title of the artists most cursed by

critical favour. In both cases, it seemed that the more review-
ers proclaimed them the way, the truth and the light, the less
people seemed moved to buy their records – which, in turn,
prompted yet more purple adulation, followed by even more
entrenched indifference. Interviewing Eitzel many years later,
I'd try to console him about his lack of guitar-shaped swimming
pool and rhinestone-studded Cadillac by reminding him that
while relatively few people had bought his records, they'd all
loved them with unusual ardour. 'Yeah, well,' he replied, 'that
and fifty cents will get you a cup of coffee.'

Electronic, *Electronic*

Little good has ever come of the supergroup: the fantasy
football-like gathering beneath one badge of assorted established talents, on the assumption that a team of champions
will naturally coalesce into a champion team. The truth is
that all great groups are that crucial, maddening quantity
greater than the sum of their parts – a theorem which can
be demonstrated by subjecting yourself to the solo works
of former members of influential outfits (one struggles to
imagine Frank Black, for example, listening to the playback
of any of his indigestibly vast solo catalogue and thinking
'Yes. Yes, this is very definitely anywhere near as good as,
say, *Trompe Le Monde*.') The debut album by Electronic, a
partnership between New Order's Bernard Sumner and The
Smiths' Johnny Marr, with occasional interjections from
The Pet Shop Boys, was one of those rule-proving exceptions.

The Fatima Mansions, *Bertie's Brochures*

Probably the oddest entry in The Fatima Mansions' catalogue – a considerable accolade. *Bertie's Brochures* propelled
Cathal Coughlan's divergent instincts to extremes. It sighed
gorgeous torch balladry – covers of Scott Walker's 'Long

About Now', Richard Thompson's 'The Great Valerio', Coughlan's own 'Behind the Moon', which should have been sung by George Jones or Roy Orbison (the latter, obviously, would have needed to live longer). It spewed bilious avant-garde dementia, most notably on a gleeful, almost-beyond-recognition desecration of R.E.M.'s 'Shiny Happy People'. Years later, I'd ask Peter Buck if he'd ever heard it, and he'd reply, 'I thought it was cool . . . and I thought, "Why would anyone want to cover that song?"'

Jesus Jones, *Doubt*

I will maintain – and not just because two members of this group ended up in my own group, the cruelly underrated Blazing Zoos – in the face of all but armed opposition that Jesus Jones in general, and this album in particular, are unfairly denied the kudos they are due. One of the defining musical motifs of the early 1990s was what was generally referred to as indie-dance – an amalgamation of the shimmering guitars and ragged tunesmithery of alternative rock with the beats and squeaks of warehouse raves. Most of the credit for this went Manchesterward – Stone Roses, Happy Mondays, Charlatans et al – but Jesus Jones had released *Info Freako* back in 1989. *Doubt* was a more polished product, but nonetheless inventive, and a nimble balance of Mike Edwards' contradictory instincts: he wanted to be a sonic adventurer, but he couldn't help writing pop songs.

15

IN WHICH THE AUTHOR GETS HIT WITH A GRUNGE ICON'S HAT

In keeping with time-honoured tradition, 1992's first issue included the results of *Melody Maker*'s annual readers' poll. This was a shameless fraud against democracy that would have been regarded as an embarrassment by the most dingbat dictatorship which ever sought to legitimise its authority by holding an election and then insisting that everyone had voted for El Presidente except one bloke called Trevor, and he hadn't been able to get to a polling booth as he'd been busy polishing the statues.

This was not entirely *Melody Maker*'s fault. Back before it became possible to express an opinion to the world by clicking a mouse, the only way to register your view in any media plebiscite was to cut the pertinent form out of the periodical in question, locate a biro, fill the ballot in, find an envelope, walk to the post office, stand – as is usually the case in British post offices – in a queue of such length that people towards the front had inherited their places from their parents, purchase a stamp and post it. The number of *Melody Maker*'s readers who could be arsed with any of this rarely cleared more than a few hundred. Our readers' poll, had its chronic under-subscription been more widely appreciated, could have been sensationally hijacked by any obscure artist possessed of the wherewithal to purchase a few dozen copies of the magazine and a quantity of biros, and organise a small circle of biddable friends.

Melody Maker maintained the pretence of a fair and representative vote for a variety of reasons. It created the impression of a journal with its finger on the throbbing pulse of its readership. It – probably more importantly – filled four pages of the magazine during the always desolate post-Christmas lull, a period in which the record companies, having flogged the thoroughbreds over the jumps during the recent festive gluttony, generally only exercised their wobbly, uncertain foals or gave the moth-eaten veteran nags one last gallop en route to the glue factory. And at the beginning of 1992 in particular, the readers' poll gave us an excuse to put Nirvana on the cover again, even though we didn't have an interview (they'd landed the rare Best Single and Best Album double for 'Smells Like Teen Spirit' and *Nevermind* respectively).

Whichever anonymous staffer knocked out the introductory copy was determined to maintain the deception. 'You wrote in in your thousands,' he lied. Other notable winners included The Wonder Stuff (Best Band) and Curve (Brightest Hope), both of whom *Melody Maker* had generally championed, and Vic Reeves (Man of the Year) and Carter the Unstoppable Sex Machine (Best Live Act), both of whom *Melody Maker* had generally affected to regard with horror and bafflement. A touching insight into the world view of our readers was provided by the results of the Event of the Year – in ascending order, the collapse of the Soviet Union, the war with Iraq and the Reading Festival (the Reading Festival, at that, which had been headlined by Iggy Pop, James and The Sisters of Mercy).

The other tradition of any calendar's first issue was a feature in which the paper's writers announced their tips, as it were, for the top (again, it filled another couple of pages at a quiet time of year). In a demonstration of my continuing apathy and ineptitude where the soothsaying element of rock journalism was concerned, I hailed Falling Joys, a fine band I knew from back in Sydney, and – again – Toasted Heretic. Cravenly if perspicaciously, I hedged vis-a-vis the latter, declaring that they were destined for 'monstrous adoration or universal derision'. Other writers did rather better – vaunted elsewhere on the same spread were Pearl Jam, The Jayhawks, PJ Harvey, Smashing Pumpkins, Tori Amos and The Verve, so early in their career that they were still known as Verve, although not so early in their career that they shouldn't have been instantly spotted as naked emperors who made King Crimson sound unassuming, and Richard Ashcroft as one of the worst lyricists of all time (Ashcroft's later solo career especially would be distinguished by rhyming dictionary doggerel that sounded like it took less time to write than it did to sing).

My first major interview of the year was with Icelandic group The Sugarcubes, with whom *Melody Maker* had conducted a somewhat tempestuous relationship. Early on, seduced by the band's unearthly, post-everything sound and Bjork's whooping whimsy, *Melody Maker* had been The Sugarcubes' most ardent champion, anointing their debut offering, *Life's Too Good*, second-best Album of the Year in 1988 (behind Pixies' *Surfer Rosa*) and featuring Bjork's porcelain elf visage on the magazine's cover almost as often as the words 'Melody' and 'Maker'. Sadly, the honeymoon had been brief. The Sugarcubes' follow-up album, *Here Today, Tomorrow, Next Week* had been declared a disaster area, obliging editors of Backlash to spend much of 1989 answering letters accusing *Melody Maker*, not for the first or last time, of building artists up just to knock them down.

The perennial dependability of such correspondence was the reason the letters page had been christened Backlash in the first place. Many readers seemed convinced of a conspiratorial undertow to *Melody Maker*'s work, as if we plotted every artist's critical trajectory in advance, calibrating exactly the most advantageous points at which we could hoist them into the firmament or dump them in the compost bin. While we weren't entirely ungratified by this notion of us as godlike puppeteers, it was absolute cobblers – as was, indeed, *Here Today, Tomorrow, Next Week*.

But The Sugarcubes' new album, *Stick Around for Joy*, seemed to be basking in the flickering warmth of a return-to-form consensus: *Melody Maker*'s Jim Arundel – formerly Jim Irvin of Furniture – pronounced the single, 'Hit', 'marvellously alive, exultant and, have mercy, sexy . . . a record about the fidgety thrill of falling in love that's both fidgety and thrilling'. The review of *Stick Around for Joy* itself, by Jon Wilde, was positive, but more measured, expounding the – not uncommon – view that The Sugarcubes, while generally marvellous, were wilfully and infuriatingly hobbling themselves (or 'pissing on their own shoes', as the ruffian Wilde had it) by indulging Bjork's co-vocalist Einar, whose surreal raps were not, to Wilde's ears, the cleverly ironic counterpoints to Bjork's breathily angelic warblings they were perhaps intended to be. ('Mumbled gibberish,' inveighed Wilde, 'that brings to mind the image of a bag lady flipping out at a bus stop.')

Mercifully, by the time this review ran, I'd already met Einar, along with the rest of The Sugarcubes, in the Kensington Gore hotel in London. Interviews in hotels with artists who are at the end of a long day at the end of a long promotional tour were rarely any fun: arduous exercises in soliciting answers to all the questions they've already heard – which were usually the ones your editor had instructed you to ask – while trying to think of enough questions they hadn't already heard to keep them, and you, awake. My stock opener in such situations was to ask if there was a question they'd always wished someone would put to them, but never had. Einar replied, 'Yes. That one.' It was a good start to an unusual interview, initially scheduled to last one hour of the early evening in a lobby cafe, but which ended up taking in several locations in West London and continuing, ever more informally, until breakfast the following morning. Though I'd never much enjoyed writing or reading interview features which are boiled down to question-and-answer transcript, I felt that a stretch of this was the best means of conveying the essence of both the night and the company, and the extent to which interviewing The Sugarcubes was akin to herding lynx on a unicycle while blindfolded.

Me (confident, taking-charge-of-proceedings tone): 'Do you think the greater British public have, at last, got over the idea of The Sugarcubes as a bunch of weirdos who beamed down from the planet Zog?'

Bjork: 'I think we've dashed all that. For me, that's sort of done. The press, and the British press especially, are finally realising – and probably not very happily – that we are human beings.'

Braggi: 'Though I think, actually, we would prefer to be from this planet, er . . . Zog?'

Me (wearily sensing yet another disappearance down a tangential dead-end, desperately wishing I hadn't introduced the whole Zog concept, even if I do quite like the idea of a world named after the former King of Albania): 'Er, Zog, yeah.'

Braggi: 'But it isn't the case. Unfortunately.'

Thor: 'That would be brilliant. We could tell you all about being an alien.'

Bjork (to me, vaguely accusingly): 'Have you been there?'

Me: 'Huh?'

Einar: 'Zog in Icelandic means "sorrow".'

Me: 'Bollocks does it.' (According to the internet, two decades later, the Icelandic word for 'sorrow' is actually *harm*, or *harmyr*, or something like that.)

Einar (unfazed): 'So if you are saying we are from the planet Sorrow, then I must disagree with you.'

Bjork (humming, kind of tunelessly, but apparently happily): 'Hmmmm mmmmm hmmmm mmmmm-mmmm hmm mmm.'

Thor: 'Perhaps we are from the planet Hap.'

Bjork (locating a melody, nodding her head): 'Hmmmm mmm hmm mm.'

Einar: 'The planet Hap, yes. Are we Hap people? Yes, we are.'

Bjork (building to triumphant finale): 'Hmmm mmm hm MMMM!'

ours of this, there was. A few years later, when Bjork had come unaccountably famous by dressing as an assortment of Christmas decorations and wittering about what washing machines do when they retire, the tapes would probably have been worth money.

My physical introduction to the frozen north came shortly afterwards, courtesy of Pearl Jam, who I accompanied to Oslo and Copenhagen for what would be their first cover story. While I hadn't been among, or anywhere near, the *Melody Maker* writers who'd actually discovered Pearl Jam, I had liked their debut album *Ten* very much, and had also been in the office when the trip was mooted; rank had its privileges. It was my first multi-country tour story, and I was accompanied by photographer Steve Gullick. I already knew Steve a bit – he'd been one of those to whom *Melody Maker* had tossed a life preserver after *Sounds* magazine, Britain's 'other' rock weekly, had sunk in April 1991, and we'd already spent time together in New York (with EMF), the Isle of Wight (with The Primitives) and Aberdeen (to review The Waterboys, an evening of which my only recollection is staying up late in the hotel bar talking to Gullick and a woman whom neither of us knew but who seemed perfectly sane and coherent aside from the fact that she was intently shrouding a suitcase in layer after layer of bubble wrap and masking tape).

Steve was a brilliant photographer and a hardened road monster, able to teach me some of the dialect I'd need to make myself understood on European tours. As I fussed with a wallet full of unfamiliar notes on the flight and fretted about the exchange rates, Steve explained that rock'n'roll already operated a sort of single European currency, long before the euro was ever seriously mooted, known to generations of musicians and road crews as the shitter. It didn't matter, Steve elaborated, whether we were actually spending Norwegian krone or Danish krone – or even, for future reference, francs, pesetas, deutschmarks, escudos or other such silly Toytown firelighter which nobody could seriously be expected to keep track of from one country to the next. As long as the tour manager had informed you at the beginning of the day how many shitters you got to the pound wherever you were, you couldn't go wrong. (Leaving aside the obvious subtext of British contempt for all things continental inherent in the name 'shitter', I remain especially fond of the verb form, with which one may, for example, declare oneself 'shittered up', i.e. in receipt of spendable local currency; I once heard Phil Nicholls, a painstakingly courteous man, forget himself slightly and ask a German bureau de change clerk to 'Shitter me up, *bitte*.').

We met Pearl Jam at Oslo's Club Alaska, a sweaty cellar stuffed to the gunwales with revellers moshing and stage-diving before the band had even started playing. Pearl Jam had already met Steve, and like almost every band who ever met Steve, had all but adopted him. Fearing for his safety amid the churning throng as he tried to shoot the show, Pearl Jam arranged for some crash barriers to be erected in front of the low stage, establishing the perimeter of an improvised photo pit. Seconds after the first chord, they were as shanties in a dam burst. In a poignant yet dignified ceremony back-stage after the show, Steve presented Eddie Vedder with the T-shirt he'd been wearing as he'd braved the mayhem: clearly visible on the back of the distended and beer-sodden garment were footprints.

I caught up with Vedder properly the following afternoon, on a tour bus parked in the snow outside a venue called Pumphuset (the band had driven, we had flown). He wasn't quite the singer in the biggest band in the world, but he was getting there. *Ten* had already sold about half a million copies in the United States; it would go on to sell nearly ten million.

Eddie, faintly aware that the prize he'd dreamt of all his life was booby-trapped, didn't seem sure whether to celebrate or brace himself.

'I don't even know,' he said, 'if I want all that to happen. I'm just apprehensive about not being able to write a serious song, or be taken seriously. That's why I fully vow to help people out with whatever comes my way, to help them get above that line. Because I went through the ice once or twice myself, you know.'

Until really quite recently, Eddie Vedder's résumé had amounted to four years of the night shift pumping gas in San Diego, spending his days surfing and playing the guitar, his evenings hanging out and helping out at local rock clubs, sleeping when he remembered to. One of the connections he forged through his pestering of passing rock groups was former Red Hot Chili Peppers drummer Jack Irons, who had passed Eddie a tape of music by former members of Seattle grunge pathfinders Green River and subsequent nearly-men Mother Love Bone. Eddie had sung some stuff over three of the tracks, and mailed it back. And here he was. It was little wonder that he surveyed his surroundings with the incredulous bewilderment of an inventor whose time-travel contraption had, against all expectation, suddenly delivered him to the court of Pharaoh Amenhotep II, or to an especially good view of the Charge of the Light Brigade.

'I just kind of came to this realisation today,' he said, 'that Pete Townshend was probably more of a father to me than anybody. And yet I never sent him a Father's Day card. I feel kind of guilty about that.'

Eddie, maddeningly, was as evasive about his history as he was expansive about his passions. He still had this option, of course – not yet at the stage where it would be financially worthwhile for tabloids to fossick in his bins, and untroubled by any notion of the existence of the internet, which would shortly make it impossible for anybody possessed of any public profile to cultivate mystery or preserve privacy.

'I mean,' he said, 'my upbringing was like a hurricane, and music was the tree I held on to. That's how important it was, and is. It's everything. If someone reads this, they'll probably think that sounds silly, but it's everything, it really is.'

He was, however, willing to concede that most of what he wrote was autobiographical to the extent that he empathised with the tottering parade of losers, loners, outsiders and misfits that populated his songs.

'I definitely identify with these people,' he nodded. 'Definitely. Without a doubt, and that's the only reason I feel like I can write about it, or sing it. Otherwise, I'd be an actor, or something.'

This begged, I suggested, any number of questions. The opening track of *Ten*, a guttural Black Sabbathesque churn called 'Once', had its narrator creeping about with a gun under his coat, threatening a non-specific but exacting revenge.

'If there is any one song that's autobiographical,' he said, very slowly, 'that's it.'

I expressed both scepticism and curiosity.

'Don't get me wrong,' he continued. 'I wouldn't want to do it. But there is a sense of – and again, I frighten myself by relating so much – a sense of, fuck it, if I'm going down, and it's not my fucking fault, and I did everything I could, and I worked with these hands, and I didn't do drugs . . . if I'm out of here, then I'm taking a few people with me. There's no logic there, it's that misplaced passion.'

Inevitably, the people who saw themselves in Eddie's songs were starting to think they understood him. Which meant they were starting to think he could help them.

'At first,' he sighed, 'I answered every letter, and I thought that would make me feel good. Then it got weird. I write back a normal letter, and find myself becoming part of their lives, a part that they need, and they keep needing more and more. I don't mind being friendly, but when it's like "Can I have your hat?" . . . No! It's my one and only hat! I love this hat! This actually comes from a real baseball player. He wore it all season.'

I asked Vedder whether he'd gone up to the player in question and said, 'Can I have your hat?'

'No!' he laughed, removing the titfer in question and swatting me about the head with it. 'I did not. He gave it to me. So I've been taking pictures of it in every city and mailing them to him. Here's your hat in London, here's your hat in Stockholm.'

Over the next couple of years, Vedder's psychological health would be a regular topic of speculation in the music press – some of it genuinely concerned, some of it hand-wringing and prurient, some of it freighted with a barely latent desire to see him enact the terminal rite of the rock'n'roll burnout, especially in the febrile aftermath of the suicide of his peer and rival Kurt Cobain. I'd see Eddie again half a year later, backstage at the Washington State instalment of the 1992 Lollapalooza festival, physically and mentally exhausted. I never really worried about him, though – partly because doing so (especially in print) would have amounted to ostentatious posturing about someone I didn't know well, but mostly because I always thought he'd be okay. He was lucky – saddled, undeniably, with that vulnerability and neediness that fame has a cruel knack for seeking out, but also mindful of where he'd come from and the knowledge that returning to it, voluntarily or otherwise, was always a possibility.

'This has happened so quickly,' he said. 'I'm still that same fuckin' surfer gas-station guy who listens to music. I'm still him.'

Later in the nineties, I would have cause to reflect bitterly on this nobly modest declaration when an assignment to interview Pearl Jam for the *Independent* degenerated into three days' idling in the admittedly tolerable surround-ings of Seattle's Four Seasons hotel, waiting to be granted a twenty-minute audience. Eddie, when the moment finally arrived, just about made up for his management's discour-tesy by spending most of the interview time apologising, and then throwing the rest of his day's schedule into disarray by phoning around Seattle record shops trying to pin down a particular Elvis Presley box set I mentioned I'd had in mind as a birthday present for my then girlfriend.

*

I never understood the romantic lustre in which rock'n'roll casualties were – and, even more mysteriously, still are – bathed. The self-inflicted death of a young person is not a statement of integrity, nor confirmation that the young person in question is somehow more than this flawed world deserves; it is never anything but a tragic abnegation of possibility. At around the same time I did the Pearl Jam story, I undertook a brief and uproarious Irish tour with Lush, whose drummer, Chris Acland, would take his own life four years later, aged thirty. Possibly because Chris was a drummer, rather than a singer, and possibly because Chris always seemed, to professional acquaintances at least, as straightforwardly cheerful a chap as one could hope to share a tour bus with, no such cult was ever convened in his honour. Everybody who knew him, or knew of him, was just sad. Which was as it should have been for Chris, and as it should be for anybody who chooses to reject the only opportunity they'll have to be themselves.

The whole point, surely, of one's twenties is to enjoy a stretch of adulthood in which the swishing of the Reaper's scythe is the faintest of noises. It may have been youthful lack of perspective on this front that caused *Melody Maker* to affront a rock colossus otherwise legendary for his equable humour and implacable refusal to take himself seriously (I'm pretty sure you can't be sued for sarcasm). Lou Reed's 1992 album was *Magic and Loss*, a sombre – and really quite beautiful – meditation on the deaths of two close friends. The trouble started when the press release announcing it arrived on the desk of Mat Smith very close to deadline. Mat bashed out a terse news story, which ran beneath the even terser headline LOU'S DEATH ALBUM.[1] Not long after, a fax arrived from Reed's management, haughtily upbraiding us for regarding the artefact so brusquely. I conceived a subtle revenge, awaiting the accompanying tour: across the bottom of a generally laudatory gig review ('a quiet, mesmeric majesty') by Jim Irvin I wrote the headline THE VELVET UNDER-TAKER. It was childish, but it made my colleagues laugh, and the singular joy of working for *Melody Maker* was that you could be reasonably sure that if something made your colleagues laugh, it would also make the readers laugh, even if it didn't have a similar effect upon Lou Reed, who I'm pretty certain never spoke to us again.

---

1   Mat would one day be responsible for what is still my favourite music press headline, ahead of a field of thousands, quite a few of which appear, I realise, at various points in this volume. One day in the production department, I perceived him squinting at a short news story he'd written about some duet Kris Kristofferson and Johnny Cash had recorded, of a song written by Willie Nelson. I all but saw a lightbulb appear above Mat's head, before he tapped out the words, KRIS COVERS WILLIE WITH JOHNNY.

Such was the passive–aggressive dynamic that governed *Melody Maker*'s coverage of its bailiwick. All of us on the paper had been propelled there by a love for music and a fascination with the people who made it – and most of us, once we'd got our names on the masthead, expended quite a lot of our passion lampooning or insulting our idols. There were several possible explanations for this – the self-impressed self-righteousness of youth, resentment that the musicians got all the girls and money, even a desire to deflect embarrassment that we all did something so bloody ridiculous for a living, but better a rumbustious and unpredictable newspaper than a meek and obsequious one. It was easy to forget, however, that the subjects of our knockabout larks were human beings – and human beings, at that, possessed of egos so fragile that they'd felt compelled to seek the approval of venues full of strangers to begin with.

Reminders of this truth could be bracing. One evening at the Astoria, I was introduced by Simon Price to Nicky Wire of Manic Street Preachers, of whom I had made a certain amount of fun. While I admired these fiercely smart evangelical autodidacts, and enjoyed their interviews, which served as excellent primers on books I should have read and films I should have seen, I thought the Manics' actual music sounded like Eddie & the Hot Rods B-sides translated into Portuguese and then back into English by someone who spoke neither language. In the course of outlining these and other reservations in one of my critiques, I had apparently – although certainly unintentionally, given the ethnic background of one uncle, several *Maker* writers and, not least, *Melody Maker*'s editor – deployed the adjective 'Welsh' in a context that made it appear pejorative. I had forgotten about this. Wire, a six-foot-and-some-change stringbean swaddled in a feather boa, had not. He declined my handshake. 'I wouldn't spit on you,' he hissed, an assurance for which I was grateful. 'You fucking racist.' At which Wire flounced, with fabulous panache. I thought this a severe, if impressive, overreaction – I'd called him Welsh, not a coal-mining, rugby-playing, holiday-cottage-burning, leek-scoffing, close-harmony-singing sheep-fondler. But it was a usefully humbling, if not always heeded, reminder that what I wrote about people might get read by the people about whom it was written.

Few artists, however, can ever have been as disappointed by their introduction to the music press as Kill Laura, an otherwise unheralded combo from Liverpool who'd had the mixed fortune to have sent the office a demo which had caught the ear of the Stud Brothers. When the Studs called the number on the accompanying letter and offered to interview them, Kill Laura pooled their resources – and, one likes to imagine, gathered their meagre possessions in a handkerchief hung from the end of a stick – and descended to the capital for a rendezvous at the legendary, or at least often mentioned in *Melody Maker*, Stamford Arms.

By calamitous mischance, the Tuesday of Kill Laura's appointment was the very one on which the Studs had returned from what had been, judging by the state of them, an arduous assignation with The Butthole Surfers in Amsterdam. Whatever they had undergone had had the effect – as extreme experiences often do – of making them even more like themselves. Which is to say that the preceding seventy-two hours had made Ben even more bug-eyed and demonstrative, and Dom even more solemn and silent. To improve matters not even slightly, a package had arrived from a reader in Bulgaria, seeking to convey his appreciation for our labours in the form of a few bottles of the output of his still. Opening one at the start of the editorial meeting, I had taken a whiff and thought it a bad sign that all the hair fell out of my nostrils. I passed it, timorously unsipped, to Ben Stud, who sank half the bottle in a swig. And the other half in another.

The ensuing conclave was one of our less productive, though more memorable, being essentially a monologue by Ben – never short of a word even at his most sober – on the subject of fuck knew what, only brought to a close by senior staff when his oration culminated, for reasons lost in the random rhetoric, with an offer to fight Ted, the features editor, in the car park. Ben was decanted by Dom Stud to the pub – where, Dom dutifully reminded him, Kill Laura awaited their big break.

One hopes that Kill Laura still speak of their encounter with the Studs to their fellow Liverpudlians as a cautionary tale, akin to Banjo Paterson's 'Man from Ironbark', of the perils that await callow hicks in the big smoke. Barely had the interview commenced than with a resounding 'thwock', evocative of a well-struck cover drive, Ben went abruptly face down on the pub table. This presented a difficulty. In contrast to Ben's habitual garrulousness, Dom was taciturn to the point of being a silent partner. Dom and Kill Laura regarded each other in perplexed hush for some minutes before Ben returned to consciousness with the suddenness of a jack-in-the-box. He vaulted to his feet and began addressing the pub at large. It became clear that he believed himself still in the Netherlands, and that the locals had a historical debt to clear.

'You fucking Dutch . . .' he began. 'Clog-wearing bastards. Where were you when the skies were dark with Dorniers? Hiding in your fucking attics, in your windmills, riding bicycles.'

Dom and I, instantly aware that this was unlikely to end well, escorted Ben outside before someone less favourably disposed to Ben offered to do the same. We hailed a taxi. Dom poured Ben into the back and pressed a twenty on the driver.

'Where do you want me to take him?' the cabbie asked.

'Away,' said Dom. 'May I have a receipt? Don't worry about filling it in.'

*

Any rock journalist gets asked – not infrequently by themselves – whether their personal proximity to people who make revered records dilutes the mystery and marvel of those artefacts. What degree of disappointment, even betrayal, might one feel upon discovering that – for example – a group one had once idolised, to a poster-purchasing degree, as profound existentialist romantics, consumptive poets and beat angels, were actually a gang of middle-class football hooligans? Backstage at the World, a 15,000-seat arena about ninety minutes' drive from Chicago, I was introduced to The Cure.

A couple of years earlier, back in Sydney, I spent little time wondering what it would be like to meet the waifish figure in the *Boys Don't Cry* poster affixed to my bedroom wall – if only because the chances of any such encounter occurring would have seemed vanishingly remote, akin to the prospects of a delegation of distinguished Tibetans appearing on the doorstep and informing me, and they were pretty sure they'd done their sums right, that I was the next Dalai Lama. But if I'd been asked, I'd probably have imagined that a late-night tete-a-tete with Robert Smith would have been longer on sips of absinthe and quips from Baudelaire, and shorter on having to yell at the sodden singer's foetal figure – over the deafening strains of Middle of the Road's 'Chirpy Chirpy Cheep Cheep' booming from the tour bus stereo – that I could see perfectly disposed to Ben offered to do the same. We hailed a taxi. Dom poured Ben into the back and pressed a twenty on the driver.

'Where do you want me to take him?' the cabbie asked.

'Away,' said Dom. 'May I have a receipt? Don't worry about filling it in.'

*

Any rock journalist gets asked – not infrequently by themselves – whether their personal proximity to people who make revered records dilutes the mystery and marvel of those artefacts. What degree of disappointment, even betrayal, might one feel upon discovering that – for example – a group one had once idolised, to a poster-purchasing degree, as profound existentialist romantics, consumptive poets and beat angels, were actually a gang of middle-class football hooligans? Backstage at the World, a 15,000-seat arena about ninety minutes' drive from Chicago, I was introduced to The Cure.

A couple of years earlier, back in Sydney, I spent little time wondering what it would be like to meet the waifish figure in the *Boys Don't Cry* poster affixed to my bedroom wall – if only because the chances of any such encounter occurring would have seemed vanishingly remote, akin to the prospects of a delegation of distinguished Tibetans appearing on the doorstep and informing me, and they were pretty sure they'd done their sums right, that I was the next Dalai Lama. But if I'd been asked, I'd probably have imagined that a late-night tete-a-tete with Robert Smith would have been longer on sips of absinthe and quips from Baudelaire, and shorter on having to yell at the sodden singer's foetal figure – over the deafening strains of Middle of the Road's 'Chirpy Chirpy Cheep Cheep' booming from the tour bus stereo – that I could see perfectly clearly that he was trying to tie my shoelaces together, so he might as well knock it off.

The Cure were twelve weeks into the epic 'Wish' tour, and had possibly spent too much time on this bus (Smith wasn't keen on flying – The Cure had crossed the Atlantic on the *Queen Elizabeth II*). They were gripped by the common tour bus syndrome of hopeless rebellion against confines one has voluntarily assumed – drinking, squirting each other with HP sauce and ketchup, wrestling with the road crew, bellowing along to daft pop music played at window-rattling volume (the playlist also included T-Rex's 'Hot Love' and Gary Glitter's 'Didn't Know I Loved You Till I Saw You Rock'n'Roll'). If it hadn't been quite what I'd been expecting, I daresay the scene inside the bus would have been an even greater surprise to the crowd gathered in the forecourt of The Cure's hotel in Chicago.

As Smith was ushered through the mascara-smeared legions of lookalike fans, Stephen Sweet, who was along to take photographs for our cover story, shot one of the best illustrations of the dysfunctional relationship between celebrity and celebrator I've ever seen. From behind Smith's shoulder, Sweet took a picture of the singer's meeting with one especially ardent adherent, capturing both the worshipper's supplicant gawp and Smith's wincing, forehead-rubbing awkwardness. The fan was sporting an impeccably composed simulacra of Smith's image – tangled hair, smeared makeup, baggy clothes, big shoes. Smith looked like someone who'd spent ninety minutes brawling and roaring Gary Glitter choruses on the floor of a tour bus while his bandmates doused him in condiments. For neither man in the photo, you could tell, was this interaction quite what either of them might once have anticipated.

A couple of nights later, backstage at the Skydome in Toronto, I found a soberer Smith in a more reflective mood.

227

The strain of cabin fever that had gripped the band in Chicago seemed now to be incubating in the tour manager, who was delighting in altering the rubber stamp with which he validated backstage passes, so that instead of the usual *Guest* or *VIP*, the after-show hangers-on were wearing stickers that read *Freeloader*, *Blagger* or *No Idea*; mine said *Poser*.

'The fans,' sighed Smith. 'I dunno. Things started bothering me on the last American tour. We'd reached a certain level, and people knew where we were staying, and they'd check into the same hotels, so I'd have people camping in the hall outside my room, not just one or two but lots, sitting in the corridor and listening through the door, and it made me very . . . uncomfortable.'

Smith sounded almost as if he thought he was being unreasonable.

'But at the same time,' he continued, 'I couldn't really go out and tell them to fuck off, because really I should be pleased. But I wasn't. So I'd just lie there and agonise over it, and it was driving me mad. So this time we're all checked in under ridiculous assumed names, our hotels aren't listed in the itinerary, so only we know where we're staying, stuff like that.'

It still must be bloody strange looking out at an arena full of people all trying their damnedest to look like you. A bit *Life of Brian*, I'd have thought: you know, 'Yes! We're all individuals!' Smith, it turned out, had given this more, and more generous, thought than I had.

'We went to this funny little diner a couple of weeks ago,' he recalled, 'somewhere between Denver and St Louis, or wherever. Anyway, horrible little town, full of people who aren't particularly friendly to people who look like us. Anyway, we went in, and what must have been the only two Cure fans for miles around arrived just as we were finishing our meal – someone must have phoned them and tipped them off. And they were all dressed up, and made up, and wearing black, you know.

'I mean, I don't know why they did it, but at the same time . . . when they walked in, everybody in the place went "Oooh", like they were obviously the local weirdos. But when those people put two and two together, they had a kind of new-found respect, like, "Oh, we know this band, and these people are fans of this band." So I think people do it for that reason, to step outside the norm. And in some of the places we're going, that must take a lot of courage. I think, really, it's just like war paint or tribal feathers or a . . . I dunno, a kilt, or something.'

In small and smallish towns in America ever since, whenever I've seen the local kooks shuffle uneasily into a bar or cafe, I've thought about that observation, and about how burdensome it must be to have your idea of yourself appropriated by strangers. I'd probably drink and fight with my roadies as well.

'The thing to keep remembering,' said Smith, 'is that we're a very foolish band. And we always have been.'

ANDREW MUELLER

16

IN WHICH THE AUTHOR ENJOYS A FIFTEEN-SECOND CAREER AS A STADIUM ROCK GOD

In a music industry environment whose sources of information and influence were still restricted by the limits of
technology, it was satisfyingly easy for a weekly music newspaper to create a fuss, when we felt like it. In the spring
of 1992, we decided to take a proper flyer, and put on the
cover a group who were not only unsigned, but more or
less unknown. They were Suede, who we'd written about
here and there, and who I'd seen play once or twice, buried
down the bill in various dumps. In yet further testament to
my unwavering incompetence as an A&R scout, I'd thought
them diverting, but no more than that.

Suede had since enticed the services of an independent press
office, the influential Savage & Best, and cobbled together
a brilliant demo tape which had united *Melody Maker*'s
office in a rare appreciative consensus – something usually
only inspired by daft novelties like twee Japanese popettes
Shonen Knife, belligerent Irish wastrels Sultans of Ping FC
or atrocious German punk rockers Die Toten Hosen, which
is to say fleetingly amusing acts who nobody really cared
about. Slapping Suede on the cover was an audacious call,

though, which Steve and Allan somehow talked each other into. My minor contribution to Suede's foundation myth was an adjustment to the cover line, which originally read 'The Best New Band in Britain?' Mindful of the rarely fallible law which holds that the answer to any newspaper headline which ends in a question mark is 'no', and believing that we might as well go hard if we were going to go, I suggested removing the punctuation.

Suede didn't let us down. The privilege of a front-row seat at the early stages of Suede's ascent really was one of those watcher-of-the-skies-when-a-new-comet-appears periods. In London, I wrote a semi-hysterical review of their show at Covent Garden's Afrika Centre which doesn't embarrass me as much now as I suspect it probably should ('Just believe us now if never again; all our alarms are ringing true'). In Newcastle, I took a friend along to see them, Phil Mitchell of Kitchenware records, who reluctantly conceded at the outset of the evening to endure a few minutes of these 'overhyped blouse-wearing nancies' (which, coming from the man who'd signed Prefab Sprout, was high-octane prejudice indeed). A little over half an hour later – Suede played brief sets with no encore, which they managed to sell as a statement of confidence, rather than an admission that this was all they knew – Phil was expressing annoyance that some other label had already snapped them up.

It was, of course, scarcely unusual for *Melody Maker* writers to proclaim barely heard of groups some measure of way, truth and light. It was, however, unusual for us to be proved correct. Probably for this reason, *Melody Maker* became somewhat possessive of Suede, to a degree which would have consequences. In May 1992, Suede opened for Kingmaker at the Town & Country Club. Kingmaker were a workmanlike indie trio who were enormously popular with the T-shirt-wearing, cider-quaffing hordes, who adored Kingmaker with a fervour which *Melody Maker* found vexing, as – in another rare consensus – absolutely nobody on the paper liked Kingmaker; we considered them duller than nine courses of lettuce. Steve Sutherland informed me that he'd review this show, and take the opportunity to draw a few battle lines. His report alternated between italics (*his rapturous admiration for Suede*) and plain type (his vicious derision for Kingmaker). It climaxed thus: 'Let's not fanny around, shall we? The Unstoppable Frank & King Carter Dustbin Stare. NME. *Suede. Verve. Levitation. Pavement. Mercury Rev. Melody Maker.* Dogshit. *Diamonds.*'

It did not require an advanced appreciation of semiotics to see what Steve had done there. The composite band name was an amalgamated reference to Carter USM, The Frank & Walters, Kingmaker, Ned's Atomic Dustbin and Thousand Yard Stare, all chirpy, grinning, self-consciously wacky acts for student discos to sing along to, and all of which the *NME*, whether out of conviction or expedience, championed heartily. The citation of such outliers as Suede, Verve, Levitation, Pavement and Mercury Rev was intended to establish *Melody Maker* as the righteous and raffishly glamorous opposition to the *NME*'s beery bumptiousness. I believe that the point stands, even if Suede are the only act in Steve's list I'd still listen to, and even if Steve was a bald man who wore shorts.

Apparently fearing the infinitesimally unlikely event of anybody missing the point, I added the headline PEARLS BEFORE SWINE (God, we were obnoxious). Steve, at least, would shortly have cause to wish that he'd taken a more equivocal view.

In the real world, things which mattered continued to occur. I was accidental witness to the guttering embers of one of these – the riots that convulsed Los Angeles following the scandalous acquittal of the four white Los Angeles Police Department officers who had, in an early forerunner of today's ubiquitous citizen journalism, been filmed beating up black motorist Rodney King. From the window of our aircraft approaching LAX, one of the first allowed to land following the reopening of the airport, I could see fires fading into the sunset. En route to our accommodations, we drove past rows of gutted, soot-stained shops and got stuck in traffic behind an armoured personnel carrier belonging to the California National Guard. Normal service was not resumed until I reached the lift in the lobby of the hotel, which had arrived from the basement car park. 'Which floor you want, man?' asked the unmistakable apparition of Eddie Van Halen.

It was hard not to feel frivolous, being nominally a journalist in that place at that time, with no more significant assignment than to spend a couple of days in a Burbank warehouse watching a rock group (Faith No More) make a rock video ('Midlife Crisis'). Watching a rock group make a rock video, it turned out – this was a first, for me – was much like watching a rock group soundcheck, except that it went on for even longer and was therefore even more tedious. It's another one of those experiences that you can recreate at home anytime you feel like it, by laying out insufficient quantities of rancid food on your dining table, then asking a few friends to charge importantly about waving clipboards and shouting, while five depressed, bored musicians mope on your sofa.

I drew some consolation from the fact that I was at least chalking off two more important rock'n'roll milestones. One, staying at the Hyatt on Sunset, where the ghosts of Led Zeppelin's televisions swooped from the balconies, and where one could – and Faith No More did, word-perfect – pay homage to one of the climactic scenes of *This is Spinal Tap* by lounging around the rooftop pool and planning a musical based on the life of Jack the Ripper. Two, under-taking a foreign trip with Andy Catlin, a *Melody Maker* photographer who, until this point, had only existed for me as a character from fable, a legend that loomed in pub myths which included phrases like 'so he set the guy's jacket on fire', 'next thing I know, he's swinging across the stage on the curtain cord', 'and he put all the damage on expenses', 'upside down in a ditch' and 'of course, we didn't get our deposit back'. Catlin never came into the office. He didn't have to. He lived, it was said, in a vast mansion block apartment in Maida Vale, reputedly the proceeds of a generous merchan-dising deal cut with an extremely famous rock star who liked his pictures (or, it was suspected, was too terrified to refuse him). He drove, it was known for a fact, a vast, vintage baby blue Jaguar, which he handled with the abandon of someone sufficiently well-heeled not to take it seriously.

To my considerable relief and comparable disappointment, Catlin more or less behaved in Los Angeles, his aspirations thwarted by Faith No More's press officer, Eugene Manzi, who had travelled with Catlin before and therefore refused to add his name to the insurance for our rented Cadillac. ('I think,' Eugene declared, 'Los Angeles has suffered enough.') Catlin would make up for it a few months later when he went back to the US to photograph Faith No More for *Melody Maker* again, this time with Mat Smith. *Melody Maker*'s contingent, along with Faith No More guitarist Jim Martin, were apprehended by police early one morning for shooting at beer cans in a Pittsburgh hotel parking lot, thereby ensuring that the Catlin Tales would now also include the phrase 'was eventually let off with a warning'.

From Los Angeles, I flew on to Portland, Oregon, to meet The Disposable Heroes of Hiphoprisy. It was fortuitous timing, in that I got to learn a lot about the Los Angeles riots that I hadn't learnt from being in Los Angeles. Hiphoprisy's thoughtful frontman, Michael Franti, had been born in Oakland and grown up in California. Though generally at ease with my middle-class white maleness, I felt out of my depth talking to Franti about this stuff; not because he was blacker than me, but because he was smarter. I provided him with the opportunity to say something daft and sentimental about the riots. He almost did, and then pivoted in the opposite direction.

'What you must understand,' he said, in his soft, measured lilt, 'is that what happened isn't a reaction, but an action against twelve years of conservative policies that have sucked the money out of those communities which rose last week.'

I wasn't sure it had been about money rather than race. I kind of hoped so, as money problems are easier to fix. But I didn't think many of the Korean–American business owners who'd clearly been targeted would have been so sympathetic.

'It was both [race and money],' said Franti. 'You can't really say one or the other. I mean, I firmly believe that if it had been a white man beaten by black cops, and an African jury had acquitted them . . .'

There'd have been trouble, I said. But probably less of it.

'So,' nodded Franti, 'it obviously is a race issue. But the economic conditions that created those conditions have been racist as well. I think this was inevitable. It reached a boiling point and, sadly, took the shape it did. But the energy released – man, that was beautiful. If we could just do something with that energy.'

Walking down the hotel corridor to the lift, we passed a vending machine, to which was affixed a sign announcing

Ice Cubes. 'Wow,' said Franti. 'Do you think he has one of these in every hotel?'

After the show, I flagged down a cab operated by a man who had no front teeth and a hook where his right hand used to be. 'Driving a taxi in Portland after midnight,' he told me, 'is like a natural drug, man.'

Repeated exposure to America was not causing me to love it less.

*

The mantra 'never apologise, never explain' is often bruited by practitioners of the critic's craft seeking to imbue the task of pecking irritably at a keyboard with a certain bullet-chewing machismo, as if slapping a two-star review on the new Depeche Mode album is an act of exemplary punitive terror akin to Sherman's march from Atlanta to the sea, or Lord Elgin's order to destroy the Summer Palace.

It is not a creed to which I've ever subscribed, partly because the people who utter it always seem to be such massive tools, but also because both apologising and explaining are often the right things to do, on the grounds that people get stuff wrong, or simply and honestly change their minds. But just as newspapers routinely punish incumbent and aspiring office-holders for 'flip-flopping' – as if it would be good, or other than evidence of a psychotic monomania, if a politician discharged decades of public service without once rethinking anything – few crimes stoked the ire of the music press like an act who deviated from the template established by their first record, as if it would be preferable for artists never to attempt to extend themselves. But there are few qualities so overrated as consistency. Or so I've always thought.

As late as May 1992, I had barely troubled to listen to U2's *Achtung Baby*, which had been released six months previously. I'd commissioned *Melody Maker*'s review of it, handing it to Chris Roberts in the expectation that he'd administer the thrashing it doubtless merited, and had been startled when Chris decided that 'U2 have, against all expectations, evoked shivers and Paradise, some anguish and much desire'. I had assumed, however, that this was one of Chris's signature perverse wind-ups, akin to his occasional attempts to make a case for, say, Queen or George Michael on the (not unreasonable) grounds that they were, whatever else one may say about them, by definition more interesting than Cud or The Senseless Things or whichever other sack of greasy-fringed never-gonna-bes the paper was pretending to care about that week.

So I first heard *Achtung Baby* played live, pretty much, in the Palau Sant Jordi arena in Barcelona. I was in town to do another feature on The Fatima Mansions, who were opening for U2 on the European leg of the 'Zoo TV' tour. I embarked thinking, essentially: 'Excellent. A free trip to a city I've always wanted to visit to see one of my very favourite bands, and I'll get to give those pompous twerps U2 another kicking into the bargain, which will not only be no less than they deserve but will make me appear even more unimpressably cool to my colleagues than I'm sure I already do, and will cause me to feel good about myself for reasons I cannot quite enumerate, but which probably have something to do with an unhealthy yearning for the regard or at least the attention of total strangers, though it'd be fair of me to observe on this front that Bono would appear to suffer from this latter one, at least, some way worse than I do.'

Initially, all went according to plan. The Fatima Mansions' Cathal Coughlan was once again an unusually forthright and funny interview subject. The Fatima Mansions had just released *Valhalla Avenue*, a seething, swearing, tieless gatecrasher of a record. 'For sheer perversity value alone,' he said, 'this whole thing appeals to me strongly. Especially since we've just released our least commercial record yet, and what do we do to promote it? A stadium tour. Makes perfect sense. It seemed like the most ridiculous thing we could do, in the circumstances. So here we all are.'

We – myself and Stephen Sweet – travelled to the venue in the Mansions' tour bus, our journey soundtracked by the stylings of the group's alter ego, The Tower of Crap. The Tower of Crap were comprised of members of The Fatima Mansions and various antique brass instruments they had acquired on their recent travels, none of which they could play even slightly. With the bus sunroof open to allow full extension of the trombone, they treated the traffic jams of U2 fans to discordant interpretations of various jazz and funk classics, including James Brown's 'Say it Loud, I'm Crap And I'm Proud', and Miles Davis's 'Sketches of Crap'.

At the venue, I discerned an early indication that U2 might have acquired a sense of humour since concluding the evangelical roadshow of *Rattle and Hum*. Sounding almost disappointed, Coughlan explained that he had not heard a whisper of objection from the headliners to the Fatima Mansions tour T-shirts being hung on U2's merchandise stalls: they read, in scrawled white handwriting on black, *Fuck Your Showbizness*. Backstage, the Mansions leafed through the tour brochure containing the names and roles of every member of U2's immense operation. 'Assistant inflight caterer,' marvelled Coughlan. 'You know you've made it when you have an assistant inflight caterer. Not when you have your own plane, or when your plane has a caterer, but when that guy has an assistant. Next tour we do, I want an assistant inflight caterer. I don't care if we have no other crew.'

Phil Mitchell of Kitchenware, also Fatima Mansions' label boss, dared me to introduce Fatima Mansions onstage. 'In,' he further goaded, 'Catalan.' Catalan is one of many languages in which I am other than fluent. I was offered help by Christina, the young woman who was, brilliantly, managing to see the world in considerable style by bellydancing during one song – 'Mysterious Ways' – in U2's show (her successor in the role would do even better, becoming the second Mrs The Edge). We wrote a brief speech that emphasised the Mansions' Irish heritage, and she disappeared in search of a translation, a responsibility I was happy to delegate, believing her more likely to be persuasive of passing local crew than myself. She returned with a scribbled paragraph. I sought assurance that it meant what we wanted it to, and not 'Fuck you all, sons of fatherless goats, and I hope Real Madrid kick your communist arses in the Copa del Rey final.' (Cathal would actually do worse a couple of nights later in Milan, almost prompting a riot by baiting the already restive crowd with some disobliging remarks about the Pope and doing something unspeakable with a Virgin Mary shampoo bottle he had purchased on an excursion to Lourdes.)

For all that rock critics are routinely accused of being frustrated rock stars, the few seconds I was up there were the only few seconds I was ever jealous of the people I wrote about. At this level, I could see, this would be aces. Even though not one of the thousands of people in the venue had the first idea who I was when I tottered onto the stage, they cheered my appearance. Though my holler of 'Hola, Barcelona!' can have done nothing to enlighten them, they roared a response that broke upon me like a wave. My hopelessly accented announcement of '*Damas y caballeros, desde Irlanda,* Los Fatima Mansions!' elicited a manmade thunderclap. This, I thought, as I glimpsed the roadie immediately stageside performing a mime which appeared to involve a shepherd's crook, would be a fun way to make a living.

To my considerable surprise, U2 seemed to have emerged from the desert they had recently been wandering with grim, dust-blown purpose, and arrived at the same conclusion. I returned to London feeling that I had no meaningful alternative but to report that the 'Zoo TV' show had been astonishing and that, on reflection, *Achtung Baby* wasn't a bad record at all. 'I can't quite believe,' I wrote, 'that the cringeworthy self-aggrandising of *Rattle and Hum* was a deliberate prelude to this spectacular slash attack on the bubble' – not one of my defter metaphors – 'and nor do Bono's witheringly ironic posturings quite seem like an apology – but as an acknowledgement of the emptiness of his creation, this is pretty damn satisfying stuff. It's like watching a bishop burn a cathedral.'

A matter of hours after the review hit the newsstands, a motorcycle messenger from U2's press office deposited on my desk a box containing the entire back catalogue and a note inviting me to change my mind still further, or words to that effect. None of which impressed Mr Agreeable (nee Abusing), a David Stubbs alter ego who dominated the TTT section of the paper with a weekly column of expletive-riddled rage: 'Andrew Mueller was definitely only there because he's a big Fatima Mansions fan and not because he'd mud wrestle his own mother for a free weekend in Barcelona, let's get that f***ing straight!'

ANDREW MUELLER

17

IN WHICH THE AUTHOR LEARNS FROM HIS ELDERS AND BETTERS

On the subject of mud-wrestling, festival season had arrived again. This was not quite the all-consuming deal it is in Britain today, when one can, if so inclined, spend every weekend between Easter and Halloween in ankle-deep mud, and stuff which you hope is mud, squinting across acres of perfectly good cow pasture at something that just about sounds like it might be Florence + The Machine (though this would almost certainly be preferable to something that sounded precisely like Florence + The Machine). For *Melody Maker*, the two festivals which counted in 1992 were Glastonbury and Reading. That year, Glastonbury was actually tolerable, which is to say it didn't rain. More significantly, as reviews editor – and therefore nominally in charge of *Melody Maker*'s coverage – I didn't have to do terribly much.

I assigned myself to review the main stage on the Saturday. My report attempted – almost convincingly, I like to think – to construct a virtue of the fact that I hadn't even discharged these light duties diligently. '[Glastonbury] is not just three gigs in a paddock,' I had the nerve to write, before listing the better things I found to do with my day than suffer through Ocean Colour Scene, The Saw Doctors, Shakespears Sister and The Fall. I at least performed more professionally than Simon Price, who wilted early beneath the combination of the warm weather, his Bolan-joins-Bauhaus ensemble, his usual three inches of makeup and as many bottles of Malibu, and who spent much of his shift dozing in a backstage hospitality tent. An American record company emissary associated with one of the bands playing approached me and earnestly asked if she might be introduced to the *Melody Maker* correspondent reviewing the day's entertainment. It was with heartfelt pride in my title and all it stood for that I gestured towards the snoring heap of fake fur, faux leather and blood-red hair extensions, and said he was all hers, if she could rouse him. Impressively in the circumstances, Pricey's eventual report prompted only one testy fax from a group complaining that he'd mixed them up with someone else entirely.

Reading wasn't bad fun either, even if it did rain – and rain, and rain, and rain, and rain, and rain. A much-abused lexicon of cliché has been too often drawn upon, not infrequently by this correspondent, to describe muddy festival sites. This leaden hyperbole usually involves reference to the Western Front, and is often accompanied by the rimshot-begging punchline that at least General Haig's sodden and terrified soldiers hadn't had to listen to Pavement. The truth is that Reading 1992 was not as bad as the Battle of the Somme, but there the praise had to end. By the third and final day, traversing the arena all but necessitated using both hands to remove alternating legs from the ooze – and it was a journey I was having to make frequently, having cunningly (or so I thought) secured my hotel room for the weekend by volunteering to help oversee proceedings in the *Melody Maker* autograph tent instead of actually writing anything.

The autograph tent had been a notion so obvious to us that we couldn't understand why nobody had thought of it before. By the end of the weekend, we realised that loads of people had probably thought of it before, but had then probably thought about it. The idea appeared dazzlingly simple – to flush artists out of the backstage enclosure for an hour or so to meet the punters and sign some stuff, which might hopefully help recruit a few readers and/or sell some *Melody Maker* merchandise. Our error was to underestimate the popularity of the enterprise. There was a two-hour queue even for an audience with fleetingly popular grunge Girlschool L7 – who had made a regrettably unforgettable contribution to Reading lore during their set on the main stage when Donita Sparks, lead vocalist, reacted to the dirt clods hailing upon the stage from the crowd by reciprocating with her tampon. Suede's appearance in the tent seemed to draw a bigger attendance than whoever was playing the main stage at the time. It is possible that the fact that we at least had a roof had something to do with this. Certainly, in the conditions, none of our gear proved as popular as the complimentary yellow plastic bags, reading *Carry Me Home, I'm Pissed*, which became the weekend's universal choice of improvised waterproof headgear.

It was chaos. The expertise of *Melody Maker* staff in crowd control did not extend much beyond periodically emerging from beneath a tent flap and yelling, 'Will you please. All. Back the fuck. Up,' at a queue of filthy, bedraggled Buffalo Tom fans. But it was also genuinely sweet. A pleasure of covering relatively obscure artists was that most of our guests were as thrilled to meet fans in concentrated numbers as their fans were to get their records signed, and many musicians stayed for ages beyond their allotted slots. Only one artist, former Black Flag frontman Henry Rollins, seemed unpleased to be there. This may have been the fault of Allan Jones, who answered Rollins' call, relayed via some minion, for an escort from the backstage enclosure to the *Melody Maker* tent. As the pair emerged into the arena, utterly unnoticed by the rabble congregated in front of the main stage, Allan handed Rollins his beer and said, 'Here, Hank. Hang on to my drink while I push a path through this adoring throng.' But even Rollins lightened up after one earnest young fan waved away Rollins' pen, announced that an autograph would hold no value for him, and that he merely wished to shake Rollins' hand.

Despite the opportunity to briefly savour the company of assorted indie rock luminaries, it feels safe to suggest that had anybody else but that year's headliners been headlining the main stage on the last day, the only people remaining on the property by the end of Reading 1992 would have been those so firmly planted in the sucking mire that they had been unable to free themselves. The place was a swamp, proceedings on the second stage had to be halted when the huge tent shrouding it threatened to blow away, and thousands and thousands of people were having precisely the same conversation, i.e. the one about how these shoes were ruined, I tell you, ruined. But we were waiting for Nirvana.

I was doing this more out of curiosity than admiration. Though I still thought Nirvana overrated, and believed their allegedly epoch-divining anthem 'Smells Like Teen Spirit' to be a flagrant rewrite of a hoary old Boston song, I'd quite liked bits of *Nevermind*, and had enjoyed their show at the Palace in Hollywood the previous year. But like everyone else with an interest in left-field rock music – and, such had been the success of *Nevermind*, millions more besides – I'd become, somewhat to my own irritation, as gripped by the attendant soap opera as anyone. A recurring theme of

Reading's backstage conversation had been the swapping of rumours of Nirvana's cancellation. This was over and above the usual Reading rumour, which was traditionally about the death, in surprisingly scandalous circumstances, of Cliff Richard. This would usually be launched by bored hacks sometime on the Friday afternoon, and would typically acquire the status of universally acknowledged gospel by lunchtime on the Saturday. Given that almost nobody had a mobile telephone with which such yarns might be checked with the outside world, festivals were potent echo chambers. Fortunately, now that we have the internet, it is impossible for complete nonsense to become widely believed.

Every appearance in the backstage beer tent by a major artist not on the bill had sparked further speculation that a last-minute replacement for Nirvana had been drafted. Nirvana's response was magnificent, if retrospectively poignant when it is considered that the young musician who began his set by mocking the prurient interest in his drug problems and mental health had about twenty months to live. Cobain arrived onstage dressed in a hospital gown and a blond wig, slouched in a wheelchair pushed by Everett True. Cobain stood, and feigned a collapse, before rising again, removing the wig and leading his group through a set which compelled me towards the never comfortable conclusion that everybody else in the world but me may have been right after all. Nirvana even 'fessed where 'Smells Like Teen Spirit' was concerned, mashing it up with 'More Than a Feeling'.

Much of the time, working as a rock journalist necessitates blocking out those voices, actual and internal, suggesting that you could probably be doing something more important with your time – like, for example, anything else at all. Some of the time, it feels like you're doing something that kind of matters. Despite the fact that I was cold, and tired, and about a foot closer to sea level than I'd been when Nirvana had started playing, I felt dreadfully envious of the writers who'd be getting to write something about this.

This was despite – or because of – the fact that I'd earlier become somewhat overexcited covering another festival that summer, the travelling rock circus Lollapalooza. I'd wanted to report Lollapalooza as if it was the 1968 Democratic Convention and I was Norman Mailer, but it wasn't and neither was I. When you're young, it's not enough merely to listen to music: you want to believe that someone, some-where, is enraged and/or alarmed that you're listening to what you're listening to. This solipsistic delusion is fuelled by the reliable willingness of nitwitted wowsers to respond in exactly this fashion. In 1992, this role was being most foolishly filled by something called the Parents' Music Resource Centre, a council of self-appointed invigilators deriving undue prominence from the fact that their leader's husband was about to become vice-president of the United States. The PMRC was the driving force behind the label-ling of albums, forbiddingly warning of 'adult content', as if there were much chance of an Aerosmith record containing any such thing.

In 1992, I thought the PMRC were a dangerous enemy to be revolted against, and that Lollapalooza amounted to a cross-country campaign that would – somehow, I hadn't quite thought the details through – gather irresist-ible momentum before smashing the citadel of the western world's uptight prigs, wherever and whatever that happened to be. I even, so help me, ennobled Lollapalooza in my report as a 'crusade'. A couple of decades later, I still think the (now apparently disbanded) PMRC and all fellow travellers are a dim, annoying claque of quacking cretins, but I also think about them what they should have thought about rock'n'roll and hip hop, i.e. that people are entitled to make whatever noise pleases them, but I'm under no obligation to listen to it. The one bankable indicator of a weak or uncertain mind is a desire to censure or censor attitudes and opinions that contradict it. Or, as Ministry's Paul Barker put it when I solicited his motivations for joining this glorious jeremiad, which would surely bring down the walls of oppression, scatter the forces of darkness and herald a new dawn of . . .

'Basically, six weeks of this equals studio. And we want a studio so bad.'

Barker, to his considerable credit, had risen above the fear that afflicted much left-field American rock of being seen to be in any way interested in acquiring wealth, or even earning much of a living, from making music. My next interview subject had not. Bob Mould welcomed me into his suite in Cincinnati's Vernon Manor hotel – previously a way station, I'd noted from the brochure in my own room, for John F. Kennedy and Nancy Reagan – with an apology.

'I don't believe this,' said Mould, wincing at accommodations indeed fit for a president, or the mad wife of one. 'I've never stayed anywhere like this.'

As far as I was concerned, it was the very least Mould deserved. In a universe calibrated according to my values, Mould would have been permanently billeted in digs of lavishness that would have overawed William Randolph Hearst, and attended by legions of obsequious serfs who competed for the honour of stringing his solid gold Flying V with the hair of unicorns' tails. Though I liked what I'd heard of Mould's new group, Sugar, the real reason I'd pitched for this interview was that Mould had once played guitar and sung in Hüsker Dü, not merely a band I'd loved to distraction at school, but a band who had recently become, despite having split up in 1987, inescapably influential: the signature schtick of Seattle grunge, of the sweetest of melodies buried beneath the filthiest of guitars, had been informed to a colossal degree by Hüsker Dü.

'I don't even think about it anymore,' said Mould, 'except when people bring it up. Which is nearly all the time.'

Mould seemed resigned to the reality that this interview was not going to be any exception. He sighed politely at my every good-hearted attempt to characterise him as some sort of godfather – or, worse, grandfather – figure to the hairy Sub Pop groups that *Melody Maker* were now smearing across the cover almost every week. 'Come on,' he pleaded, 'I'm only thirty-one.' Out of chronic modesty, or the desire to stop another journalist blithering on and on about his old group, Mould also attempted to spread the credit. 'Oh, I hear it, I do,' he said of Hüsker Dü's influence. 'And I know Nirvana admit to it. And yeah, I think it's cool. But it wasn't just Hüsker Dü. It was The Minutemen, Meat Puppets, Black Flag, Circle Jerks. I think it may have a lot to do with the fact that Hüsker Dü were kind of the first to start and the last to quit.'

Mould was more gracious about fielding Hüsker Dü-related enquiries than his erstwhile collaborator Grant Hart had been when I'd met him the year before. But he was nevertheless straining perceptibly against the same dreadful punishment that rock'n'roll visits upon its most important figures – that of being defined forever by something you did in your twenties, of playing through your thirties, forties, fifties and maybe beyond to audiences who, whatever regard they may have for your newer material, are fidgetingly anticipating the encores, while you wonder if you can bear once more to crank out a song written half a lifetime ago, for reasons you might barely remember. When I saw Sugar play that night, to a two-thirds-full house at Cincinnati venue

Bogart's, it was impossible to avoid noticing that they barely drew breath, let alone spoke, between songs. This was, Mould later explained, so nobody would have any opportunity to holler any annoying requests for old Hüsker Dü songs.

In a coincidence that would, many years later, prove useful for seamlessly stitching together two paragraphs in a book I was writing, Mould had also recently sung a duet on one track on *Red Heaven*, the new album by Throwing Muses, my next interview. I flew from Cincinnati to Newport, Rhode Island. I was met at the airport by Billy O'Connell, manager of Throwing Muses, and husband of Throwing Muses song-writer Kristin Hersh. Contributing further to the happy families vibe was the fact that I was, at the time, going out with a press officer at Throwing Muses' record label, 4AD. My doing this story was obviously, therefore, an appalling conflict of interest, which I can defend only by observing that i) this sort of thing really did happen quite a lot, the music business being no less incestuous than most, and ii) I had been listening to Throwing Muses since I'd had to spend a fair chunk of a day's pay to purchase imported copies of their albums back in Australia. Billy drove me to the lovely house that he and Kristin shared with two preternaturally pleasant children, Dylan and Ryder. Kristin made me soup and worried that I looked tired.

I was pleased to meet Kristin, as she was one of my favourite songwriters, and I thought Throwing Muses were just astounding: flailing to explain why in the introduction of the feature I eventually wrote, I described them as 'one of the most compelling, unsettling and discomfiting groups extant', which was true as far as it went, though it made a canon of exquisite melody, wonderful singing and giddy, gleeful rock'n'roll sound much harder work than it is. But

I would remain ever after glad that I met Kristin, not merely because of my limitless appetite for the conversation of smart, funny, kind people who make excellent soup, but because her example would serve as a useful prophylaxis against one of the more pernicious strains of rock'n'roll bullshit, that of the tortured artist.

Kristin was, in this regard, the real thing. The year before, she'd explained in an interview with the Stud Brothers that her extraordinary songs were substantially the product of a bipolar personality disorder – that, indeed, she often felt less like the composer of them than the messenger who merely delivered the works of the characters who'd taken up lodging in her head. She named three of her tenants: She-Wolf, Bee and Fear. She regarded this, rightly, as nothing to boast about, but as something that could be talked about, ideally with a certain wry candour.

In rock'n'roll as elsewhere, the most dramatic claims of – or most tantalising allusions to – psychological disequilibrium are usually made by people who are merely vain, silly, spoilt and badly behaved, and are seeking to excuse their wilful nonsense as symptoms of a glamorous and intriguing affliction, rather than evidence of self-absorbed fuckwittery. Hersh, like most people who are coping successfully with an actual problem, thought about and discussed her illness with logic and clarity.

'It has been,' she said, 'a really long process. About ten years long, I guess. The biggest difference was meeting Billy. I was really embarrassed that I was pretty crazy, and I didn't want anyone to know. I mean, I'd have seizures, I've knocked teeth out, talked in these other voices, gone into trances. Billy was the first to be with me through all that and to talk to all those other voices. And it had to be done. Now, I have a very normal life, and I think I'm doing a good job at it.'

Her relationship with the rest of her group, especially with long-serving drummer David Narcizo, also seemed to help. In any crisis, there are few things as useful as someone who knows and loves you sufficiently to tease you.

'Just looking out the car window driving around the other day,' said Kristin, 'I realised that I see songs everywhere. Spirits in the bushes and stuff.'

'See,' said David, 'she's not a songwriter at all. It's just that Rhode Island is crawling with the things.'

'So all I do,' laughed Kristin, 'is go out every morning, and rake 'em in.'

ANDREW MUELLER

18

IN WHICH THE AUTHOR IS UNABLE TO AVOID NOTICING THAT THINGS, ON A NUMBER OF LEVELS, ARE NOT WHAT THEY ONCE WERE

'I've a favour to ask,' whispered Roddy Frame. It was near the end of a long and lavishly lubricated lunch in a Swiss restaurant – we must have been drunk – in Soho, and I had been spending the afternoon trying to interview Roddy about Aztec Camera's new single, a semi-flamenco shimmer called 'Spanish Horses'. It had gotten out of hand quite early on, when we'd been interrupted by Edwyn Collins, who'd been passing, tapped on the window, and invited himself in – although not before Roddy had imparted what may be the most succinct summation of the artist's creed I have ever been offered: 'To write something nice you've got to take a chance, you know? I wanted to sing something beautiful, and I tried my hardest, and if I fall short and offend some people . . . fuck 'em.'

But now, it seemed, he needed me to do something for him. I leant forward, and solemnly, slurringly promised that I'd do my very best, whatever it was.

'See,' he continued, 'every Friday, I like to buy *The Spectator* and *Melody Maker*, and I go and have breakfast and I read Jeffrey Bernard in the *The Spectator* and Mr Agreeable in the *Melody Maker*.'

Mr Agreeable was the present by-line of the former Mr Abusing – a much-beloved fixture of the TTT pages. At some point in 1991, a reader's mother had happened upon her young son having a chuckle at one of Mr Abusing's expletive-riddled indictments, and had declined to share the merriment. She wrote not to Allan Jones, our editor, but to the chief executive of IPC, *Melody Maker*'s publishers, who demanded that Mr Abusing's tenure be immediately terminated. David Stubbs, Boswell to Mr Abusing's Johnson, replaced the choleric savant with Mr Agreeable, who started out blandly jaunty, grew gradually more backhanded and sinister and finally, when Stubbs perceived that the smoke had finally lifted from this particular clash, resumed the previous asterix-scattered service, while maintaining the cautious facade of the less confrontational name. When Roddy brought him up, I was pretty sure I knew what was coming.

'I've never been in Mr Agreeable's column,' he fretted, 'and I think it's long overdue, man. Do you think you could have a word?'

When I returned to the office, I did exactly as requested, and Mr Agreeable duly whaled upon 'Spanish Horses' as a 'clod-hopping crock of cloppety crap'.

The end of the summer of 1992 was echoed by a slight chill in the atmosphere of the office. There had always been factions and cliques at *Melody Maker*, as there have always been in every organisation ever, but in our office at least there had been a general assumption that we were all essentially on the same team: for a rabble of disparate unemployables, we had a remarkably hardy esprit de corps. The cause – or at least the frontline – of the eventually quite sour schism that developed was Riot Grrrl, a zealously feminist tributary of grunge (this description is offered with total indifference towards the prospect that high horses may be mounted, in some quarters, at the insinuation that Riot Grrrl was spliced from grunge like some surplus rib).

Riot Grrrl shared with the Nirvana-dominated zeitgeist a principal spiritual homeland (the Pacific North-West, specifically Portland, Oregon, and Olympia, Washington), a lofty disdain for all things corporate, and a dogged do-it-yourself punk ethic. Riot Grrrl differed, however, from the lank-fringed, plaid-wearing Seattle groaners that had been dominating *Melody Maker* the last couple of years in that the groups which drove the scene – Bikini Kill, Bratmobile, Sleater-Kinney, among others which *Melody Maker* had covered to a limited extent – had largely female memberships.

Riot Grrrl didn't interest me. I didn't – and don't – have much time for anyone who thinks that their gender, skin colour or sexuality are, in and of themselves, any more fascinating than which hand they happen to hold a plectrum in. I thought the music sucked – witless, tuneless, graceless and hapless, a dreary canon of tone-deaf tantrums. (Sleater-Kinney, in fairness, would later perform sterling service as a pick-up band on The Go-Betweens' lovely 2000 comeback, *The Friends of Rachel Worth*.) I thought that the Riot Grrrl groups' attempts to make a virtue of incompetence – they seemed to believe that such things as an elementary ability to play one's instrument were stifling and outmoded 'male' concepts – were cheap and lazy. And I thought the personalities associated with the movement came across, even in pieces written by their most ardent champions, as pompous martinets suffering the common misapprehension that loudly claiming to be a repressed voice is the same as actually having anything useful to say.

On top of which, pretty much every woman in my immediate social circle that I asked – none of whom, just so we're clear on this, were simpering, housewifely mannequins whose primary animating impulse was the reinforcement of my paranoid male ego – thought the whole thing was abject and cringeworthy bullshit. As one of them observed, rather wearily, the Riot Grrrl eruption had occurred at almost precisely the instant that the last boneheaded male chauvinist dinosaur had ceased thinking it remarkable if women chose to play in rock groups. It all struck me, at least, as akin to a militant suffragette movement emerging in, say, the 1960s and demanding the vote they already had on the grounds that they refused to learn anything about politics.

Which is not to say that the music business in the early 1990s – and, I daresay, the music business now – was not institutionally sexist. It was: as could be assessed, among many other measures, by comparing the gender ratio of music journalists to that of record company press officers. And sexism is a pernicious, corrosive debility everywhere, to a degree that I wouldn't appreciate properly until I started writing about things other than music, which gave me the opportunity to visit a few less reconstructed societies. There is, indeed, a plausible case that complete female emancipation is the most urgent cause facing humanity.

However, I didn't see that caterwauling over ineptly performed indie rock was going to help with this, much. But Riot Grrrl was clearly going to be a thing, not least because a few *Melody Maker* writers had decided that it would be. In the issue dated 3 October 1992, Everett True and Sally Margaret Joy, a recentish recruit to the paper, wrote a double-page spread on the most significant British response to Riot Grrrl's war cry, Brightonian quintet Huggy Bear. Though Huggy Bear, like many of their comrades, feigned abstemious disdain for the brutalising machinery of patriarchal oppression that was the music press, Everett managed to land the interview – a few embittered sceptics would suggest that this scoop had been facilitated to an unfair extent by the fact that two of the group lodged in his house. In Huggy Bear's wake followed Voodoo Queens, Mambo Taxi and other kindred British spirits. I thought them all terrible, but was happy to allot them space on the reviews pages in proportion to the enthusiasms of our writers – especially Everett, who was possessed of the rare gift for being entertaining however risible his subject. Besides, he was on staff, so it didn't cost any extra.

More exciting to me was the chance to interview the standard-bearers of an earlier British rock'n'roll insurrection – one which had, I suspected, greater resonance than anything Huggy Bear were ever likely to perpetrate. I received a call from a press officer trying to interest me in the news that the release was imminent of the first authoritative Sex Pistols retrospective, an artefact entitled *Kiss This*. Send it over, I told her, I'm sure we'll review it. She thanked me for this courtesy, but explained that she was calling to offer an interview – the first formal Sex Pistols interview since they'd split in 1978. John Lydon, she explained, still thought fondly of the Australian who'd teased him about his outfit a couple of years ago, and had asked her to ask me if I fancied it. I said that I imagined I'd find the time. In late 1992, the memory of The Sex Pistols remained an almost palpable inspiration: not a few commentators had suggested that grunge was, pretty much, America's own punk rock, as if the echo of the last chord thrashed from the Pistols' guitars at San Francisco's Winterland Ballroom in January 1978 had somehow bounced back.

For the purposes of this interview, The Sex Pistols were Lydon and drummer Paul Cook. I began by asking if they could remember the last Sex Pistols interview.

'Er, yeah,' said Cook. 'Probably in San Francisco, just before our last gig.'

'Except,' cackled Lydon, 'we weren't really talking to each other at the time. I think the word "cunt" passed between us a lot.'

Being in the Pistols must, I thought, have been incredibly exciting. I was, frankly, envious – not necessarily of John and Paul, but of the writers who'd got to report on this hurricane which had so dramatically uprooted the fixtures and fittings. Back in the office before the interview, Allan Jones and I had been looking through some contemporary editions of *Melody Maker*, with a view to using them as illustrations in the feature. The other headlines on Pistols-related front pages from 1976–78 illustrated what Lydon and Cook had taken on: [PETER] GABRIEL TO TOUR, YES TO TOUR, DAVID SOUL ON STAGE, GENESIS BONANZA, MCCARTNEY'S 'MULL' – IT'S A RECORD! Allan had been there, though – actually on the Pistols' infamous Jubilee Day boat trip on the Thames. I, by way of contrast, had been aboard the previous week's recreation, in which *Kiss This* had been launched by a Sex Pistols tribute act playing to a crew of hacks who were, it had to be suspected, more interested in the free drink and an afternoon out. The comparison felt an overwhelming metaphor for the waning potence of rock'n'roll (though it is probably the case that every generation of rock'n'roll listeners since the first has been torn between believing that the old folks just don't get it, and seething jealousy at missing out on what their elders had).

Lydon and Cook were at pains to observe that it hadn't always seemed like that much fun at the time.

'[It was] very frightening,' said Cook. 'None of us could walk the streets. And there was no money for us to be taking cabs, so it was buses and subways, and it was just a constant battle. Someone would always want to smash your face in.'

'I got torn to pieces with knives one night,' said Lydon, flourishing a scar on his wrist, 'by one particular group who said, "We love our Queen." Look, right through there. Severed two tendons. I'll never play guitar again, maaaan. Ha ha ha.'

'And I got beaten up just down the road, in Shepherd's Bush,' said Cook. 'You don't expect it, you're not used to it. You try to keep a distance, and maybe that's where you get that rock'n'roll arrogance from. You're not sure about this middle-class business you've been dumped in, and in 1975 it was ten times worse than it is now, people in their big kipper ties and flares and everything. And you can laugh now, but that's what we were up against.'

Lydon spent much of the interview cheerfully pitching the best-known texts of the Pistols' legend into the fire. He described Jon Savage's *England's Dreaming* as 'a non-book', Greil Marcus's *Lipstick Traces* as 'just absurd' and Alex Cox's film *Sid and Nancy* as 'Spiteful . . . it trivialised very important work'. (Lydon would eventually tell his own story, with characteristic aplomb, in the tremendous *Rotten: No Irish, No Blacks, No Dogs.*) It seemed fair enough to ask, especially given what was going on in Seattle, and back at the office, what he now thought of punk's crucial credo, that Anyone Can Do It.

'Unfortunately,' Lydon said, smiling, 'we didn't expand on that. Anyone can do it – if they put some effort into it.'

'And,' added Cook, 'they've got a little bit of talent.'

*

At an editorial meeting in October, Steve Sutherland made what may have been the only nervous statement he'd ever uttered in the direction of *Melody Maker*'s writers. 'As you, uh, know,' he said, 'IPC have been looking for a new editor for the *NME* recently. Anyway, they've made their decision, and, well, it's me.'

At that instant, the room may briefly have been a perfect vacuum, as everyone in it inhaled a stunned lungful simultaneously. Steve hadn't always been the easiest bloke to work with, but he'd also been the main reason that an office populated by such a cast of deadbeats and screw-ups had managed to put out a paper every week. He had served, effectively, as sergeant major to *Melody Maker*'s motley company of irregulars – a personage every outfit needs, to ensure that the people gathered beneath your colours at least look like they're marching in some sort of step some of the time. He was also a great writer and a fine editor, and occupying the cubicle next to him had been a priceless education, in both journalism and swearing.

One of my favourite relics of this period is a photograph of the pair of us agreeing a truce to conclude an arms race of Lego. This had begun when some poor press officer, blissfully unaware of what they were about to unleash, had sent me a record by some now long (indeed, probably instantly) forgotten group, and included, by way of enticing trinket, an individual Lego pirate. Steve – it must have been a slow day – phoned the PR in question, reminded him of his superior rank and suggested, none too subtly, that a Lego acknowledgement of this should be dispatched. Enraged by Steve's gloating at the small Lego pirate ship that subsequently adorned his desk, I reminded the PR that though Steve might technically have had more stripes on his sleeve, as reviews editor it was my decision whether the band in question

were ever mentioned in the paper at all. This escalated for
weeks, and ultimately resulted in the office containing more
pirate Lego than Hamley's, including a galleon and an island
fortress. People attempting to fathom the current parlous
finances of the music business should bear in mind that this
sort of thing used to happen quite a lot.

So I was sorry – indeed, quite bereft – to see Steve go, even
if his departure meant that my name was now second from
the top of the *Maker*'s masthead (Ted, the features editor,
had left in the summer to return to his native America, and
hadn't been replaced, Steve taking charge of his brief as well).
The mood in the Stamford Arms immediately following the
announcement was strange. It wasn't just that Steve was
leaving, it was where he was going. *Melody Maker*'s rivalry
with *NME* was usually waged with the weapon of sulky
silences during shared lift journeys, but Steve could usually
be perceived in the vicinity of the middle of the trouble when
things did kick off. ('When things did kick off' should obviously be read, in this context, as 'When sarcastic sneers were
uttered in the queue for the bar' or 'When glibly derisive
quips about the opposition were made in a downpage review
of Bum Gravy'.) Though the rich pageant of *MM/NME*
hostility had included a few instances of chest-prodding and
drink-throwing, it had never, to the best of my knowledge,
gone anywhere close to actual fisticuffs. Partly because we
weren't, you know, savages, but mostly, I suspect, because
of a shared, unspoken recognition that a proper all-in biff
between the two troupes of puny flaneurs which constituted
the papers' writing rosters would have been a wretchedly pathetic spectacle, if one which might have interested
physicists curious to know what happens when a resisti-
ble force meets a moveable object. It was, of course, Steve
who had unambiguously declared, in his infamous review

of Suede and Kingmaker just months earlier, that the difference between *Melody Maker* and *NME* was the difference
between diamonds and dogshit.

I didn't think Steve was doing anything wrong; it was
a promotion, and he'd have been crazy not to take it.[1]
I certainly didn't see it as any sort of betrayal – he was leaving
one music magazine to start work at another music magazine,
not grassing up MI6 assets to the Kremlin. But I did wish
he wasn't doing it, because it meant that I would now be
obliged to make decisions. Allan offered me the position of
features editor and rather to my surprise, to say nothing
of the appalled astonishment of the ghost of my teenage self,
I found myself equivocal about the prospect. I liked things
just fine as they were. I had the job of my dreams, a wonderful girlfriend, and had moved into a lovely flat in a Muswell
Hill mansion block with an old friend from Sydney and a
new friend from London. I was not at all receptive to the idea
of change. I jammed my thumbs firmly into my ears, and
loudly hummed a happy tune.

This was a mistake, of course. It almost always is. When
you avoid making decisions, they have ways of making
themselves. Though this at least affords one a gratifying
opportunity to feel self-righteously aggrieved at what results.

---

1   The aghast view of this tumult from the *NME*'s office may be gleaned from
    the concluding chapters of Stuart Maconie's rock journalism memoir, the
    unbetterably titled *Cider with Roadies*. It's a charming book, and I for one
    prefer to believe that Maconie's mistaken insistence throughout that he
    worked on the 26th floor of King's Reach Tower – that was us; the *NME*
    were a floor below – is a Freudian slippage of an unrequited yearning.
    Maconie was one of several *NME* types who reacted to Steve's appoint-
    ment by quitting the paper to pursue careers reminiscing whimsically about
    bygone children's television and chocolate bars on nostalgic clip shows. This
    is obviously a childish, gratuitous slight upon a respected broadcaster, but
    old enmities die hard.

Melody Maker's Album of the Year for 1992 was R.E.M.'s *Automatic for the People.* I voted for that, and others which did less well.

R.E.M., *Automatic for the People*

Stately and magnificent, by a band who had yet to be anything but either. It's arguable, though, that this was the first R.E.M. album on which their influences blended entirely seamlessly, without revealing any tension between Stipe's rootless, forces-brat, art-school inclinations, and the arse-kicking southern rock instincts of Buck, Berry and Mills. It would be another seventeen years until I visited R.E.M.'s home town, but seeing the original slogan that became this album's title, on the sign outside Weaver D's soul food restaurant in Athens, Georgia, was surprisingly thrilling. Although not as much as seeing, that same week, Berry, Mills and Buck playing an encore of garage rock favourites ('Ballad of John and Yoko', 'Hang on Sloopy') after a Minus 5 show at the 40 Watt (Stipe, though on the premises, declined to join in).

Pearl Jam, *Ten*

Wasn't a patch on Pearl Jam's live shows at around this period, but then nothing much was. Was also, especially in retrospect, somewhat burdened by a surfeit of intensity, even by the zealous standards of grunge. This was probably due to Eddie Vedder's incredulity at his good fortune in being delivered to this group, and concomitant panic that it might all end tomorrow, and that he therefore needed to say everything he'd ever wanted to RIGHT NOW AND LOUDLY.

Buffalo Tom, *Let Me Come Over*

A stone classic in its own right, the mopey fury of north-west grunge met halfway by the wry self-deprecation of north-east college rock. But much though *Melody Maker*, as a publication, loved Buffalo Tom, we nevertheless gave them way more press than their modest profile merited due to the El Dorado that their name represented to our headline-writers: NEVER MIND THE BULLOCKS, SHOCK OF THE GNU, HOW SOON IS COW?, OF BISON MEN, CATTLE & STRUM, et cetera ad infinitum. Few groups realised how much they could have saved on retaining press officers simply by naming themselves after some species of ruminant.

Moose, *XYZ*

See above. That said, this Mitch Easter-produced debut possessed sufficient deadpan charm that it wouldn't have wanted for space even if it hadn't given us the opportunity for puns of the order of TOUCHED BY YOUR PRESENCE, DEER, and so on.

The Rockingbirds, *The Rockingbirds*

My love affair with country music was still, at this relatively early stage, being conducted somewhat furtively, on the grounds that I still didn't feel quite able to admit to myself that I was experiencing these strange stirrings on perceiving the whine of a pedal steel. Stupidly, I'd somehow persuaded myself that if I was listening to country music made by people who could be mistaken for hipster indie musicians, ideally from somewhere other than the sort of places where people actually made country music, then that was okay. I was too dim to understand that the reason this self-titled debut by a bunch of Brightonians was such a ripper was that they suffered no such foolish uncertainty: they simply embraced what they loved, and held it hard. It is a monstrous shame that so much of a person's youth is consumed by the curse of cool.

The Jayhawks, *Hollywood Town Hall*

'Yes,' I probably reassured myself, 'while there are twanging guitars and keening harmonies and yearning lyrics, they're from Minneapolis, and on Rick Rubin's label, so they're probably not really a country band, so I reckon I can just about get away with this.' Really, I didn't deserve this record. I eventually interviewed Gary Louris and Mark Olson in 2011, in Chicago, on the occasion of their reunion beneath the Jayhawks banner. It was some consolation that they recalled undertaking a similarly confused journey to country, something that didn't come naturally in a town whose local scene was defined by The Replacements and Hüsker Dü.

Lemonheads, *It's a Shame About Ray*

It was virtually illegal not to love this album in 1992. In retrospect, it seems an unlikely hit. The production is wan and washed out, forcing the melodies to struggle through the murk. Though the songs are lovely, especially 'Turnpike Down' and 'Kitchen', it's difficult not to think that *It's a Shame About Ray* benefited unduly from the fascination that the world's more overcharging photographers conceived for Evan Dando shortly after its release. Many years later, I asked Dando how odd this got. 'I don't know where the fuck that came from,' he said, sitting amid the detritus of a London hotel room he'd occupied barely thirty-six hours, but which looked like Keith Moon had been resident for a month. 'Maybe if I hadn't done those pictures with Bruce Weber . . . but you're not gonna say no to the cover of *Interview* magazine if you're trying to sell your record. Everyone's looking for someone to point to and say "Aren't they great?", and they happened to pick me on me for a second.'

Throwing Muses, *Red Heaven*

There's a revealing moment in Kristin Hersh's poised memoir *Rat Girl* in which she concludes a bemusedly horrified description of 'ambitious' musicians with the important caveat: 'But the musicians who make noises for noise's sake fascinate us. Their vocabulary is slamming joy and desperation, lethargy and force.' The chronically self-effacing Hersh would never presume to fascinate anybody, but the rampant and scabrous *Red Heaven* was yet another demonstration of exactly why she does. 'I can see what gets famous in the world,' she once told me. 'Not only is that a crowd you don't want to hang with, but I think [Throwing Muses] are too confusing or something, too real. People who get famous really want everyone to love them a lot, and I'm sure that takes up hours and hours of their time, making that happen. Our concerns are making the records, and playing them. If they made me famous, I'd make some huge mistake, like saying the wrong thing, or wearing the wrong thing, and just blow it. And then I'd be a failure, instead of whatever it is we are now.'

Sugar, *Copper Blue*

A more cynical artist would have cashed in on the zeitgeist he'd inspired by re-forming the old group. Bob Mould returned to the fray with this beautiful album, which managed to encompass the Pixies pastiche of 'Good Idea', the breezy hood-down pop of 'If I Can't Change Your Mind', and the extraordinary 'Hoover Dam', on which Sugar might well have invented the (probably mercifully) underexplored genre of prog-grunge.

The Fatima Mansions, *Valhalla Avenue*

Cathal Coughlan once claimed that The Fatima Mansions had lived by the exemplary creed: 'If that looks like the right thing to do, let's do the opposite.' Whatever else *Valhalla Avenue* might have been – and it was plenty – it was not a career move.

ANDREW MUELLER

19

IN WHICH THE AUTHOR QUITS, THEN UNQUITS

I've never been any good at office politics. I'm too lazy and/or grandiose to get involved in petty intrigue, picayune alliance-building, the crawling up poles nonetheless greasy for their lack of height. This is certainly part of the reason that I've constructed my professional life so that, in the general run of things, the only meetings I ever attend are a daily morning get-together with the coffee pot in the kitchen, at which I gawp vaguely out of the window and try to think of something interesting to do with the day.

But there was politicking being done at *Melody Maker*, by people who were better at it and cared more about these things than I did. At the risk of giving away the ending of this particular episode, in early 1993, I lost my job. Jim Arundel, who'd been doing terrific work enlivening the front portion of the magazine, had some ideas for cheering up the live reviews pages – annoyingly good ideas, for the most part. However, rather than take them to me, Jim took them to Allan, who decided to promote him to live reviews editor.

All of which was perfectly fair enough – Allan was the editor, and therefore perfectly entitled to reorganise matters as he saw fit, and was also tired of my vacillating about the features job, which he awarded to Paul Lester, another long-serving writer. And an effort was made to do the right thing by me – the plan was that I'd be kept on as album reviews editor with no reduction of my retainer, so in theory would be getting the same money for half the work, and more opportunity to write.

My response, to summarise the longish and indignantish speech I made over the phone to Allan, was that they could cram it. This was informed by three key factors: one, your basic wounded pride; two, a nagging sense that I didn't think I really wanted to be a full-time music journalist anymore – an instinct which I clearly lacked the courage to act upon, and which my display of self-righteous ire was probably intended to sublimate; three, and most elevating of my dudgeon, the fact that nobody had told me. I had heard of the reshuffle from my girlfriend, Colleen, who'd heard it from someone in the *Melody Maker* office, where I hadn't been that day because I'd been preoccupied with having my flatmate, my old friend from school in Sydney, interned in a psychiatric facility.

The first weeks of 1993 were, to understate matters auda-ciously, difficult. My old friend – I'll call him Martin – had always been eccentric, but always affably so, and at any rate really no more so than most of my circle. I don't recall exactly when it became clear to myself and my other flatmate, Vicki, that we had a major problem – mental illness is a stealthy stalker. That cruel fact, coupled with the general human tendency towards denial when confronted by difficulty, meant that by the time Vicki and I admitted to each other that we were miles out of our depth, Martin was going days at a time without sleep (which meant that we were, too), was in regular conversation with the radio, and was convinced that the Virgin Mary had taken up residence in the attic (to be fair, I never looked).

It was incredibly difficult to get Martin the help he needed. He wasn't capable of acting for himself, and I had no legal right to act on his behalf, but he had no family in the United Kingdom – and none in Australia who seemed inclined to help (his mother sent a Get Well card, a memory which can still, I notice, cause me to type with unnecessary forcefulness). As I floundered in medical bureaucracy, Martin became ever more consumed by whatever it was. He assumed the entranced air of a man wandering about inside his own head, wondering why nothing was quite where he recalled putting it.

The doctor who eventually visited the flat didn't require much of Martin's company to make a diagnosis. 'Bottom line,' she said, after noticing that the jargon about schizophrenia and psychosis was causing my eyes to glaze somewhat, 'is that the poor fellow is really quite crazy. And,' she continued, 'by the look of you, you're getting there yourself, right?' I may have tried to hug her. She agreed that Martin should be in hospital, but said she wasn't going to force the issue right now – taking paranoid people to mental hospitals after dark was best avoided, if possible. She assured me that Martin was probably no threat to himself or to others, and that he certainly wouldn't be after he'd taken the horse-stunning sleeping pill she was about to give him. We agreed that I'd take Martin where he needed to be the following morning.

Martin seemed to understand what was happening, enough at least that we both laughed out loud on passing through the gates of our destination. I had paperwork admitting him to something called Friern Hospital in Barnet, which we were both probably picturing as a clean, modern, antiseptic set-up – or what two young Australians would think of as a hospital. What we saw was the forbidding Victorian visage of a building which had originally been known, upon opening in 1851, as the Middlesex County Pauper Lunatic Asylum. 'Bloody hell,' said Martin. 'If you pay them three groats, they'll probably let you poke the inmates with sticks.'

Inside, the staff confirmed that Martin would be with them for a while, by the looks of things. I went back to our flat to fetch him some clothes and books. I'd get to know the journey well over the coming weeks, spending most evenings talking to Martin in the common area of his ward, often accompanied by Colleen, who did a sterling job keeping me sane. Sometimes Martin would be almost uncontactable, for all that he was sitting a few feet away. Other times he'd be on sufficient form to take the piss, beginning one visit by solemnly whispering, 'My armies are stranded at the gates of Moscow, and I fear the coming winter may defeat me.'

I decided to make some sort of accommodation with the changed circumstances at *Melody Maker* – Martin was going to need an uncertain amount of looking after, which meant that I was going to need money. I dismounted my high horse, and accepted the offer to stay on as album reviews editor. The distance between my heart and the proverbial in it at around this period can be measured by my tips of acts to watch in 1993 in the year's first issue, which were desultory even by my lackadaisical standards in this arena. I endorsed The Auteurs, who everybody already knew were going to be at least a biggish noise in coming months, and The Moles, a Sydney group whose singer, Richard Davies, had recently been resident on our sofa. This wasn't quite the outrageous act of nepotism it appeared. The Moles were a great group, and Richard would go on to form half of enigmatic duo Cardinal, who released a stone classic self-titled debut in 1994 – and followed it up with the no less obliquely tuneful *Hymns* a full eighteen years later. (Richard is now a trial attorney in the Boston vicinity.)

Everything seemed suddenly to have acquired a valedictory tone. Pete Paphides, who'd recently taken over the gossip column, True Stories, instituted a new section called the True Stories Masterclass, in which he daringly proposed to reveal to readers the writing secrets of various *Melody Maker* writers by composing a parodic pastiche of their work. I was Pete's first subject, and he was unnervingly accurate. The fictional review was riddled with the arch-namedropping of a certain Irish rock singer – who I'd met once, by this point, and I can't believe I'd gone on about it that much – plus gratuitous references to The Go-Betweens and overlong multi-clause sentences overburdened with deadpan negatives like 'not inconsiderable' and 'not unbegrudgingly' – of which I remain, not unadmittedly, not unfond. It was not unfunny, but it felt at the time not unlike a send-off, a gift to a not un-departing colleague.

Which was, I'd decided, exactly what I would be, once Martin had been stabilised sufficiently that he could be flown home to the care of his family and the Australian health service. I'd no idea how I'd pay for this, but as I wondered vaguely if there was some semi-prominent indie artist I'd championed to the extent that they might be emotionally blackmailed into a benefit gig, it was explained to me that sending Martin home would be much less a drain on the Exchequer than keeping him indefinitely. So his return to Australia, with a doctor accompanying him, would be done on the NHS. This still seems to me emblematic of Britain at its greatest – generous, civilised and pragmatic. Invigorated by the prospect of walking out of Friern's gates for the last time – and by my plans to leave Britain to spend some time meandering in Eastern Europe and the Middle East – I set about enjoying the time I had left at *Melody Maker*.

This probably wasn't as hard as I felt it was. I was daily toting a heavy burden of worry and sorrow into a place where the emotional acoustics were unreceptive, as if I'd been sauntering every morning into the offices of *Which Hearse?* magazine wearing a Wonder Stuff T-shirt and exhorting 'Yowsa! Let's rock!' I was miserable and sullen, and all the more miserable and sullen because I was being miserable and sullen at *Melody Maker* – a place which, back when I couldn't imagine I'd ever get in, I imagined I'd never want to leave. It didn't help my mood that the tiresome inanities of Riot Grrrl were being squawked louder and louder over more and more pages of the magazine. During one rancorous post-work session at the Stamford, Caitlin Moran – who was, it is important to remember for the purposes of the upcoming punchline, barely of legal drinking age – ventured some reservations of her own about the shrill, cultish aspect of the Riot Grrrl revolt. 'Your problem, Caitlin,' thundered one of *Melody Maker*'s holiest Riot Grrrl warriors, a balding male comfortably into his thirties, 'is that you don't understand what it's like to be a teenage girl!'

My disagreement with Riot Grrrl was substantially one of style, rather than content. Rock'n'roll, an arena to some extent constructed as a space in which men could not only behave like priapic boors but be applauded for it, was certainly way overdue some sort of feminist comeuppance. I just thought then, and think now, that such points are ultimately made more forcefully when the work speaks, rather than the gender (or race or sexuality or whatever other inherent trait) of its creator. In general, however, I am ceaselessly surprised, and endlessly grateful, that all women are not completely bloody furious with absolutely bloody everything all the damn time.

A rummage of my memory and of the archive yields the retrospectively startling conclusion that during the Riot Grrrl Wars, as this irruption became known, I never fired a shot – did not write so much as a syllable of discouragement of the literally several dozen young women, from all points Camden to Brighton, who during this brouhaha formed bad and unpopular rock groups. Like many ordinary, solid citizens I would later meet in such crossfire-streaked crapholes as Gaza, Baghdad, Kabul and Sarajevo, I kept my head down and went about my business (I am aware that the comparison is so melodramatic as to verge on the offensive). It is hard to entirely avoid trouble in such an environment, however, especially when one party to the conflict is suffused with the crusading zeal that interprets anything less than complete fealty as counterrevolutionary treachery. My girlfriend was among a few female music business employees of my acquaintance whose reluctance to take the Riot Grrrl pledge was rewarded with abuse and threats on their answering machines.

*

It felt like a small victory, in this context, to secure two pages of the paper for a feature announcing the return of Wendy James, former Transvision Vamp diva. Transvision Vamp had been cheered heartily along by *Melody Maker* on the grounds that they made great singles, annoyed all the most gratifying people and that Wendy gave entertainingly vainglorious interviews. However, the Vamp had run out of road and careened into the ditch a couple of years previously. The final wheel had fallen forlornly off when *Melody Maker*'s Paul Lester had reviewed Transvision Vamp's third album, the intriguingly titled *Little Magnets vs the Bubble of Babble*, and dealt it a sustained and gleeful (and, to be honest, deserved) battering. Transvision Vamp's record company, reasoning that if even *Melody Maker* weren't going to play along, yanked the woebegone offering from the schedules (it was, however, a minor hit in Australia, peaking at number twenty-five).

As my introduction acknowledged, that should really have been it for Wendy. But she'd fashioned a second coming by observing the always useful principle that luck is there to be pushed. She'd written a long letter soliciting guidance to Elvis Costello, of whom she'd long been a fan but had never met. Costello had responded by dashing her off an album's worth of punky vignettes and neurotic ballads which lyrically related the hubris and nemesis of an ambitious starlet bearing more than a passing resemblance to Wendy James herself. Once endowed with the brash production of Chris Kimsey, the frantic drumming of The Attractions' Pete Thomas and Wendy's breathy yelp, the record approximated an overwrought hybrid of *This Year's Model* and *Evita*. Wendy had titled it *Now Ain't the Time for Your Tears*, after a line from Bob Dylan's 'Lonesome Death of Hattie Carroll', though parallels between Transvision Vamp's demise and the limply punished murder of a barmaid by an arrogant young plantation owner were bewitchingly unapparent.

It's common enough to hear undue portent in a particular album that finds you at a moment congruent to your circumstances – say, Bruce Springsteen's *Born to Run* when you're trying to summon your courage for a shot at the title, or Leonard Cohen's *I'm Your Man* when you've reached the stage of deriving amusement from your own failings. It is the privilege of the rock journalist that you can sometimes find yourself hearing the right things at the right time from rock stars in person. This paragraph may well stand alone in the canon of western thought as unique in referencing Wendy

James alongside Bruce Springsteen and Leonard Cohen, but *Now Ain't the Time for Your Tears*, as Wendy explained, was a parable about 'the pomposity of the music business, the pomposity of the stars within that business, how brilliant – in quotation marks – London is . . . these are all things that are, at the end of the day, bullshit. And it's a healthy thing to be reminded of the bullshit factor on a regular basis. Otherwise, before you know it, you're believing in it, subscribing to it, and becoming it.'

Wendy was more certain about this than I was, but then we'd had vastly different experiences of the music business. For her, the bullshit had been the prime, uncut stuff: money, minions, acclaim, applause. For me and my fellow hacks, bullshit was certainly available, but it was of a much lower grade, adulterated with resentment and poverty. When Wendy – or someone in the position she had once occupied – went on tour, it would be a months-long carnival of privilege and attention and exotic derangement, for which there would be abundant remuneration on offer. I could see how that could get to people. It was harder to have your head turned when your usual experience of the rock'n'roll bacchanal was three days of being stuffed around by the management of whichever artist it was and ignored by everyone backstage before returning home to find that the gas had been cut off again. Maybe I just hadn't yet got close enough to whatever it was to understand that there was really nothing there.

And maybe you can only see that clearly from a distance. At around the same time, I interviewed Luke Haines of The Auteurs for their first *Melody Maker* cover. The Auteurs' extraordinary debut album, *New Wave*, was a withering, unforgiving survey of fame, and of the absurd expectations and imaginations of it harboured by the unfamous, Luke himself then among them. Prior to forming the suddenly successful Auteurs, Luke had spent long, ill-rewarded years toiling in indie journeymen The Servants.

'I'm not eaten up by bitterness,' he said, 'and I don't have a chip on my shoulder about not being famous. It's rather a weird situation, at the moment. I'm being questioned about this album that's getting attention from people, and it's all very much about a time when nobody was paying attention.'

Providing fate with irresistible temptation, I started my Auteurs feature with a vignette from the photo shoot. While Luke had been perching on a ladder at the behest of *Melody Maker*'s resolutely old-school lensman Tom Sheehan ('Come on, me laddo, throw us a few shapes'), the dreary account-ant rock of Del Amitri had issued from the radio, eliciting the only proper response, i.e. a trio of defeated groans. But Del Amitri, I goadingly reminded Luke, had been on *Melody Maker*'s cover once themselves. Sheehan, who had been *Melody Maker*'s staff photographer long enough to have been party to more than one such fiasco, took the cue, reciting the roll-call of artists whose first *Melody Maker* cover had coincided precisely with their last. Any Trouble. The Pop Tarts. The Jo-Boxers. Raymonde. Stump. Attila the Stockbroker. Skinny Puppy. The Farm. Thousand Yard Stare. King, verily and forsooth, Trigger.

Some of these had cost me, such was the faith vested in the music press by its readers. In 1988, I'd paid twenty Austra-lian dollars for a Skinny Puppy album. According to the Reserve Bank of Australia's inflation calculator, that shakes out at about forty dollars. It would now be regarded as an act of lunacy akin to declaring oneself Pope to spend a third of that on a record, even one that didn't sound like a toolkit in a tumble dryer.

'Raymonde!' whooped Luke, both aghast and impres-sed. 'Jesus, how did that happen?' Raymonde were an unnecessarily fey mid-eighties indie act lumbered with the twin burdens of being compared to, and championed by, The Smiths – an act that Raymonde were as unable to follow as pretty much every other British rock group since.

I explained to Luke the collective, catastrophic dementia that sometimes possessed editorial meetings, and ended up affording, for one week only, the undeserving the unwarranted. The first *Melody Maker* editorial meeting I'd ever attended had been largely consumed by the paper's senior staff – who I presumed had played some part in the decision-making process – asking each other how the living, breathing fuck we'd come to put The Soup Dragons on the front. The Soup Dragons were a group, heavily inspired by the early works of fellow Glaswegians Primal Scream, who spent the late eighties making tinny, dinny records beloved by music-press-reading boys to whom girls would not speak. In the early nineties, after Primal Scream rather unexpectedly released the triumphant indie/dance crossover masterpiece *Screamadelica*, The Soup Dragons decided, with almost endearingly unabashed shamelessness, that they fancied a bit of this action themselves. They suddenly affected bowl-shaped haircuts and baggy, stripy clothes, and released a feeble cover of The Rolling Stones' 'I'm Free', which sounded like Primal Scream trying to sound like The Rolling Stones (as would, indeed, quite a few subsequent Primal Scream records). It was at this moment that The Soup Dragons disgraced *Melody Maker*'s cover, behind the admittedly ingenious strapline 'From indie to ecstasy'.

Fearing that myself and Tom were making Luke nervous, I reassured him of my own certainty that this cover shoot was but the first of many for The Auteurs on *Melody Maker* (I was wrong, but that's showbiz). However, it was instantly, intriguingly and thrillingly clear that Luke really wasn't bothered either way. This was, after all, a singer in an up-and-coming rock group who'd apparently been utterly untempted by the recent offer of a support slot on a Duran Duran stadium tour.

'Nah,' shrugged Luke. 'They're kind of like a wonderful cartoon, incredibly rich, privileged, very, very dim cunts who think they're wonderfully artful, and who think it'd be wonderfully artful of them to have The Auteurs support them. No thank you.'

Luke appeared on the cover of *Melody Maker*'s edition of 20 February 1993, behind the boast 'Last year we brought you Suede, now get ready for THE AUTEURS – the new saviours of UK rock'. (This description reappeared many years later as a chapter title in Luke's splendidly choleric memoir *Bad Vibes*, and was irritably deconstructed in the ensuing text: 'Why would I want to save rock? The damn thing has been stumbling around like a wounded donkey since 1981. The only thing I want to do with rock is kick the fucker to death and put it out of its misery.')

The line was somewhat gracelessly self-promoting on our part, but we were, as a title, still fearfully pleased with ourselves about Suede. The last major feature I wrote before leaving *Melody Maker* was a Suede cover story – their sixth in twelve months. I followed their tour to Coventry and Sheffield, which at least made the thought of my imminent departure from Britain that little bit easier to bear. In a subsequent long, reflective interview at the untidy Camden Town flat that Suede singer Brett Anderson was sharing with bass player Mat Osman at the time, it occurred to Mat that they might, that evening, have opened their doors to a dangerous man. 'This is your last story for *Melody Maker*, right?' said Mat. 'You're leaving the country. Christ, you could write anything.'

Inspired, while writing the piece up, I mentioned in passing that Brett and Mat were not the only occupants of the apartment, and that also about the premises was a small goat named Kevin. This invention either eluded or – more likely – was waved merrily through by our subeditors, and duly appeared in print. A little less than a year later, after I'd changed my mind about a few things and returned to London, I would perceive, loping through the fog of cigarette smoke and self-regard at some after-show wing-ding, the vengeful visage of the lanky Mat above the shoulders of the other revellers.

'You utter, utter bastard,' he spluttered. 'We had to do a European promo tour just after that piece ran. Three fucking weeks of fucking Pepe Le Punk[1] asking me about goat husbandry.'

*

I spent the rest of 1993 waltzing my matilda, negotiating an overland route which began in Finland before descending south through Estonia, Latvia, Lithuania, Poland, Hungary, Romania, Bulgaria, Turkey, Syria, Jordan and Israel. It's a trip that couldn't be done now. While the physical journey could be retraced, allowing for the odd war here and there, what could not be replicated was what I found most valuable – the experience of being alone in the world, reliant on my

---

1   Pepe Le Punk was a newish character introduced to the TTT pages by David Stubbs. An awesomely well-observed caricature, Le Punk was a Belgian rock journalist endowed with the qualities that often distinguished our continental brethren, which is to say that he was earnest, tireless, humourless and possessed of an overthought haircut, stupid glasses and a face it would take a long time to tire of punching (in Le Punk's case, one snipped from an ancient press shot of A Flock Of Seagulls). Le Punk blossomed into one of Stubbs' best-loved creations, forever lurking backstage at Antwerp's Rock Till You Are Hot! club, poised to belabour another unsuspecting star with the wrong end of the stick.

wits and the kindness of strangers. I didn't have a mobile phone, and nobody I knew even knew what the internet was. My only indication of what lay up the road was a travel guide of such fabulous unreliability that, on discovering that the youth hostel in Gdansk was actually a brothel, or that the next train to Istanbul wasn't until Tuesday, I developed sympathies for those indignant Backlash correspondents who used to end their critique of some or other live review with the furious rhetorical flourish 'Was [insert name of *Melody Maker* hack] even at the gig?' For days, even weeks, at a time, even those closest to me would only have had the vaguest notion of my location. I kept in touch with people by sending postcards. They replied by sending letters and parcels Poste Restante to the central post office nearest where my most recent card had said I was likely to be.

My consumption of music during this interregnum was also something that could only be experienced now by someone determined to embrace retro technology to a frankly self-punishing degree. An entire compartment of my rucksack was consumed by a library of mix tapes – each of which had, of course, been laboriously and time-consumingly compiled, and each of which palled gradually as I became familiar with their running orders. The rectangular plastic cases which clattered and rattled with every step I took amounted to a library of, I suppose, maybe 400 songs – or about 16,000 fewer than the collection I travel with now, all stored on a device the size of one C90 tape.

*

I returned to Australia late in 1993 assuming that I was returning to Australia. It turned out that what I was actually doing was realising that I didn't really want to live in Australia anymore, selling my record collection to raise a one-way airfare, and returning to London. I had nothing against the old country, a beautiful and agreeable place in which I was fortunate to be born and raised. Australia was just in the wrong location, at least for my purposes. I wanted to see more things, meet more people and write more stuff, and these ambitions seemed much more attainable from London than from Sydney or Melbourne.

I made what I intended to be a couple of conciliatory calls to *Melody Maker*. These were received with the sort of enthusiasm which might have attended Leon Trotsky's application for a podium seat in Red Square at the 1929 May Day festivities. The victors in the Riot Grrrl Wars, and the opportunist collaborators who had benefited from their triumph, were in no mood to be magnanimous, and my exile was to continue – as, I began to presume, an armband-wearing cadre trawled through *Melody Maker*'s archives, meticulously plastering laudatory reviews of Bikini Kill and Huggy Bear over everything I'd ever written for the paper.

We are all most vulnerable to entreaties from the dark side when we feel rejected or betrayed. Steve Sutherland got wind of the approaches I'd made to *Melody Maker*, and the fact that they'd received a response unlikely to be mistaken for a tickertape parade. He got my parents' number in Melbourne from a mutual friend, and called me.

'Come and work for the *NME*,' he said.

*

As I was, by the end of 1993, a rock critic of no fixed abode, nobody asked me for my opinions about the year's best albums. If they had, I'd have voted for these.

Suede, *Suede*

More for what it represented than what it was. Though *Suede* was everything a debut album should be – feverish, audacious, sky-high on its own supply of talent and promise – it also sounded like it had been recorded in a bucket. This may have been an attempt to bottle the punky furies of Suede's live performance, but it failed. Suede on record should always have been grand, melodramatic, dicing with folly. They would realise this on *Dog Man Star*, by far their best album.

Belly, *Star*

Debut album that wasn't quite a debut album. Belly's Tanya Donelly already had significant form with Throwing Muses and The Breeders before putting her own band together. *Star* was massively hyped by a record company which wanted to turn Donelly into a thing, and by a music press which was happy to help – *Star* finished third in the *Maker*'s end of year critics' list, ahead of Suede, Pearl Jam and indeed everyone except Afghan Whigs and Tindersticks – but it never quite happened. None of which made *Star* any less pretty a record. Belly's version of The Flying Burrito Brothers' 'Hot Burrito No. 1', which appeared as a B-side at around this time, is one of the decade's supreme pinnacles of human accomplishment, at the risk of overselling it.

Grant Lee Buffalo, *Fuzzy*

I was suspicious of GLB's debut album for far too long, on the grounds that it almost felt like someone had gone to the unlikely trouble of assembling a group and a record out of absolutely all the things I might be expected to like.

The Breeders, *Last Splash*

'Cannonball' was *Melody Maker*'s Single of the Year, ahead of Radiohead's 'Creep' and Pulp's 'Razzamatazz'. *Last Splash* as a whole was one of those records which radiated an unselfconscious glee, as if The Breeders had, while wreaking the laughing-gassed surf rock of 'Cannonball', absorbed the revelation that remarkably little in this life is worth taking seriously, rock'n'roll least of all: even the heartbroken 'Do You Love Me Now?' sounded only a beat away from collapsing into giggles.

The Lemonheads, *Come On Feel The Lemonheads*

At its best ('Great Big No', 'Down About it'), a better album than *It's a Shame About Ray*, and I didn't just think that because of a significant Australian input. Much of it was co-written with Tom Morgan of Smudge, and the single 'Into Your Arms' by former Hummingbirds bass player Robyn St Clare. Too much of it, unfortunately, is consumed by point-free instrumental noodlings, slapped in by a distracted Evan Dando in order to fulfil the terms of his publishing contract.

PJ Harvey, *Rid of Me*

I've never had much time for music – or literature, or visual arts, or anything at all, really – which could be described as hard work. *Rid of Me* is an exception to this rule. Harvey's second album, by almost no measure pleasurable, is nevertheless brilliant. A few years later, I interviewed Polly Harvey near her home in Dorset, circa *Stories From the City, Stories From the Sea*. During the mumbling-while-putting-new-batteries-in-tape-recorder stage of proceedings, she asked the always appalling question, 'Do you like my new album?' I replied – truthfully – that I did, very much, while I merely admired most of her others, *Rid of Me* among them. She seemed pleased enough with this.

The Posies, *Frosting on the Beater*

Right place, wrong time. Though it was difficult to be in a rock group in Seattle in the early 1990s without becoming more famous than the president, The Posies managed it by disdaining the flannel shirts, goatees and then-profitable temptations of grunge in favour of a breezy, upful, old school power-pop. Music press chin-strokers noted a resemblance to Alex Chilton's doomed, lost and legendary 1970s power-pop outfit Big Star – roles in whose relaunched line-up, from 1993 onwards, would be congruently occupied by The Posies' Jon Auer and Ken Stringfellow. The same music press chin-strokers were less enthusiastic about acknowledging The Posies' debt to Cheap Trick, whose critical stock had crashed following the oppressive success of turgid 1988 ballad 'The Flame', which sounded like Bon Jovi singing Celine Dion, but whose late-seventies albums are fantastic, delirious, joyous celebrations of melody and electric guitars. As is *Frosting on the Beater*.

Teenage Fanclub, *Thirteen*

Another group on whom Big Star had exerted an irresistible gravitational pull – to the extent, indeed, that the headline above *Melody Maker*'s review of Teenage FC's previous album, 1991's inescapable *Bandwagonesque*, had declared it THE GREAT TUNE ROBBERY. Though *Thirteen* was named after a Big Star song, it sounded less like a Big Star album than other Teenage Fanclub albums. Wilful underproduction – by Teenage Fanclub themselves – lent it such a potent melancholy that even a tune as colossal as 'Radio' sounded elegiac. In its own messy way, as bilious a statement of post-success disillusion as Radiohead's still-two-years-away *The Bends*.

The Auteurs, *New Wave*

All debut albums should sound like they think they're doing you a favour by existing. *New Wave* opened with 'Showgirl', a song which started with a progression through the chords from which it was constructed, announced 'I took a showgirl for my bride', and then stopped for a few seconds, as if waiting for the thick kid sharing the desk to catch up. *New Wave* remains an astute meditation on fame, the most over-valued commodity of an indiscriminate age, wrought from a semi-amused appreciation of the irony that celebrity tends to gravitate towards those who deserve it least, and will handle it worst.

American Music Club, *Mercury*

Hopelessly enthralled music geek that I was, I had a tendency to regard great songs as all but graven commandments conveyed from a mountain by some infallible oracle in the employ of a divine power. It wasn't until years later, when attempting to make an album of my own, that I was struck by the thought that every single recording I've ever heard and loved is just one of infinite possible variations on itself. Every great chorus I can hum might have been deflated by a misjudged chord, every sumptuous production ruined by too heavy a hand on one of those unfathomable knobs on the control desk, every lyric which seems a decoding of the chaotic transmissions of the heart and/or soul about an elephant decamping a subcontinental circus. This belated revelation only caused me to appreciate much more, in retro-spect, such ideas as framing, as Mark Eitzel does here, a song expressing concerns about one's professional inadequacy as an imaginary conversation with Johnny Mathis.

ANDREW MUELLER

20

IN WHICH THE AUTHOR ENJOYS INTERVIEWING THE UNCOOL

Working for the *NME* wasn't easy. This was because almost nobody at the *NME* wanted me to work for it. Everyone in the office still resented Steve, but there wasn't much they could do about him, because he was the editor. They could, however, vent some of their frustration on the only hireling he'd brought from the floor above, so they did (the possibility that some *NME* people independently conceived a dislike of me or my writing must also be admitted, barely credible though it seems). In five months of contributing, I wasn't assigned any of the traditional benchmarks of acceptance – cover stories, the singles or the letters. My name never appeared among those of acknowledged regular writers on the masthead.

Nobody was actively malicious, or least not to my face, and I wasn't ostentatiously obnoxious, or at least not to their faces. It wasn't them, or me. I just didn't belong there. I'd been a *Melody Maker* person from the day I'd first bought the two rival titles from that newsagent in Crows Nest, and I'd never felt more like a *Melody Maker* person than I did at the *NME*. I'd find myself calling record companies and announcing myself as 'Andrew from *Melod* ... *ME*,' then looking guiltily around the office, afeared that someone had overheard.

They – and I never managed to stop thinking of my new colleagues as 'they' – were different. More serious, more studious, much harder-working. They seemed to believe that, where the weekly music press was concerned, the *NME* was the grown-up journal of record, a distillation of the deliberations of sages, while *Melody Maker* was a pamphlet of footling frivolity produced by a creche of giggling yahoos. At *Melody Maker*, of course, we'd always thought that our paper was the fulgent outpourings of raffish, dashing intellectual boulevardiers, while the *NME* was gimmicky populism produced by people too thick to get jobs on *Smash Hits*.

The differing approaches to the propagation of profanity struck me as significant. *NME* were bound by the same IPC edict disallowing the unadulterated printing of swear words, and reacted by warning contributors off using them – and, when they absolutely had to be used because they'd been dropped by interviewees, drawing lines through them, so that 'fucking' became 'f---ing', and so forth. *Melody Maker*, on the other hand, had generally taken the no-swearing rule as encouragement, choosing to replace the offending letters with asterisks ('Sting is a f***ing c***,' etc), happily aware that this only drew attention to them.

The *NME*'s editors wanted to do things like discuss assignments in advance, in detail, which was all very proper and professional, but I missed the *Melody Maker* approach of launching hacks at stories like semi-trained human cannonballs. And the *NME* appended marks out of ten to its album reviews, and took the calibration of these very seriously – so seriously, in fact, that the verdict of the reviewer would often be adjusted by the editor, if they felt it askew (the abundantly merited nine out of ten I bestowed on *Love of Will*, the debut solo album by former Triffids frontman David McComb, appeared in print, literally overturned, as a six). *Melody Maker* had always disdained such ratings, regarding them as an inexcusably self-important exercise in making the subjective appear objective – and, worse, an invitation to not bother reading the review. *Melody Maker* were right. Though such indicators are now almost universal, they're not only self-important, but dishonest. A truthful distribution of marks out of ten or stars out of five would mean most of the records reviewed in a given publication in a given week or month would be lucky to get four points or two stars each, on the grounds that the overwhelming majority of records released pitch somewhere between blandly competent and no use at all. A three-star review should be a rarity, a four-star review a miracle, a five-star review as rare and portentous as the birth of a three-headed goat.

I was eventually permitted to conduct a few interviews for the *NME*, though in a couple of cases I suspected that the assignments were, if not outright exercises in hazing, then possibly indicative of the fact that nobody else had been available or interested. John Mulvey, *NME*'s features editor, dispatched me to Warners' offices in Kensington to interview former Van Halen frontman David Lee Roth, who was in town promoting his fourth solo album, *Your Filthy Little Mouth*, which was every bit as bad as I'd imagined it might be (though I concede that there exists a theoretical possibility that *Your Filthy Little Mouth* suddenly blooms into majesty at some point past the three and a half tracks I endured). *NME*'s review of *Your Filthy Little Mouth*, by Stephen Dalton, declared, 'The chrome may be polished and the paintwork immaculate, but there's nobody behind the wheel,' before awarding it one out of ten, which I felt was harsh. What I'd heard of it deserved twice that.

I was nevertheless happy for the work, and not just because I didn't have any money. One of the grubbier secrets and more amusing ironies of rock journalism is that you almost invariably get the best interviews from the least cool artists. If you are dispatched to interview a giddyingly erudite song-writer, or dazzlingly brilliant sonic architect, chances are high of emerging with a tapeful of defensive mumble and/ or boneheaded cliché. If, however, you are allotted a rendez-vous with some preening heavy metal pantomime dame and total critical punching bag, your story will write itself, for the true showman realises that he's never off duty (others of this type I'm grateful to have interviewed since include Slash, Ian Gillan and Alice Cooper, erudite and charming gentle-men each).

Approximately forty-five minutes into our interview, Roth contemplated the period immediately after he left Van Halen to reinvent himself as camp cabaret crooner 'Diamond' Dave Lee Roth, a sort of day-glo Tom Jones.

'Well,' said Roth, 'it turns out that people take it all a little bit more seriously than I thought. I mean, I do take this stuff seriously, and I laugh to win, but . . .'

He was interrupted by a click. After logging a whole side of Roth's aggrandising anecdotage, the tape had run out. Roth arched an eyebrow and gestured at my Walkman. I fumblingly turned the cassette over and pressed the red button. Roth counted down from five to one with the fingers on his right hand, to allow for the tape to wind on, and returned to the thought precisely where he'd left it.

'. . . this is part of the way I take it seriously. I used to work in surgery in a hospital, for two years right out of high school. I know how to laugh to win. It's a necessary part of your arsenal when you work nightshift in emergency. This is the way I deal with serious things, with a little tequila wisdom, you know?'

The Nile Rodgers-produced *Your Filthy Little Mouth* was an earnest attempt at a grown-up artistic statement, as befitted a man who had recently undertaken the rites attending a desire to be taken seriously budding in the heart of a peroxide-maned, spandex-clad, Hollywood rock'n'roll harlequin. Which is to say that Roth had pruned his hair, dressed down, and moved to New York – a city he described rather well in one couplet on his otherwise wretched album as a combination of Dante's *Inferno* and *The Price is Right*. With what struck me as touching optimism, Roth now wished to be considered part of Gotham's rich underground heritage, a descendant of The Velvet Underground, Warhol and Ramones, about as plausible from Roth as a claim to be related to the royal family of Tonga.

'[New York] is in contrast with the way we've come to think in most of the United States,' he asserted, 'where we equate great work with success. To my way of thinking, it's more often than not the exact opposite. A best-seller in the United States is the tomb of a mediocre talent, but these are the kind of philosophies they have in LA. Are you telling me that Jane Fonda's workout video is the best film ever made?'

Or, I mused, possibly rather tactlessly, that 'Jump' is the best song ever written.

'HA HA HA!' whooped a fortunately delighted Roth. 'Yeah, okay.'

The cover of *Your Filthy Little Mouth* would remain substantially unsullied by the grubby fingers of the megastore masses, who aren't wrong all the time. Roth would, in due course, return to Van Halen (and then quit again, and join again, and quit again, and then tour with Sammy Hagar, who'd replaced him in Van Halen in the first place, then join again, and so on). At this juncture, however, Roth and Van Halen were on firm non-speakers. Roth seemed kind of down about this, but not sufficiently to prevent him bitching amusingly, and at length.

'I ran into Edward with his wife, Valerie, on the street a few months ago,' he said. 'It went just like this. I said, "Ed?" because I didn't recognise him right away, he's changed some. I said, "Oh, my life in front of my eyes, man, how you doing?" And she says, "He's fine." That was it, man. It's all in the subtext there, I guess.'

Roth was not regarding his former band's fortunes with fraternal solicitousness.

'I think,' he says, 'they're experiencing a situation like Raiders merchandise. The most popular merchandising item in the world is LA Raiders logos. But the Raiders haven't won shit for nine years! They didn't even get into the playoffs!'

In a flagrant effort to flatter Roth into further hissing and scratching, I asked, with all the fraudulent solemnity I could muster, if he ever felt sorry for his successor in Van Halen, the sweaty groaner Hagar. Big – and vertiginously high-heeled – boots to fill, and so on.

'He lives with a horrifying nightmare,' grinned Roth, answering in kind, 'that most frontmen do not even have to begin to approach. Every time Sam looks in the mirror he has to say to himself, with absolute surety, "I can be replaced instantly. And to the tune of seventeen times the business, seventeen times the attention." That's a horrible thing to be chased by. Every time you show up at work, you have to address that.'

Meeting Roth was less like interviewing a musician than being importuned by a politician running for office:

the immovable smile, the relentless charm, the exaggerated laughter, the protestations of a bright, bold future, the sly rubbishing of former allies turned current enemies.

'As an artist,' he declared, 'I can think of a million more kinds of icing to add to the cake. Do you really want to be the guy tomorrow you are today? It's not a bright future. It's certainly predictable. And that's never been my way.'

Aside from the bit in which the guy who wrote 'Hot for Teacher' had breezily declared himself 'an artist', this struck me as wisdom with the quality of mantra. I thanked Roth for his time, and added that I did not always end interviews by so doing.

'Stellar stuff, kid,' Roth assured me. 'Write a good one.'

The good thing about the *NME*'s solemn, curatorial culture was it meant that most of the paper's writers devoted considerable energy to the aspect of rock journalism which had always bored me most thoroughly: discovering, nurturing and promoting new artists. This, in turn, meant that I was permitted to get on with interviewing the has-beens. I deploy the phrase without pejorative intent: 'has-been' implies a past of accomplishment and notoriety, which is always worth hearing about. I would, for example, much rather interview someone who Has Been to the moon than interview someone about why they'd like to go.

Bob Geldof lived a cruel paradox. He was one of the most famous musicians in the world, but his actual music was, by this point, barely known. His record company were trying to rectify this by issuing a compilation called *Loudmouth*, which gathered the best of The Boomtown Rats and Geldof's solo career, such as it had been. I was interested to see how someone of Geldof's legendary irascibility would cope with journalists who were – understandably, given his other accomplishments – unlikely to be keen on discussing what he was supposed to be promoting. I asked his record company if I could sit in on a day of him being interviewed by other people before I picked up the whip and chair myself. They agreed that I could do this. In Brussels.

The succession of Pepe Le Punks who entered Geldof's hotel room at half-hourly intervals did not disappoint. Nor did Geldof. He amused himself with the first few by cheerfully confessing that *Loudmouth* had been conceived, selected, titled and packaged with absolutely no input from himself beyond the new single, 'Crazy', which was a coldly calculated attempt at a hit co-written with Dave Stewart (it spent a week at number sixty-five). His good humour ebbed with the day, however. By mid-afternoon, he was greeting quivering supplicants with: 'Right. One fucking question about Live Aid, one fucking question about Paula [Yates, then Geldof's wife], that's your fucking lot.' By day's end, one hapless inquisitor was having his – rather too detailed – enquiry about Geldof's views on the latest developments in Belgium's Flemish–Walloonian schism answered with a singsong, 'Don't fucking know, don't fucking care.'

By the time I renewed acquaintance with Geldof in a King's Road cafe the following week, he had, according to his press people, given 104 interviews in seven countries in twelve days. The prospect of a 105th did not appear to enthral him.

'Go on,' he began, nodding towards my tape recorder. 'Do your fuckin' job.'

I was faced with the same difficulty as my continental colleagues. I didn't really want to ask him about *Loudmouth* either. It turned out that Geldof didn't really want to talk about it.

'Any Irish band you meet,' he said, 'will talk about anything except their records. They all have an opinion on fuckin' everything. A lot of it is naive, but God bless 'em because they kick up a fuss. They piss people off, they provoke them. Really, Bono and the guys don't have to do anything. Yet they never fuckin' shut up, you know, boring the hole off all and sundry. Sinead [O'Connor] never shuts up. It's a confused railing, sure, but if 0.5 percent of it irritates and prickles, God bless her! Fair fucks to her! She doesn't have to. And it's better than "Hey, man, let's talk about my record, what I was trying to achieve was . . ." FUCK. OFF. You know?'

It was getting on for ten years since Bob Geldof, then a somewhat adrift and fading rock star, had watched a BBC news report on an Ethiopian famine. Everybody knew what had happened next. As the *NME*'s standfirst reminded, the orchestrator of Band Aid and Live Aid was now a rarefied eminence, rock'n'roll's own snarling conscience, Sir Bob Geldof. (In fact, Geldof, a citizen of the Republic of Ireland and therefore not a subject of the British crown, was awarded an honorary knighthood, which does not entitle the honouree to style himself 'sir' – not that Geldof has ever shown any inclination so to do.)

'Also,' he noted, in tones more bemused than boastful, 'I'm a Prince of the Tuareg, a Sheik in the Order of the Two Niles, a Chevalier in the Order of Leopold II, a Doctor four times and a freeman of more cities than I could ever hope to fucking visit.'

I wondered how Geldof felt about what Band Aid and Live Aid had done to music: in the time since, it had barely been possible for a child to fall from its bicycle without being immediately surrounded by a troupe of the other year's chart stars bellowing a Beatles song.

'Farm Aid, Secretary Aid, Petrol Pump Attendant fucking Aid,' nodded Geldof. 'It couldn't do any harm.'

I was surprised, however, by what he said about Band Aid and Live Aid. Back in Australia, I'd bought the record and watched the concert like everyone else I knew. And, like everyone else I knew, thought it a stirring, thrilling triumph of idealism. Geldof didn't.

'That's the great mistake,' he said. 'I saw it clearly as a pragmatic thing. Look how pragmatically we set about it. Here we are. The Rats don't sell records at the moment. I can write songs, but my confidence is waning. I need someone with a name, who is also a friend, who can write with me. So, Midge [Ure], you know. And then anyone else we can think of. Anything to make it work.'

He emphasised the last three words with gentle raps of a fist on the cafe table. Geldof clearly thought them the difference between Live Aid, and the well-intentioned posturing of which rock'n'roll was generally fond. He was right: the wisdom of judging people by what they do, rather than what they say, is especially useful in a milieu in which the standards of behaviour are less than stringent.

'I was always very pragmatic,' he said. 'Songs about here and now, real people, real life. So I got involved in pragmatic things from when I was very young. What was the point in sitting around fucking Dublin singing fucking folk songs? That wasn't going to stop apartheid.'

But Live Aid, I felt it fair to suggest, hadn't stopped famine – still less the crooked and vicious African governments which used it as a weapon of war, or regarded it as a vaguely regrettable by-product of ideological progress. Had Live Aid worked? Had it really changed anything?

'For those we touched,' Geldof replied, 'it changed their lives utterly. They were allowed to live. You can't have a more profound change than that.'

There were, I supposed, worse things a bloke could be remembered for. Like most rock'n'roll records.

'Don't care,' he snapped. 'I'm not interested in the least in being remembered. I'm dead, goodbye, blessed oblivion, you know?'

ANDREW MUELLER

21

IN WHICH THE AUTHOR CONTRIBUTES NOTHING TO THE BIGGEST ROCK STORY OF THE DECADE

Another artist I interviewed for *NME* around this time had also been contemplating his epitaph.

'Reznor,' mused Trent Reznor, for it was he. 'Died. Said "fistfuck" and won a Grammy.'

The Nine Inch Nails songwriter had become an extremely unlikely rock star. Reznor had spent five years, we calculated, doing everything you would do if determined to doom yourself to obscurity and ridicule, and had accomplished precisely the opposite. Nine Inch Nails' 1989 debut, *Pretty Hate Machine*, had been a howl of uncompromising adolescent fury, riddled with profanity, blasphemy, obscenity and – possibly most provocatively, in an American context – synthesisers. It had sold, at the time of our meeting, more than a million copies. In 1992, Reznor had followed that with two mini-LPs. One, *Broken*, was a salvo of scabrous disgust which should have been one of the great suicidal career moves, Reznor's own 'Metal Machine Music' or 'Don't Stand Me Down'. It went platinum. The other, *Fixed*, was a collection of remixes from *Broken* which ran the gamut from the confrontational to the unlistenable. For one track on this – 'Wish' – the National Academy of Recording Arts and Sciences had indeed awarded him one of its gramophone-shaped bookends.

'Go figure,' he sighed. 'I'm sure it's the only time ever the word "fistfuck" will appear in a Grammy-winning song. That's my true accomplishment.'

By the time we had this conversation, in the bar of the Phoenix Hotel in San Francisco, I'd spent three days with Reznor and found him to be a number of things that his records and reputation had not encouraged me to expect: wry, self-mocking, awkward. Myself and *NME* photographer Derek Ridgers had certainly, if unwittingly, given him ample reason to unleash upon us some of the hell bottled in his records (and therefore, one assumed, his psyche). When we'd first met him in Los Angeles, a combination of a fortuitous hire car upgrade (to a bright red Mustang convertible), Ridgers' brilliant idea for a photo location (Watts Towers, the junkyard playground built over thirty years by Simon Rodia) and a chronically inept map-reader (your correspondent) had caused us to blunder interminably about South Central, uncannily resembling three lost white men in an expensive car with no roof. Reznor, dressed for the pictures – which is to say slathered in mascara and swaddled in leather – had been remarkably patient.

'Guys, come on,' had been the eventual extent of Reznor's tetchiness, 'this is a bad neighbourhood to be driving around looking like two English weirdos and their gimp.'

One of the weirdos, I reminded him, was Australian.

'I believe,' he muttered from the back seat, 'the point stands.'

Reznor had been living in Los Angeles until recently. He'd recorded Nine Inch Nails' new album, *The Downward Spiral*, at his home at 10050 Cielo Drive, Benedict Canyon –

infamous as the house in which, on 9 August 1969, dopey followers of ridiculous racist doom-prophet Charles Manson murdered five people. *The Downward Spiral* had impressed me. It had, I thought, the gleeful sonic inventiveness of, say, Ministry, but was unhampered by Al Jourgensen's tendency to retreat into frat-house buffoonery, and it summoned something of the grandeur of Depeche Mode without being burdened by Depeche Mode's lyrics. The birthplace of *The Downward Spiral* impressed me rather less. Going out of one's way to make a record at a crime scene seemed dismally crass, the sort of thing people do before growing up suffi-ciently to appreciate that affronting elementary decency is not a worthwhile end in itself.

I knew I'd have to address all this. But by the time we sat down for the formal interview in San Francisco, I'd also been within microphone-stand swinging range of Reznor's pugnacious stage incarnation at a couple of chaotic Nine Inch Nails warm-up shows in claustrophobic clubs popu-lated by the sort of people who regard rubber as evening wear. On stage, Reznor was a human wrecking ball. He'd covered himself in bruises and cuts, and had gener-ally conveyed the impression of being capable of doing the same to anybody else who tempted his wrath. But any aura of malevolent portent he may have acquired since our excursion to Compton dissipated a short walk out of the Phoenix's lobby in search of an interview location in San Francisco's Tenderloin district – which was, at the time, the sort of neighbourhood that estate agents describe as 'up and coming', shortly before handing you the house keys and saying, 'No, you go on ahead. I'll, uh, stay here and watch the car.'

I was anxious about the crack-crocked zombies congre-gating on the street corners, but did not wish to betray my nerves to the fearless bringer of doom strolling alongside me. Happily, the fearless bringer of doom spoke for both of us.

'Man,' said Reznor. 'This is horrible. Let's go back to the hotel.'

It was a cue, of sorts. So Reznor had found walking a few blocks of Tenderloin grim beyond endurance. Living and working in the Hollywood house whose walls had once borne taunting slogans daubed in the gore of the recently slaughtered tenants, on the other hand . . .

'We had one day to look for a place,' Reznor sighed, 'and it was just the coolest house, the location was awesome, and the view . . . well, wow. And then, at the end of the night, I heard it was, like, the house. I thought, well, freaky, but that it was kind of cool, in a way. I wasn't thinking in terms of press or anything like that. I just thought it was a cool place. I wasn't afraid of ghosts. If anything, I was interested to see if there was anything there.'

This seemed disingenuous, if just about believable. But there seemed to be little question that Reznor had allowed the location to inform the work. The very title *The Downward Spiral* was surely an allusion to 'Helter Skelter' – the name the Beatles-obsessed Manson gave to the race war he intended the killings to provoke. Two of the songs on the album deployed variations of the word 'pig' in their titles – this was the insult that the Manson family had smeared on the front door in the blood of one of their victims, Sharon Tate. Reznor had also named his home studio 'Le Pig'.

Reznor reacted to this indictment with the sheepish air of a man up a tree in a lion enclosure explaining to an irritated zookeeper that it had all seemed like a terrific jape at the time.

'"Piggy" was written before I was even in California,' he said. 'And it wasn't, in my mind, in any way about the murders. "March of the Pigs" was formulated [at the house], but not consciously about killing Sharon Tate. I guess I just used that word generically, as a metaphor for people I don't like, or myself, or things I don't like. Naming the studio "Le Pig", well, obviously.'

Reznor didn't need to be as bright as he was to see where I was going with this. Charles Manson had, over the preceding quarter-century, acquired a certain cachet among hard-of-thinking rock stars who affected to perceive him as an indefatigable avatar of mystic counter-cultural integrity, as opposed to a nasty, bigoted clown who had orchestrated the murder of a lot of people for no especially good reason (Manson's lousy songs have been covered by The Beach Boys, Guns N' Roses and Lemonheads, among others). I wondered if Reznor was among them.

'No,' he replied flatly. '[But] I think he's a charismatic character. I think the media created him, the embodiment of evil that the people wanted to see, the ultimate terrifying bad guy turning our hippy children into killers.'

In fairness, I noted, he was a terrifying bad guy who'd played at least some part in turning someone's hippy children into killers.

'I do tire,' continued Reznor, 'of the sub-groups of people who really look up to the guy, and I've met 'em all, because they all come up to the house, and I'd let 'em in, you know, but after a while . . .'

. . . you find yourself wondering, I'd imagine, why you've let a bunch of boring dickheads into your house.

'The turning point,' Reznor continued, 'was that we became pretty good friends with the woman who was staying in the guest house before we moved in. And one of her best friends is Sharon Tate's sister . . . And that gives you an odd perspective. I don't think people think what it must be like to have your sister senselessly murdered and have the whole world know. It made me feel kind of weird about the whole thing.'

Reality will do that. Shock for the sake of shock is a shabby refuge, crowded with bounders and chancers who'd struggle for attention if compelled to rely on their wits. *The Downward Spiral* was a shocking album in that it was shockingly bleak: essentially a chronicle of the momentum of suicidal despair. But it was also clearly the product of an agile and articulate mind, one which must have been slightly concerned at the prospect of such a thoroughly diseased piece of work being purchased by at least – it seemed reasonable to assume – a million American households.

'Yeah,' he said, shifting uneasily. 'I've thought about that. The danger of it?'

Not, I said, the danger of the record inspiring someone to pull a Chapman or a Hinckley – or, come to that, a Manson. Anyone crazy enough to kill for a record is crazy enough to kill, full stop. More in the sense of what the popularity of such a record would say about the way a lot of people were thinking. Reznor's reply was an eloquent summation of the purist rock artist's frustrations with a western world which had, in the twenty-nine years of Reznor's life to this point, gone out of its way to accommodate rock'n'roll's every last inchoate demand, even to the extent of presenting Grammys to people who say 'fistfuck'.

'I wanted to make a record about something,' he said, 'and what it was about was a fairly bleak set of issues. And I knew that it wasn't going to be the kind of record you could listen to in your car, or throw on at a party. I just think music today is – and this is a very general statement, unfair to some – somewhat uninteresting. It's force-fed and accepted, and saying you want to be a rock star is as legitimate a career aim as saying you want to become a doctor. I mean, I've relied on shock tactics in some of the lyrics on this record, being quite aware of that, to slap some people in the face, or at least affect them in some way, whether they're relating to it, revolted by it, or reading something completely different into it.'

American music at this time was still dominated by the miserabilist furies emanating from Seattle – to the extent that it was becoming slightly fashionable to mock the grunge groups for so loudly protesting their anguish at a society which appeared completely content to revolve admiringly around them. I wondered if Reznor – though nobody's idea of a grunge artist – had taken a deliberate decision to up the ante by making a record which admitted no light to the end of its tunnel. Reznor protested slightly, referring to a song which would, some years later, and in circumstances which would have seemed beyond incredible at this point, cement his reputation: 'Hurt' would be made properly famous in 2002 by Johnny Cash's stunning interpretation.

Reznor said, 'I think there is a slight bit of optimism – "slight" being the key word – thrown in there. Because though [the album] does examine completely giving up, that's why I put the song "Hurt" on the record, which was the last song written, I might add.'

Album finale 'Hurt' was, I agreed, a marginally elevating song in the context, but it wasn't exactly 'Somewhere Over the Rainbow'. The only redemptions it seemed to offer were drugs and flight.

'Well,' Reznor said, 'I think it offers redemption through the desire for it. By the end of that record, everything has been discarded, and things that I'd looked for hope in have failed me – belief systems, religions, drugs, power, leading to the fantasy of suicide in the song "The Downward Spiral" But, with "Hurt", I think I address something that . . . there was a certain feeling that I didn't think I'd conveyed anywhere else, which was one of melancholy, not definite anger, but sadness and loss. But also a kind of wish that things could have been better if I'd known how to do things differently. Which I think is at least a slightly positive thing, as opposed to, you know, my head's blown off and I'm bleeding on the carpet.'

*

Funny he should say that. On a Friday night a little over a month after having this conversation with Reznor, I was watching the news in the Wood Green flat I'd rented with my friend Vicki when the newsreader, in the furrow-browed tones of someone pronouncing new words for the first time, announced the breaking story of a body being found at the Seattle home of Kurt Cobain, singer with Nirvana. This was shocking without being surprising. Four weeks previously, the *NME* had devoted a cover and a three-page news special to the near-fatal overdose Cobain had taken in a Rome hotel; the portrait on the front of the issue had shown the singer, rendered clammy and cadaverous by stage lights, gazing heavenwards.

It probably requires journalistic and/or youth-grade narcissism to believe that the suicide of someone you once met briefly necessitates any response on your part, but I felt impelled to leap into action, pausing only when I realised I had no idea what to do. I tried to call Everett, then realised that i) I hadn't a clue where he was, and ii) the whole world would now be trying to call Everett, whose friendship with Cobain had suddenly become an extremely valuable commodity (to the eternal credit of Allan Jones, his response to having this colossal scoop dumped in the lap of his paper was to tell Everett to take his time, to go wherever he needed to be, do whatever he felt he had to do, and not worry about *Melody Maker*).

I also left a message for Steve Sutherland, volunteering my services in what was now obviously an all-hands-to-the-pumps situation (the latest deadline for both papers was usually mid-morning on Monday, though everything but late-breaking news stories and reviews of especially important weekend gigs was expected to be well and truly in by then). As it happened, the *NME* decided that they could assemble their tribute without my input, and they were right. The four-page report at the front of the paper was exemplary, and bundled beneath what endures as the most iconic music press front page of the 1990s: a black-and-white portrait taken during an *NME* shoot a few years earlier, showing Cobain's mascara-shrouded eyes gazing reproachfully from beneath a peroxide mop.

The delirious weeks following Kurt Cobain's suicide now feel like the last time that rock'n'roll could have been mistaken for any sort of counter-culture. At the time he died, Cobain wasn't merely a member of some barely regarded punk outfit, known only to people who wrote things on their clothes: he was the singer in the biggest rock group in the world. But it wasn't just the BBC newsreader who appeared baffled – none of the mainstream media seemed to have any understanding of what had happened, and why it mattered. It also says much about the difference between then and now that the day after I'd seen Cobain's death reported on the BBC, I had lunch with a few friends, mostly employed in the music business. They'd all been out the night before, and had heard nothing about it until I told them.

My only contribution to the turmoil of this period was as the bearer of glad tidings. A few weeks after Cobain's

death, I was on the Isle of Skye, where the *NME* had sent me
– again, malice cannot be completely dismissed as a motive –
to review The Proclaimers (it was a great show, truth be told,
and the highlands and islands of Scotland in spring were
beautiful, still iced with the most tenacious of the winter
snows; getting to Skye had been like driving through a
country-sized lime meringue pie). In the hotel restaurant the
morning after, I was attempting to distract myself from the
internal showdown between a heaped Scottish breakfast and
a hideous Scottish hangover with that weekend's edition of
the *Guardian*. The *Guardian* was among those mainstream
media outlets still trying to get to grips with Kurt Cobain's
passing – at the time of his death, they'd run his obituary
smaller than that of Dan Hartman, marginally remembered
for 1978 disco hit 'Instant Replay'. Now, they were compensating, running several thousand words of beard-scratching
punditry in the colour magazine, which was adorned with
a Warhol-ised treatment of the same haunted, haunting
picture the *NME* had run on its cover immediately following the news, and which was already appearing on T-shirts
and coffee mugs hung amid the usual Princess Diana tat on
London souvenir stalls.

Sitting across from me was a grey-skinned, limp-haired
figure bearing the unmistakable demeanour of someone who
had slept in the clothes he was wearing, if he had slept at all.
He squinted at the magazine cover.

'God,' he said, 'it's turning up everywhere.'

Indeed, I agreed. An ill wind, and so on, but some
photographer somewhere has won the damn lottery.

'Do you think so?' he asked.

Good gravy, I replied, or words to that effect. It's this
generation's John Lennon in the sleeveless New York City
T-shirt, or Paul Simon on piledriving his bass into the stage of

the New York Palladium. It's going to be one of the defining images of the decade.

'Ah,' whimpered the wreck opposite, stifling an involuntary retch. 'That's interesting. I took it.'

Martyn Goodacre had clearly committed whichever infraction the *NME* punished by sending photographers to remote windswept islands to take pictures of unfashionable groups in the company of unwanted writers. Not unreasonably, in the circumstances, he was drunk. It would have been difficult to properly impress on him, in his state, the urgency of reacting to an escaped gorilla upending the furniture, never mind establishing the whereabouts of a four-year-old photograph, but I asked Goodacre who owned the negative. He said he was pretty sure he did.

I informed him that he was buying breakfast.

ANDREW MUELLER

22

IN WHICH THE AUTHOR GOES TO THE WORST THING EVER

Goodacre was unusual – indeed, rarer than a three-eyed unicorn – in becoming enriched by working for the music press. When anyone did strike lucky, it tended to be photographers, who earned repeat fees every time a picture was reused, and could parlay their connections into merchandising, advertising and record-company-sponsored promotional shots. For we hacks toiling for a fraction less than ten pence a word to create work unlikely to be featuring on T-shirts decades hence, maintaining a comfortable distance between door and wolf was more difficult.

I had been supplementing the crumbs which fell from the *NME*'s table with day shifts in the music section of London listings weekly *Time Out*, where I wrote album reviews, previews of upcoming gigs and the occasional music-related opinion column. Between these two sources, and the fact that it was still possible to hint record companies in the direction of regular free lunches – and subsequent ransackings of their stock cupboards, the contents of which could be exchanged for convertible currency at second-hand record stores in Soho – I just about covered rent, and food, but had little left for such luxuries as anything else at all.

In your mid-twenties, your attitude to money changes. People – at least, people with no responsibilities – don't mind being broke in their late teens and early twenties. By your mid-twenties, it's not that you mind being broke, as such, but you do start to mind the idea of being broke forever. At some point, you think, you'd quite like to have things in frames hanging on the wall, a sofa that didn't disassemble every time someone sat on it, and a bedroom in which you didn't have to begin winter mornings by chipping a quarter-inch of ice off the inside of the windows. You might even, you reckon, enjoy feeling a blithe confidence about the prospects of laying in sufficient groceries for the week regardless of whether or not you are okayed to get the train to Manchester on a wet Tuesday night to watch The Posies play in some university rec room.

It was becoming as clear as the scarlet ink on the bills that such workaday middle-class comforts were an unlikely consequence of persisting at the *NME*, where I was not growing on the section editors. Nor, however, did I much fancy asking the folks for the loan of a return airfare – while I didn't doubt they'd have helped out, I also took the view that they'd fed, clothed and housed me for nineteen years, and so were probably off the hook.

One summer morning, at around the point at which I'd begun seriously considering the profoundly unpalatable option of getting a job or something, I heard the phone ringing in the lounge room. It was Everett, which wasn't entirely surprising: it probably hadn't helped my prospects at the *NME* that I continued to socialise with my former comrades.

'How's it going at the *NME*?' he asked.

Really pretty badly, I told him, which was nothing he couldn't have guessed if he read it every week.

'Well then,' he said, 'I think you should come back to *Melody Maker.* Take some time to th–'

Okay, I said.

The *NME*'s efforts to retain me fell short of exhibiting the merest suggestion that they cared in the slightest, and I returned to the twenty-sixth floor with such dispatch that I joined a select coterie to have had their by-lines in both papers in the same week. It was good to be back in and of itself, but it was a good time to be back, too. The Riot Grrrl Wars were over: the great crusade's most zealous shock troops had calmed down, or gotten bored, or gone elsewhere. On the paper's masthead, my name was shoehorned onto the end of a list of contributors which had been joined, in my absence, by some tremendous new talent, most notably the prodigiously gifted angry popinjay Taylor Parkes, and Coventry-based diatribist Neil Kulkarni. Even more happily, the reviews sections were now overseen by Sharon O'Connell, who'd edited some of my earliest scribblings back at *On the Street* in Sydney, and Simon Price, who seemed to have forgiven me for the whole Go!-Discs-coach-trip-to-Liverpool thing.

More importantly, the British music press was about to embark on what would become its valedictory hurrah. The eventually stultifying dominance of rock'n'roll enjoyed by Seattle – and, by extension, America – over the last few years was being answered by a startlingly cocksure British backlash. The phenomenon became known as Britpop, which was a slight misnomer – none of its principal artists (Blur, Suede, Oasis, Pulp, Elastica, Sleeper, Supergrass) or any of their legion coat-tail riders were ever likely to be taken for being Welsh, Scottish or Northern Irish. Britpop was a specifically, even parochially, English irruption, interestingly and ironically defined by a near-total lack of what middle-class English people usually feel most acutely about the very fact of their Englishness: embarrassment.

Britpop was a fabulous boon for the music press: a home-grown explosion of great music and entertaining characters, to all of which we had barely fettered and almost exclusive access, the internet being a barely noticeable rumble in the distance, music television hardly extant, mainstream radio labouring under the misapprehension that the 1980s hadn't ended, and newspapers still largely uninterested in modern popular culture. If people wanted to keep up with the Britpop acts – and a lot of people did – they had to buy *NME* and/or *Melody Maker*. Or, it should be ungrudgingly conceded, *Select*, a generally very decent – not that we'd have admitted as much at the time – music monthly which was launched shortly before Britpop flowed, and which folded shortly after Britpop ebbed. *Select*'s April 1993 cover, featuring Suede's Brett Anderson posing in front of a Union Jack and behind the caption 'Yanks go home!', had been an audacious herald-ing of the imminent new dawn.

All this had some pleasingly surreal consequences. Colleagues turned up on grown-up news programs to explain the difference between Oasis and Blur. I was invited to debate at the Cambridge University Union, arguing – alongside a classical music critic from the *Guardian* and former Sigue Sigue Sputnik agitator Tony James – in favour of the proposition that 'Today's music is better than ever'. It said something about the prevailing zeitgeist that we were voted victors by a vast margin. That is, it must have said something about the prevailing zeitgeist, because it can't have had anything to do with our debating skills, which had not been sharpened by the post-prandial sherries at the pre-debate dinner: for reasons no clearer to me now than they were then, I spent much of my allotted time lecturing a baffled hall about the Suez Crisis. It was a tremendous time to be a rock journalist. On occasion, girls even spoke to us.

The first two cover stories that *Melody Maker* ran after my return were an aghast five-page special on Bernard Butler's departure from Suede, and four exultant pages reporting Oasis's tour of America. These were followed, illustratively if not deliberately, by a cover story on hitherto venerated grunge godheads Soundgarden, which spent much of its considerable length mocking them for being a bunch of spoilt, petulant, paranoid prima donnas: Mat Smith's report included an excruciatingly detailed recollection of the half-hour of manouevres necessary to get the tour bus bearing Frowngarden, as Mat renamed them, from their hotel in Phoenix to the venue, which was across the road – the group being far, far too grand to do anything as plebeian as walk.

*

If I had any doubts of my own that America's music business had reached some apex of decadent foolishness, they were dispelled shortly afterwards.

People who attended Woodstock – the 1969 beano convened on Max Yasgur's farm in upstate New York – have never shut up about it. We veterans of Woodstock II – the 1994 revival held in a mosquito swamp near Catskill – rarely speak of it. Granted that the weather that weekend – which you may recreate by having a shower – wasn't the fault of the organisers, but everything else was, including a line-up of bands who should only ever have been gathered in one place to make it easier for the air force. With what felt like deliberate cruelty, alcohol was banned from the site. With ingenuity which had inevitable consequences, people realised that the only way they could get booze into the premises was by drinking a lot of it before arriving. Mud, drink, bad music and boredom are a terrifying combination: I saw humanity returned, physically and spiritually, to the primeval ooze.

Despite the trauma engendered by Woodstock II, I agreed to participate in *Melody Maker*'s reporting of the 1994 Reading Festival (I was young, impressionable, needed the money, etc). My contribution ended up amounting to a review of the proceedings on the main stage on the Saturday – highlights, Pulp; lowlights, pretty much everybody else – and a bestowal to the mythology of incompetence which forms the cornerstone of every decent magazine's vernacular of most-treasured in-jokes. On the afternoon of the final day, looking for excuses to avoid returning to the site, I dropped by *Melody Maker*'s temporary production suite in the Ramada Hotel, festival flophouse of choice for hacks and artists. I volunteered to write captions to the pictures that would accompany our report. Stumped by an image of a cropped-haired female lead singer in a silver dress, I typed 'Who the f*** is this?' into the allotted space at the bottom of the shot, imagining that I'd come back to it when my memory found second gear, or that some other writer would later atone for my ignorance, after pausing to chuckle at my punctilious use of the asterixes, in these circumstances. Altogether inevitably, my caption ran as it was.

It was in many respects an entirely standard Reading: the Cliff Richard death rumour did the rounds as usual, and the Ramada was evacuated at three o'clock one morning as usual when the fire alarm went off as usual, either because someone had fallen asleep smoking, or because someone had thought it might be amusing. Everett True and Simon Price almost came to blows over which of them was the bigger fan of Dexy's Midnight Runners, and – probably not coincidentally – Everett ended up in hospital suffering alcohol poisoning (or, as our own report put it, 'being too soft to hold his lager'.) But proceedings were enveloped by a pall quite unlike the traditional Reading fug generated by bad fast food, worse toilets and dim students attempting to smoke the parsley they'd been sold by chortling, grey-goateed bikers in Tygers of Pan Tang T-shirts. As Caitlin Moran's report from backstage noted, 'It would be crap to say that the spectre of Kurt Cobain hangs over the site like the smouldering copies of the *NME* being burnt in the main arena – but it does.' Cobain's widow, Courtney Love, played with her band Hole on the Friday. I didn't watch them; I felt a bit weird about it. And, as an unintentional but retrospectively poignant precursor of rock'n'roll's next great self-inflicted tragedy, Manic Street Preachers appeared as a three-piece, Richey Edwards absent, suffering from nervous exhaustion. I did watch them, because they were playing the day I was reviewing, and I was being professional (also, it was harder to desert your post at Reading than at Glastonbury, as Reading only really offered a choice of the main arena, where the bands were playing, and backstage, where your editor and/or one of the featured artist's people might see you). I described the Manics as 'lousy rock'n'roll, but great theatre' and further declared, 'I do love them and everything they stand for; I only wish I could stand their music.' I stand by both those judgements: Manic Street Preachers, grim gruel though their records are, were a treasurable reminder that rock'n'roll can be, or at least should be, about so much more than music.

With apologies to Caitlin, and indeed to the reader, it would also be crap to report that the spectre of Kurt Cobain hung over my immediately subsequent assignment, to Los Angeles to interview Grant Lee Buffalo, but it did, sort of.

I had been entranced – indeed, utterly besotted – by Grant Lee Buffalo's second album, *Mighty Joe Moon*. One song from *Mighty Joe Moon* in particular nagged at me. This was 'Happiness', a gorgeous essay in despair, narrated from the point of view of someone clearly unable to find much of worth in the riches he'd accumulated: the motif of starting each line with the words 'never mind' seemed an obvious giveaway. I began the interview with GLB songwriter Grant Lee Phillips by remarking on this incorporation of Nirvana's story into the album's wider narrative of America's knack for destroying its mavericks even as it celebrated them, from Kennedy to Koresh to Cobain.

'Oh, no,' said Phillips, evidently appalled. 'No. It was written a long time before that. We were playing it last year.'

Ah, I said. Bugger. That's a whole new angle I'm going to have to throw together quickly.

'Well,' said Phillips, perhaps trying to be hospitable (I'd come a long way), 'it is kind of freaky, though. I did think about it later, after we'd found out [about Cobain's death]. But yeah, when I listen to 'Happiness' these days, it does kind of make me think of that.'

Phillips was obsessed with America: its madness, its possibility. This was fair enough: so is everyone else. He wasn't sure about this assessment.

'I'm just writing about the four walls that surround me, in that sense,' he said, a neat if inadvertent summation of the unfair advantage that is the birthright of the American songwriter. 'But I feel like an ant trying to figure out the workings of a jet engine.'

*

Back at the office, it was still pleasantly unlike being back at an office.

Melody Maker had a real brio about it at this point, born of a largely justified belief that the best way to produce a paper that might amuse other people was to amuse ourselves as thoroughly as possible. Even the artists we wrote about seemed willing to buy into it, and even when the amusement was at their expense. Simon Price delivered a slapping unto The Wonder Stuff's *If The Beatles Had Read Hunter* singles collection, establishing his credentials by noting that, in various bygone seizures of now-recanted fervour, he'd probably spent about £35 on Wonder Stuff records and gig tickets; later, in the week of publication, his post included an envelope containing a cheque for that amount, drawn on the account of Miles Hunt.

Record companies, too, seemed happy to underwrite our indulgences. Caitlin Moran's twenty-four-hour assignment to Paris with fleetingly fashionable teenage popstrels Shampoo ended with the presentation of a hotel bill – once the wholesale looting of minibars, annihilation of fixtures and fittings, and clean-up costs had been assessed – in the vicinity of £4000.

Shampoo, at least, got a cover – and probably, therefore, a better return on their investment than whatever was spent on flying me and a photographer to Dublin and putting us up for the night so I could write a 500-word gig review of The Fatima Mansions, or sponsoring a similar expedition to Glasgow to do the same for Elastica, or another one back to Dublin for Counting Crows, or another one back to Dublin for Schtum or another one back to Dublin for Brendan Perry. My reward for each of these outings, incidentally, even after billing *Melody Maker* for the requisite tube and taxi rides and a modest dinner, wouldn't have exceeded £70 a time. Idiotic.

But altogether amusing. We put relatively minor Britpop acts like Gene and Echobelly on the cover, and still sold papers. We decided that there was a Mod revival, and dedicated a vast multi-part cover story to it, despite the fact that the only evidence supporting the proposition was the recent opportunist founding of a lightweight Britpop troupe called Menswear, who made a point of wearing suits.

Menswear were an instructive illustration of what can be accomplished when boneheaded determination is blended with total shamelessness. Despite the fact that they never once sounded in danger of writing a halfway worthwhile song, Menswear attracted a record deal, a publishing advance of half a million quid, audiences and press coverage simply by deciding that all these things would happen, and refusing to be daunted by any rebuff. At a very early stage of their existence, one of their number, not yet of voting age, approached Allan Jones at 1994's Reading Festival, and introduced himself with a drippy smile, a meerkat pup attempting to befriend leonine royalty. 'Shouldn't you be in bed, sonny?' asked Allan, squintingly.

This should, really, have been as calamitous for Menswear's relationship with *Melody Maker* as had been an earlier ill-advised attempt by tedious Canadian novelty act Barenaked Ladies to serenade *Melody Maker*'s staff as we enjoyed our production-day libations at the Stamford one afternoon. A few bars into their first number, Allan had interrupted, saying, 'Sorry, chaps, you do realise that this place doesn't have an entertainment licence?' And then, after a meticulously timed pause, sighing, 'Though as I suppose nobody here is being entertained, carry on.' Barenaked Ladies were barely written about by us again. Menswear were on the cover twice within the year.

And we continued regarding rock's sacred cows as creatures to be teased and tormented. It is all but unimaginable now, but it was pretty much routine then that, say,

Taylor Parkes could review, say, the generally venerated Kate Bush and describe her as 'the epitome of all those awful, pretend-ethereal, rich-daddy, piano-lesson, "I'm-so-f***ing-weird-arf-snork-hey-have-you-ever-read-'Winter Trees'-by-Sylvia-Plath" spoilt-bitch sixth-form pains in the arse' before noting that 'the sooner the witch gets her tits caught in an accordion, the better,' and, furthermore, 'Get outta here, f***pig.' This assessment of Bush, while intemperately phrased, was spot on in every important respect: in terms of inspiring generations of over-indulged, simpering, wilfully kooky semi-posh women in lacy dresses to perch at their fucking pianos and trill their high school English syllabuses to cloying tunes while batting their eyelashes, Bush has a deal for which to answer.

Taylor's indictment of Bush elicited the all-time best ever Letter To Backlash From An Angry Foreign Person. These, with all due humble acknowledgement that facility with other languages is something I do not possess myself, were always a joy, the giddy consequence of fury overspilling the limits of vocabulary. In this particular instance, one Tommy Bohman, of Vasterhaninge, Sweden, accused Taylor of 'throwing up his bullshit', of being 'filled with hatred and all horsed up,' further said of him that 'he fucks around in all directions,' and declared that 'Mr Parkes reached the bottom all by himself.' 'All horsed up' was instantly seized upon by David Stubbs as a new catchphrase for Pepe Le Punk.

Even a debacle concerning the cover of our Christmas issue did not knock us off our swagger. We had planned – and been promised – a major interview with Oasis. Shortly before the last possible moment, Oasis's press officer, Johnny Hopkins of Creation Records, informed our intended reporter, Everett True, that the interview would not be occurring, leaving *Melody Maker*'s panicking design department to patch together a collage of Britpop-related headshots so that we had something to put on the front of what was supposed to be our year's crowning achievement. Other magazines, or the same magazine at a less confident moment, might have accepted the defeat and cravenly hoped to leverage it into a favour further down the track. *Melody Maker* at the end of 1994 did not. ET filed what he had, which was an almost suspiciously lengthy – and somewhat curiously structured – review of Oasis's performance at the Hammersmith Palais. Read from right to left, it was an interesting, interested, impressionistic and generally laudatory piece of rock journalism ('There's plenty I dislike about Oasis, much of which is periphery. Their live show is another story altogether'). Read from top to bottom, if anyone cared to, the first letters of Everett's paragraphs spelled 'J-O-H-N-N-Y-I-S-A-C-U-N-T.'

We were making hay, and gathering rosebuds. We should have studied more closely an article by Jennifer Nine on page 40 of the issued dated 8 October 1994, which provided an introduction to something called 'the internet', in much the same way that the merrily gambolling diplodocus and triceratops of yore should have paid more attention to that strange new star that seemed to be getting brighter and bigger by the day.

*

Melody Maker's Album of the Year for 1994 was Portishead's *Dummy*. Mine were these.

R.E.M., *Monster*
Widely regarded, unfairly, as the beginning of the end of R.E.M.'s regal procession from *Murmur* onwards. *Monster* is actually a brilliant and gaudy bauble in their crown, a

rhinestone-studded phoenix rising from the ashes of *Automatic for the People*, a riot in a funfair, and an occasioner of overexcitably mixed metaphors.

Blur, *Parklife*

Christmas Day in 1994 was actually, if you read/worked for/cared at all about the preferred subject matter of *Melody Maker*, 7 October, when Blur headlined Alexandra Palace with Pulp and Supergrass (and Corduroy, of whom we sadly hear so little these days) as their opening acts. *Parklife*, unusually for a record which defined a moment, has aged pretty well, thanks to its astute balancing of boisterousness and melancholy. 'Girls & Boys', the emblematic lead single, is at once a raucous celebration and terribly, terribly sad.

Jeff Buckley, *Grace*

Like everyone else at the time, I fell for this quite hard. Like everyone else now, I never listen to any of it except his lovely, fragile version of Leonard Cohen's 'Hallelujah'.

Nirvana, *Unplugged in New York*

A taste of a future that never was. Cobain would have become one of those songwriters who got more interesting as he got older. Most rock musicians – and many rock fans – are driven by a desire to preserve their youth. Cobain, as he'd made heartbreakingly clear, was in a desperate hurry to put his youth behind him. On the evidence of this album, Nirvana were about three releases away from making a truly great country record.

Suede, *Dog Man Star*

Preposterous. Magnificent.

327

Kristin Hersh, *Hips and Makers*

First instalment of a solo career yet, at time of writing, to yield something that wouldn't have made my list this year, or most years.

Nick Cave and the Bad Seeds, *Let Love In*

Glorious melodrama is what we pay Cave for, of course, and it has rarely been more glorious or melodramatic than on *Let Love In*, an epic study of diseased desire. It's great, obviously, but it has to be wondered how much damage has been inadvertently wrought by Cave – and other songwriters similarly inclined – ennobling romantic dysfunction by elevating it to such tremendous artistic heights. Cave could do humanity an enormous favour by making just one great album about meeting a girl who was basically quite nice, and seemed to like him okay, but with whom things just didn't work out, as sometimes they don't, and with whom he still catches up for lunch every so often.

Johnny Cash, *American Recordings*

Though I still harboured some feelings about country music which confused me, I probably had Cash written off as a shelled-out cabaret turn chiefly of interest to bussed-in tour groups eating dinners which began with prawn cocktails. It's little consolation that this is pretty much how Cash himself felt about Cash before Rick Rubin hove into view to produce this first instalment of an astonishing late-life renaissance, convincingly casting Cash as the supreme oracle of American music, the all-seeing eye at the top of the pyramid.

The Fatima Mansions, *Lost in the Former West*

In 1995, the 4 March issue of *Melody Maker*, with The Beastie Boys adorning the cover, gave away a small paperback titled *Unknown Pleasures*, in which the paper's writers were permitted 2000 words a time to make cases for albums whose reputations, they believed, had lapsed into unmerited disrepair. It says much for The Fatima Mansions' continuing atrocious luck that while most other writers focused on albums entombed by decades of cobwebs, I felt it timely to make a case for *Lost in the Former West* a matter of months after it had been released.

Liz Phair, *Whip-Smart*

The only thing wrong with Phair's fierce and funny second album was that it had to follow Phair's arguably fiercer and funnier debut, 1993's *Exile in Guyville*. Like few other artists in history, Phair's career can be plotted as an almost kink-free downhill trajectory, beginning at a vertiginous peak and bottoming out somewhere near the earth's core around the release of 2003's *Liz Phair*, an album so hog-whimperingly bad that I rather pulled my punches in my review of it, for *Bang* magazine, vaguely concerned that I was the victim of some sort of prank.

ANDREW MUELLER

23

IN WHICH THE AUTHOR DOES LITTLE TO IMPROVE *MELODY MAKER'S* CHANCES OF EVER INTERVIEWING MORRISSEY AGAIN

Another year, another readers' poll. The Best Album and Best Single categories were won by exactly the records that might be expected to win a mid-nineties British music weekly's readers' poll, i.e. Blur's *Parklife* and Oasis's *Live Forever* respectively. Possibly for this reason, a late surge of entries in suspiciously similar handwriting – handwriting suspiciously similar, that is, to the handwriting of Taylor Parkes, Caitlin Moran and Simon Price – ensured that the rival godheads of Britpop were beaten to the Best Band accolade by Manic Street Preachers. This appalling act of electoral chicanery would prove retrospectively, if inadvertently, fitting: the Manics would become, if for the grimmest imaginable reasons, the single act that would have the most impact on *Melody Maker* and its readers in 1995.

Again, I rather phoned in my tips for the proverbial top in the year looming. Unbothered by the fact that my 1993 prediction of Brobdingnagian success for Australian indie group The Moles had proved mistaken, I announced – with the dauntless insouciance of one of those doomsday prophets who keeps announcing new apocalypses and summoning his purple-robed followers back up the hill regardless of previous anticlimaxes – that 1995 would be the year of Cardinal, the new concern forged by Moles songwriter Richard Davies. I also enthused about Schtum, a pugnacious, punky outfit from Northern Ireland who were, I said, 'reminiscent of Steve Albini's Shellac with a latent pop sensibility' – for all the good it ever did them. At least I wasn't playing it quite as shamelessly safe as David Bennun, who boldly vaunted briefly incandescent indie poster girls Veruca Salt – who were on the cover of that week's issue. (This Christ-January's-quiet front page aside, *Melody Maker* generally regarded Veruca Salt as suspiciously pretty piñatas, whom we thrashed mercilessly for being a callow corporate facsimile of the obviously superior Breeders. In general, to the exceedingly limited extent that I cared, I agreed. I thought Veruca Salt's minor debut hit 'Seether' sucked, and that their debut album, the admittedly brilliantly titled *American Thighs*, sucked worse by dint of going on for longer. However, Veruca Salt's second album, 1997's Bob Rock-produced *Eight Arms To Hold You*, is a ripper.)

I was, at least, trying to imbibe the spirit of the times elsewhere in 1995's first issue. My review of that week's singles enthused over voguish British artists McAlmont, Sleeper and Tricky. The live pages contained my longish dispatch from the previous month's Transmusicales festival in Rennes – which, if it had been a review of any other festival in any other country at around this point in human history, would certainly have been a review of a festival dominated by the Union Jack-spangled zeitgeist. However, the French are as French – that is, pointlessly and aggressively contrary – about booking rock festivals as they are about everything else, and so the star attractions of Transmusicales, in the year of *Parklife* and *Definitely Maybe*, had been Beck, Massive Attack and The Prodigy. None of which thrilled me half as much as the stylings of Mieskuoro Huutajat, a Finnish shouting choir – which is to say forty or so young men in suits who, marshalled by a conductor, shouted. In Finnish. It was curiously invigorating, though I couldn't imagine that they picked up much pocket change playing weddings. That said, I don't know what Finnish weddings are like.

In a year in which England and things English were clearly going to be widely discussed and admired, I thought it'd be interesting to undertake about the most English expedition imaginable: to Blackpool, in winter, to see Morrissey play. The northern coastal hovel was, by this point, Morrissey's municipal equivalent, something he even seemed to have acknowledged on 'Every Day is Like Sunday', his beautiful elegy to the oxymoronic notion of the English seaside resort. Morrissey and Blackpool had, I thought, things in common – cold, wet, shabby and past it, dealers in nudges and winks towards something that maybe was great, once, if not really in the lifetime of anybody I knew, but which nevertheless retained a dilapidated grandeur.

I wanted to enjoy it, albeit in the same way that you want the 50/1 nag you've put a fiver on to win the race. I liked the idea of Morrissey assuming the role of an exacting, curmudgeonly tribal elder, reminding the cocky upstarts of Britpop who was really in charge around here, who was the one who'd actually defined a specifically English pop lexicon. I also, despite having heard his solo albums, felt vaguely sorry for him. By 1995, the guitarist in the biggest band in the country – a band who shared Morrissey's Manchester Irish heritage – was making a point of slinging an Epiphone Sheraton emblazoned with the Union Jack, and everyone appeared to find this wonderful. In 1992, Morrissey had carried Britain's flag onto a stage in Finsbury Park, and prompted several pages of characteristically sanctimonious *NME* arse-ache about whether or not this marked him as some daintily goose-stepping strain of racist (I am aware that the case against Morrissey on this front has more heft than this, and includes one or two lyrics which are at best woefully maladroit. 'Bengali in Platforms' is the one most often cited, and while it's a silly and patronising song, only those determined to take offence could fail to see that Morrissey is attempting to offer sympathy from one lifelong outsider to another – he blows it by failing to acknowledge that to a large extent he chose to be perceived as he is, while his awkward, friendly protagonist didn't.)

The concert, as it turned out, was incredibly boring – but it's some small tribute to Morrissey that it was boring in an interesting way. As a musical event, it was at least as lacklustre and predictable as my review's observation that his backing troupe of bequiffed rockabilly plodders would have been more appropriately employed plying their trade at the end of one of Blackpool's seafront piers. As a study in the ennui engendered – in both performer and fans – by a mutual accustoming to adulation, it was riveting.

> The stage invaders [I marvelled] start appearing towards the end of 'We'll Let You Know', and continue appearing at regular intervals throughout . . . They climb on stage, grab him briefly, and then walk off in an orderly fashion, as if only doing it for form's sake rather than out of any genuine infatuation. Morrissey, in turn, ignores every one of them. It's a little like watching an elderly, dysfunctional couple continuing to enact the motions of married life because they know that, at this late stage, no one else would have them.

None of which should be interpreted as a suggestion that I didn't bitterly resent every second I stood amid the dismal tat of the Empress Ballroom. I did, never more so than when photographer Steve Hall made the altogether sensible suggestion, about four songs in, that we call it a night and go and play bingo, or perhaps get comprehensively hammered in some dolorous, damp and vaguely hostile pub and wonder what the fuck we were doing with our lives. Tempting though it was, I was compelled to remind him of the sub-clause of Sod's Law that pertains specifically to music journalists: the night we bunk off a Morrissey show, I said, is obviously the night he returns for the encore and says, 'Ladies and gentlemen, please welcome Mike Joyce, Andy Rourke and Johnny Marr. You call 'em out, we'll play 'em.' (This did not happen, but a nonetheless stunning reading of The Smiths' 'Shoplifters of the World Unite' did.) With truly fabulous cruelty, *Melody Maker* ran my disdainful notice of Morrissey ('a show which he can hardly be bothered to perform of songs he can hardly be bothered to sing') as the bottom half of a split page, beneath Sharon O'Connell's report of a triumphant Hammersmith Palais show by his upstart heirs, Suede.

*

Morrissey has not, in the years since, done much to dispel the perception of him as a miserable, prurient, purse-lipped Little Englander (David Stubbs was already writing semi-regular sketches for TTT which depicted Morrissey as a batty old woman in quilted dressing gown and hair curlers, mithering about the weather and the minutiae of tea-making in dialect borrowed from Alan Bennett). And Morrissey has not, since the mid-nineties, made a record that hasn't sounded like Ena Sharples covering Shakin' Stevens, and has made several Duke of Edinburghish quips about various strains of foreign person.

His opinions are nevertheless still sought and printed (very often under the in-no-way crashingly obvious headline BIGMOUTH STRIKES AGAIN). It can only suggest that, barely explicable though it seems, there are people who still care what Morrissey thinks about anything. My theory is that Morrissey does indeed speak for, and to, a disenfranchised sector of British society. Morrissey's people are English people so convulsed by their self-loathing ambivalence about their nationality that they can't quite bring themselves to admit that they hate everybody else even more than they do themselves. It's at least arguable that Morrissey's post-Smiths popularity – which surely can't have anything to do with his solo records – flourishes because of his graceless judgements on Johnny Foreigner, not despite them. He says out loud what many of his fans dare not: he's a *Daily Mail* tucked inside an *NME*.

The same cognitive dissonance was also discernible at *Melody Maker*. Most of my colleagues had come of age in the 1980s, during which the music press had, like most media, braved the brisk self-scouring of Political Correctness. Political correctness was not altogether a bad thing; to believe otherwise is to yearn for the halcyon days of the 1970s, when bullying jokes about race and rape were staples of mainstream entertainment. Political correctness is also not, despite the claims of various professional bores and blowhards, an orchestrated campaign of Maoist repression. There is still bountiful opportunity for the outrageous and provocative to be outrageous and provocative. It's just a little bit more difficult for dim, mean-spirited arseholes to get away with being dim, mean-spirited arseholes.

At any rate, it had hardly stopped *Melody Maker* making fun of foreigners. There were rules about this, undefined but understood. The Dutch, the Belgians and the French were all obviously fair game. The Germans were largely left alone, probably out of a fear of looking like the sort of people – English football fans, English tabloid newspapers – who make fun of the Germans. Eastern Europeans were rarely targets for mockery, earning a pass under the more-to-be-pitied-than-blamed clause. As for the home nations, it was permissible to make fun of the Scots only in exceptional circumstances, the Irish never, and the Welsh as much and as often as one felt like it. In *Melody Maker*'s case, however, the most frequently punished targets were continental. This was less a reflection of any innate belief in the inherent superiority of Anglo-Saxon stock than it was an honest reflection of the self-evident truth that Europeans are completely hopeless at rock music (in one of Mr Agreeable's more perceptive outbursts, he reacted to the news that the French government had awarded a cabinet minister special responsibility for French rock by predicting that the politician in question would be kept 'About as f***ing busy as the f***ing squadron leader of the f***ing Royal Dutch Mountain Rescue Service!').

I had the opportunity to put this point to one of the exceptions to this rule: Antwerp quintet dEUS, who had just released one of the very greatest singles of the decade, 'Suds & Soda'. My introduction to my account of my meeting with dEUS in Strasbourg laid out the case against: 'When numbering the great European rock groups, an inability to count beyond nought has scarcely been a disadvantage. When you think Euro-rock, you think mistimed gestures, badly copied poses, lyrics that would make a cat laugh, and white socks.' (The colossal popularity enjoyed by Depeche Mode in Europe strikes me, in this context, as significant; they really might as well be German.) What, I asked dEUS's wondrously named singer Tom Barman, made dEUS the first decent rock band in European history? His answer was both more polite than I deserved, and more perceptive than I'd been expecting.

'A lot of it,' explained Barman, who'd acquired a pleasing trans-Atlantic drawl, 'has to do with having a good accent.'

Really?

'Really. A lot of people take that very seriously outside Belgium. I've given tapes of other Belgian bands – and there are some other good Belgian bands – to my friends, and they've just gone "Jesus, the accents".'

'Also,' elaborated bass player Stef Carlens, 'English just goes well with the music. When people sing in their own language the music that goes with it, like Spanish or Japanese with Spanish or Japanese folk music, it does work well within those limits. But when I hear, like, some Italian singer doing crossover rap/jazz/funk in Italian, I'm, like "Oh, no".'

'Then again,' said – that name again – Barman, with the sudden animation of a man about to make a palpable point, 'Italian and Spanish are world languages that people will recognise, and they might sound at least exotic. But Flemish doesn't sound exotic at all.'

Barman's point about languages being naturally more suited to their indigenous music was both good and intriguing, if rather undermined by the lessons derived from another assignment I undertook at around the same time. The cloying, adenoidal whine that is the accent of England's Black Country would seem, in theory, to be about as well-suited to hip hop as, well, Belgians would seem to be to rock'n'roll. In Chicago, however, I beheld an arena full of Americans propelled to exultant transports by exactly this proposition, in the riotously unlikely form of Stourbridge's own Pop Will Eat Itself, who were touring the United States opening for Nine Inch Nails.

PWEI were interesting to me at this point mostly because they still existed. They'd been going for ten years, during which they'd been part of (or associated with) at least half a dozen discrete zeitgeists – and, as such, had become routinely derided as unprincipled and incorrigible chancers, ever-eager to salute whichever flag happened to be flying. Among other reasons why PWEI weren't taken seriously was a refusal to take themselves seriously – on their record sleeves, PWEI's songs were credited to one Vestan Pance – and a certain lack of decorum about the public airing of soiled laundry. During the 1991 Reading Festival, after-show revellers at the Ramada Hotel – which is to say pretty much everyone of any import in the UK music business – had been treated to a drunken punch-up between two of the group's members, climaxing in a loudly slurred announcement by singer Clint Mansell that he was quitting, and that PWEI were, as of this moment, over. It says much about PWEI's critical standing that Mansell's valediction was greeted with sustained, spontaneous applause from all present.

And yet PWEI were still going. Without anybody really noticing, they'd had more than a dozen Top 30 hits in the UK (this was, circa the mid-nineties, still an accomplishment). They were about to release an album of their works remixed by such luminaries as Alex Paterson, Jah Wobble, The Prodigy and Apollo 440, all of whom had asked to be involved. Nine Inch Nails' Trent Reznor, the singer in plausibly the coolest band in the United States at this point, had declared himself a fan – even cited PWEI as an influence – and signed them to his record label and taken them on tour. This was how PWEI and myself came to be gliding to an enormous venue on the outskirts of Chicago in a tour bus not noticeably smaller or worse-appointed than the suites in the not-at-all-mangy hotel in which we'd all been staying.

'I don't understand it either,' said Mansell. 'The only reason I can think of for why we keep managing to transcend things is that somewhere, some way, we must be doing something that somebody wants that nobody else is giving them. Maybe it is that ability to be receptive to what's going on around us.'

Or, I suggested, what is more commonly regarded as a shameless predilection for scrambling aboard any passing bandwagon.

'Well, possibly,' allowed Mansell.

I recited a – necessarily incomplete, we didn't have all week – list of all the groups that had, at one time or another, been identified as peers or inspirations of PWEI, all now licked while PWEI kept ticking. Talulah Gosh. Gaye Bykers on Acid. Zodiac Mindwarp and the Love Reaction. Age of Chance. Ned's Atomic Dustbin. There were dozens more: PWEI had been, by now, shamblers, greboes, agitpoppers and rappers, everything but a massed pipe marching band. I wondered if Mansell was embarrassed by any of it.

'No,' he beamed. 'It's just something you did, isn't it? I mean, ten years ago I was going out with such-and-such a girl. I'm not going out with her now, but I don't regret that I did. It's a phase of your life. You know, like getting out your old snapshots of when you were a New Romantic.'

This observation prompted the inevitable enquiry.

'I'm sure we must have had a go,' pondered Mansell. 'No, actually, I don't think we were. I think we were a bit late. The first band we were in was very sort of Bauhausish, all makeup and goth stuff.'

Humbler beginnings were difficult, if not downright disturbing, to imagine. But PWEI had signed a Faustian mortgage, I thought. They were successful, by most measures applied to rock bands – people wanted their autographs, and one assumed they'd made a few quid, if probably less than the people who wanted their autographs imagined. But PWEI were all but seen as a cartoon strip in human form. By which I meant that if the bus on which we were riding was to knock over Trent Reznor in the backstage car park, the Nine Inch Nails auteur would be remembered as an artist. If, however, the bus plunged off a bridge before we got there, PWEI would be remembered, at best, as entertainers. Clowns, not poets.

'I don't know if I'm very entertaining,' said Mansell. 'I suppose your ego would love to be remembered as an artist, but I don't think people view us as artists. Or, if they do, it's only as piss-artists.'

Journalists have a tendency to insist that things are more complicated than they appear to be. We do this so we'll look – and, perhaps more importantly, feel – cleverer than our readers. We also do it because writing of Situation X or Person Y that it or they is or are 'pretty much exactly what you'd reckon' tends to leave us a way shy of our word count. Still hoping to prompt some revelation, some visitation from the hidden depths of Pop Will Eat Itself, I noted that for all Mansell's affability, he was nursing a self-inflicted injury: he had, last night, vented some sort of frustration on a lift at the hotel, which was why his left hand now resembled an udder.

'Oh,' said Mansell. 'I just get drunk.'

ANDREW MUELLER

24

IN WHICH THE AUTHOR ENDURES A BRIEF TURN AS SPOKESIDIOT FOR A GENERATION

The instant interactivity of modern publishing has much to commend it – journalists have to be sure they have their facts in order, and polemicists need to be confident that their arguments are competently marshalled, lest their work get duffed righteously up by an avenging online posse.

However, the instant interactivity of modern publishing often just means in practice that several dozen dickheads, none of whom have been required to do anything beyond open a laptop, or learn anything beyond a few phrases of rudimentary playground abuse, call you a Nazi within three minutes of your article going live. Old-school postal contact was slow and cumbersome, but it did at least dissuade all but the most determined, in one sense or another. When that enthusiasm was deployed in the cause of sustaining a running joke, *Melody Maker*'s readers could be positively inspirational.

Rummaging through the Backlash folder one evening in February, I found a couple of letters enquiring, yearningly, about the relationship status of *Melody Maker*'s demo reviewer, Holly Barringer. Holly had arrived in the office a

couple of years previously, on some or other sort of intern-
ship, and absolutely everybody had – not unreasonably, as she
was smart, nice, dumbfoundingly beautiful and had the filthiest laugh in Christendom – fallen hopelessly in love with her.
She had been assigned a weekly column, Holly's Demo Hell,
in which she reviewed the tapes submitted to the paper by
budding new artists, generally in the unforgiving tones they
deserved. As we were not utterly insensitive to the proclivities
of our readership – largely hopeless young men whose first
words upon actually meeting Holly would be, as mine were,
'Hmphrggggnnnnnmph' – this column was adorned with a
portrait of Holly, embellished with clip-art devil horns.

This picture used to generate a fair bit of post in itself,
some of it best handled with tweezers. However, this particular week, a few correspondents had noted the recent change
in Holly's by-line from Barringer to Hernandez, and were
wondering if congratulations – or, perhaps, a mournful
plunge from Beachy Head – were in order. While I was pretty
sure she hadn't got married, the truth was that I had no idea
why she'd adopted this nom-de-plume – and finding out, with
deadline looming, might have involved, like, calling her or
something. So I decided to run with it. I replied: 'No, chaps,
you weren't the only ones left crying into their snakebite as
the delectable Holly strolled down the aisle with Rafael "El
Burro" Hernandez, a dashing young matador from Cadiz. If
any of you are interested, we're chartering a plane to his next
fight in the Madrid ring, where we'll be cheering on the bull
for all we're worth.'

To my delight, readers responded in similar spirit, in some
volume. Editing Backlash again a few weeks later, I was
compelled to report a mixture of blessings. The good news,
I invented, was that young Rafael's first bull of the afternoon had collected him square amidships, and gone tearing

around the arena spooling his major intestine off one horn like tape from a shattered demo cassette – which meant, of course, that Holly was, or would be after a discreet interval, back on the market. The bad news, I continued, was that Holly had interpreted our three raucous cheers for the bull as a mite insensitive, in the circumstances, and that the ears of his last kill, which she was insisting on wearing around her neck, were starting to hum a bit. This update only piqued further curiosity, and over ensuing weeks I was obliged to invent an entire family of Hernandez brothers, all of them engaged in dashing and potentially hazardous occupations, all of whom met calamitous ends shortly after stepping up to take Holly's hand – among them Miguel, a keen amateur balloonist, and Pietro, a trapeze artist. I shall not dignify with a response suspicions that I made some of these letters up myself and that they were in fact a series of ardent but cunningly veiled declarations at one remove. Though we did go out for a bit about a decade later. Still friends, etc. There's a lesson here, I think. A beautiful woman will swiftly forget most of the grovelling losers who present her flowers, jewellery, and other such tawdry and cliched votives, but she'll always remember the guy who ghostwrote fan mail about her to music papers, manufactured several Spanish husbands for her, and then had them all killed.

Not all submissions to Backlash were idle whimsy. By April 1995, indeed, the idle whimsy was becoming overwhelmed by a gathering cascade of unhappiness and desperation. It had begun late in 1994, in response to Simon Price's extraordinary interview with Manic Street Preachers' troubled totem Richey Edwards, which had been the cover story of the 3 December issue. This was scarcely the first music press interview in which a rock star had discussed his demons, but it might have been the first like this.

Edwards' self-mutilation had appeared to many – certainly to me, anyway – a particularly wretched form of attention-seeking, most notoriously when he had carved the slogan '4 Real' into one arm with a razor blade to prove his integrity to Manics-sceptical *NME* journalist Steve Lamacq. By the time Edwards sat down with Simon on the Manics' tour bus in Paris, he seemed to have grown either i) tired of being perceived as another self-destructive rock'n'roll clown, a Sid Vicious for the 1990s, or ii) up, just a little bit. Edwards spoke humbly, sensitively and with bleary wit about his struggles with anorexia, alcohol and depression. He absolutely refused to romanticise any of it: 'Mental institutions,' he said, and he knew from first-hand experience, 'are not full of people in bands.' The feature was accompanied by a brilliant sequence of portraits by Tom Sheehan of Edwards clad in a white jumpsuit even paler than himself, excerpts from Rimbaud's *A Season in Hell* daubed across the back. On the cover, Edwards appeared set against a wall of human bones, somewhere in the Paris catacombs. He looked, as Tom intended, like a ghost.

We always got a lot of letters from Manic Street Preachers fans – a lot of letters, that is, from chronically self-dramatising adolescents determined, as chronically self-dramatising adolescents are, to perceive their workaday vexations as epic existential trauma. Generally, the replies we printed in black type beneath their wittering and (on a few excruciating occasions) poetry, tended towards the patronising. The ones that started filling the file in the weeks after Pricey's piece ran were different – sufficiently so that even I, who rarely needed much provocation to make fun of maudlin teenagers with maladroitly applied eyeliner, noticed. There was a lot of identification with Edwards, specifically with his self-harm. People wrote in who did it themselves and were ashamed and, perhaps more worryingly, people wrote in who did it themselves and couldn't see what was wrong with it, so there.

The Backlash editors who answered the first wave of these responded by suggesting, as kindly as possible, that the anguished correspondents probably needed help from people better qualified to assist them than rock journalists – i.e., almost all of humanity aside from rock journalists. Our responses at around this period also included a few weary reminders that, you know, we're only young once, worse things happen at sea and so on, and that maybe lightening the fuck up might be a tack worth considering. It rapidly became clear that this wasn't enough. We got more letters about Richey Edwards, and still more letters about the letters about Richey Edwards. And then, one day in February, Richey Edwards was reported missing, and *Melody Maker*'s postman became the hardest-working person in show business.

When a famous and adored musician comes to grief now, there are any number of means by which the bereft can share their agony. In 1995, the letters pages of the music weeklies were pretty much it. I happened to be editing Backlash the week that news of Edwards' disappearance broke. I decided not to turn the page into a requiem for Richey for two reasons. One was that I had to allow for the possibility that by the time the paper hit the newsstands, he might have reappeared, or otherwise explained himself. The other was that a lot of the letters were just horrible – clearly disturbed, certainly disturbing, and I was as qualified to answer them as I was to field the distress signals of astronauts adrift in a malfunctioning spacecraft.

I printed one of the more straightforwardly concerned and plaintive Richey letters, from a Jo in Billericay ('Shit, I don't understand, Richey, I don't even know why I'm writing this letter'). The rest of the page I filled with more traditional Backlash correspondence – querulous Morrissey fans, angry Sleeper fans, humourless dullards who thought Caitlin Moran should wind her neck in, thwarted suitors anxious for the latest news of Holly's progress through the ill-starred Hernandez clan – aside from the Viewpoint, the editorial penned by each week's Backlash superintendent. After consulting with Allan, and with a couple of mental health charities, I suggested that anyone having serious difficulty coping try calling the Samaritans, and that anyone who wanted to talk about this stuff in an upcoming *Melody Maker* feature write directly to me.

I had no idea if anyone would reply, or what I intended to do if they did. I'm slightly baffled now that I felt so intensely that it was the place of myself or *Melody Maker* to get involved at all. But I felt, as I think we all did, protective of our readers – they paid to read our blathering every week, thereby permitting us to continue our blathering. And I was, as I know we all were, shocked by the worst of what we'd been getting – a few had not only explained their self-harming routines in excruciating detail, but enclosed illustrative photographs of the damage (which, in the era preceding digital photography, intimated a worrisome degree of determination). Plus, to a very small and semi-detached extent, I empathised. Not so much with the garment-rending over the (probable) death of a pop star – I tend towards the belief that if Dead Person X wouldn't have cared overmuch if I died, I've a limited right to discombobulating grief where Dead Person X is concerned – but with the pervasive sadness of people who were, on the face of it, strapped for things to be sad about.

Ridiculously, despite the friends, opportunities and adventures chronicled in this book, I didn't enjoy quite a lot of my twenties. Indeed, I spent (far too) much of the decade in which you're probably supposed to be concentrating hardest on having a good time enveloped in a disagreeable fog of discontent and bewilderment. A couple of doctors diagnosed this as depression, and they might have been correct, but even if they were, it was never the danger-to-self-or-to-others variety, and so I was left, probably quite rightly, to try to make sense of it myself. I don't really know if I did that, but I do know that the mist began to lift in my early thirties, and has now all but evaporated. I mean no disrespect to those burdened by blacker dogs with bigger teeth when I say that I believe that this process has mostly been a consequence of assimilating the realisation that I just don't have time for this crap anymore. There are, it turns out, some consolations to growing older: indeed, I'm now a practical optimist that my half-a-lifetime-younger self would find unrecognisable, and possibly unbearable. (In which case, get stuffed, you moody little twerp. I've got more money than you and I've gotten laid a lot more, plus I've been all over the world, written three books and made two albums. What have you ever done, eh? Go on, fuck off.)

At the time, anyway, I thought I got it. I wrote a slightly overwrought confessional piece for the 1 April issue – I felt the date offered me an escape clause – outlining my personal view from inside a mind that contrived to refuse every fine thing laid upon its table (you kind of have to forgive The Eagles everything else for 'Desperado'). I accompanied this with another piece about the letters I'd received in response to my Viewpoint of a few weeks earlier. They were, I noted, surprising.

All bar two out of dozens were from women – though statistical wisdom holds that self-harm is as predom- inantly a female trait as suicide is predominantly a male one, the intensity of identification with Richey expressed in many of the letters turns over a few ideas about the fan/star relationship (traditionally, boys are supposed to aspire, girls to admire). The letters were also noticeably better spelt, punctuated and expressed than the semi-literate invective that is the usual diet of the pop paper mailbag. All were thoughtful and polite, and a couple were even bleakly witty.

On the facing page, we ran pieces by the Samaritans' press officer, and a clinical psychologist. All of which, naturally, did as much to stymie the flood of tear- and blood-stained letters as offering £20-pound record vouchers for each one we received (which, just to be clear on this, we didn't – although a couple of years later, at the behest of some genius in marketing, Backlash did begin offering record store vouchers for the Letter Of The Week. It was astonishing how many poised and witty missives *Melody Maker* suddenly began receiving from the flatmates of its contributors).

There was another response to our coverage, and one that was, in its way, even more disconcerting – from the rest of the media. Someone in a newsroom saw the issue, and called us. Then someone else saw the story that resulted from that, and called us as well. And so on. For a deeply strange week or two, *Melody Maker* was the desired quarry of a full-scale global clusterfuck. I did more than forty interviews, including with every newspaper in Britain, several in the United States, the evening news on the BBC and ITV, and Radio 4's *Today* program. I found this exciting, of course: along with a rarely satiable appetite for the sound of my own voice, I had aspirations of one day working for such august institutions as these. I was therefore thrilled by the opportunity to be of some help to these indefatigable pursuers of truth as they went about the serious business of responsibly imparting an important story to their trusting viewers and readers.

And I was swiftly baffled and bemused by the incompetence and irresponsibility of what they reported. Interestingly, the best of the television reports were worse than the worst of the print equivalents, aside from the write-up in one of England's putrid tabloids, which strongly insinuated that I'd shown their reporter the letters we'd received, which I wouldn't have for money. In general, there was a boneheaded determination to put the effect cart before the cause horse, to declare that Cobain and Edwards had inspired a copycat cult of semi-suicidal slashers, when the obvious truth, at least to anyone with half a brain who thought about it for five seconds, was that their public discussion of self-harm and depression had encouraged others, long silent, to believe that it was okay to speak – hopefully to someone who could help them. The BBC's *Six O'Clock News* filed a hilarious report from the Slough of Despond, gravely intoning that a group called The Smiths had had a hit with a song called 'Heaven Knows I'm Miserable Now' (which they had, in 1984, and it had been more than half a joke), observing with horror that there was a band called Suicidal Tendencies – a sack of dreary skate-thrash bozos who had precisely nothing to do with anything – and completely neglecting to mention Kurt Cobain at all.

The frustration I expressed at this in a follow-up article did at least afford one of *Melody Maker*'s regular victims a measure of spiteful satisfaction. Years before I joined the paper, some reviewer or other had found fault with 70 Gwen Party, purveyors of inferior industrial electronica to the small audiences which gathered – or were stuck to the carpet – in such venues as the Sir George Robey in Finsbury Park or the White Horse in Hampstead, among others unlikely to be mistaken for the London Palladium. 70 Gwen Party's singer had taken issue with the consequent write-up in *Melody Maker*, inscribing a lengthy exposition of his displeasure, and signing it Victor Ndip. The combination of Victor Ndip's indignation and Victor Ndip's name had tickled *Melody Maker*, with the result that the poor bastard became a fixture as a stooge in the TTT pages and as a personality in the gossip columns, where we regularly linked him romantically with fashionable indie singers of the moment, inventing fleeting relationships with Carrie of Shampoo, Louise Wener of Sleeper, most of Elastica and Zoe Ball, among many others. During my stint as Reviews Editor, I regularly used 70 Gwen Party as a punishment detail, compelling errant writers who'd missed deadlines, mixed metaphors or otherwise displeased me to redeem the debt by enduring the Gwen's racket, which further swelled Ndip's bulging file of disparaging notices, and seemed to do similar for the veins in his temples. Ndip wrote still more voluminous and furious letters, briskly trimmed precises of which we ridiculed in Backlash until he began suffixing them with legalese clauses insisting that his thoughts be published unabridged or not at all (Everett ran one such diatribe with everything deleted except the words: 'No editing, please.').

'All I can say,' Ndip smirked from the Letter of the Week eyrie in the 29 April issue, 'is, Andrew, welcome to the "real" world. Not so cosy on the other side of the media fence, is it? So you were misrepresented and edited, were you? Doesn't feel good, does it? Does it surprise you to hear that your own paper is responsible for such crimes, week in and week out?' This epistle went on a lot longer than that, but in keeping with the relationship Ndip and *Melody Maker* enjoyed, I've cut most of it.

It was a considerable relief when, a few weeks later, Backlash became substantially overrun by an impassioned dispute about whether or not chickens can fly. What happened was this. At a more than usually hungover editorial meeting, two or more *Melody Maker* contributors became – for reasons lost to memory – embroiled in an argument about the aerial abilities of hens. This spilled into the paper's gossip column, where a call for informed input from the readership prompted dozens of responses, none better – for no letters ever were better – than the one we headlined LETTER OF THE CENTURY.

This was from one Femke Engelse, a resident of Rotter-dam, who had the inestimable advantage, in divining the truth of this matter, of owning a chicken, named Kip. Femke enclosed a photograph of said bird, along with some hand-drawn graphs sketching trajectories which varied according to the reason for flight, for example, escaping from a vacuum cleaner or foraging for food. Her conclusion was: 'Yes, chickens can fly, but it requires an enormous amount of flapping, which tires them out after about ten seconds, at which point they give up, unless there's some nice yummy rice on the table.' It remains one of my favourite demonstrations of my belief that magazines attract the readers they deserve. We called Ms Engelse and asked her to name her reward. She expressed a desire to feature as Mr Agreeable's Cretinous, Useless, Neglible Tosser of the Week, the write-in section of Mr Agreeable's column, in which readers submitted themselves for a dressing-down from the great sage. Mr Agreeable lit scornfully upon her admission that she edited a fanzine: 'What the f*** is there to write a fanzine about in Holland? What's your fanzine called? 'There's a Lot of Tulips Around Here and F*** All Else'?'

A few weeks later, an envelope bearing Dutch stamps turned up at the office, containing the latest issue of said journal, renamed *There's a Lot of Tulips Around Here and F*** All Else*.

25

IN WHICH THE AUTHOR ELICITS A REMARKABLE CONFESSION FROM THE JESUS & MARY CHAIN

Writing for *Melody Maker* was, as ever, richly rewarding in every respect save for the sort of recognition of one's efforts best appreciated by landlords, publicans, grocery store proprietors and so forth. The freelance writer's life inspires enormous gratitude for humankind's development of a system of convertible currency. My sort would not long survive in a barter economy, in which we would be compelled to stand at a counter trying to exchange a 300-word review of 70 Gwen Party for a week's worth of frozen pizza and beer. For this reason, I began making an effort to write for other titles. I was briefly adopted by *Top of the Pops* magazine, about which I felt sheepish to a degree that now strikes me as unseemly – like the pompous twit I was clearly capable of being, I think I considered *Top of the Pops* somehow beneath me. Surveyed again today, *TOTP* was a very sharp read, a plausible attempt to recreate the alternately breathless and sardonic glories of prime mid-eighties *Smash Hits* for the Britpop era.

I wrote one emblematic cover story for *TOTP*, overseeing an interview of Kylie Minogue by Jarvis Cocker of Pulp.

355

It was a typically astute summation by *TOTP* of the unusual pass British music had reached, where artists like Pulp, who would once have been the exclusive concern of the readers of *Melody Maker* or *NME*, were now proper pop stars, recognised in the street, never off the television. That same issue of *TOTP* saw nothing wrong with assuming that its readers would be as interested in The Boo Radleys and Shed Seven[1] as they were in Take That, Wet Wet Wet and Whigfield. On balance, Jarvis's questions ('Have you ever had a Saturday job?', 'Do you have any phobias?', 'If you had to kiss one of Take That, which one would it be?') were better than Kylie's answers. Though Minogue was perfectly pleasant, she at no point threatened to break her already impressive – and to this day unblemished – record of never saying anything interesting or even memorable, an astonishing accomplishment for someone who has been so famous so long. She'd have made an ideal royal wife.

I also started writing, with rather more enthusiasm, for a newly launched – and swiftly doomed – monthly called *Ikon*. It was edited by *Melody Maker* colleagues Chris Roberts and

---

1 The Shed Seven feature was also mine, a somewhat contemptuously dashed-off account of a few days spent in Italy with a group I really couldn't have cared less about, even if I undertook a three-year, full-time, degree-level course in Caring Less About Shed Seven. The jaunt was redeemed by the company of fellow *Melody Maker* moonlighter Tom Sheehan, he of decades of service as *Maker* house photographer and of the dialect of rhyming slang spoken by nobody but himself. As we finished our final lunch and prepared to head for Milan's airport, Sheehan threw back his post-prandial espresso and said to an Italian record company operative, with a complete lack of self-consciousness, 'We're late for our Thomas. Can you get on the dog and call us a sherbet?' I very much enjoyed explaining that my colleague was observing that that the departure of our flight home was imminent, and that we would be obliged if she could employ her telephone to summon us a taxi (Thomas Paine = plane, dog & bone = phone, sherbet dab = cab).

Ian Gittins, and proposed to cover music, film, sport, books and other stuff besides. It permitted an exciting spreading of journalistic wings, allowing me to interview racing drivers, and to take my first tentative, thrilled, terrified steps into something resembling a war zone (Bosnia and Herzegovina), even if this was largely by accident.[2]

By the time the sun came out in 1995, Britpop was embarking on its period of peak imperial pomp. Even allowing for the self-regarding insularity of youth, it probably wasn't entirely wrong to feel that something important, or at least interesting, was happening, and that a regular writer for a music weekly had some part to play in it. It certainly felt like, say, a ticket for a secret Blur gig at Camden Town's Dublin Castle – a venue that held about eight people in any kind of comfort – was a scrap of paper worth more than any with the Queen's head on it.

Ah, Camden Town. When I'd first visited NW1 in 1990, as a wide-eyed greenhorn fresh off the plane, it had struck me as a reeking slum heaving with terrible pubs, aggressive drug dealers, snotty record shops, absurd goths and bad-tempered market stallholders selling overpriced junk to dim Japanese tourists. Five years later, Camden Town still struck me as a reeking slum heaving with etc, but it had somehow become the designated centre of the universe. Even more bizarrely, the centre of the centre of the universe had been pinpointed as The Good Mixer, a bedraggled old man's pub on the corner of Arlington Road and Inverness Street, whose clientele of bedraggled old men had been steadily crowded out by fashionable musicians, and those who derived some

---

2 An account of this journey appears in *Rock & Hard Places*, a book described as 'insightful reading' by no less an authority than the *Biloxi-Gulfport Sun-Herald*.

sort of thrill from being beneath the same ceiling as fashionable musicians.

The Good Mixer's stature had nothing to do with its innate charms, as it possessed none, and everything to do with its location. As the helpful map in *Melody Maker's* 17 June Camden Town special made clear, the Mixer was but a short stagger from the offices of all of MTV, Food Records (Blur's label), Creation Records and Savage & Best PR (representatives of Suede, Elastica, Menswear and Pulp, among many others they've been less keen to boast about). The inevitable cover stars of this issue were Menswear, who not only drank in the Mixer, but had formed the group there. Our strapline asked 'Do Britain's best-dressed band justify the hype?'; attentive readers will recall the rule about newspaper headlines which end in question marks.

I visited the Mixer most Sunday afternoons to rendezvous with a group of hacks, industry types and musicians for beer and toasted sandwiches before adjourning to Regent's Park to play inept, hungover football, often in front of small groups of dim Japanese tourists wearing overpriced junk who squealed reprovingly whenever someone kicked Damon Albarn. We did this less often than might be imagined of a bunch of men of roughly Damon's age who were acutely aware of the extreme unlikelihood of ever being as desired, acclaimed, rich or famous as Damon already was. For the duration of these fixtures, he appeared altogether unaffected, and when he did flex a degree of rock star largesse – occasionally inviting some of us for champagne and oysters at Maison Rouge studios in Fulham, where Blur were recording *The Great Escape*, before taking everyone to see Chelsea next door at Stamford Bridge – he did so with what was at the very least a convincing impression of guileless generosity. These expeditions were always treasurable for the manner in which the few rows in front would turn quizzically around upon hearing the 'Parklife'-familiar voice of Phil Daniels yelling at Paul Furlong.

It was such a heady summer that I even forgot my post-Woodstock II horror of mass live events sufficiently to go to more of them: Blur at Mile End stadium, the Reading and Glastonbury festivals. Our coverage of Glastonbury '95 was partially reported by Paul Mathur, an ebullient former reviews editor who by this point was a semi-permanent member of Oasis's entourage, in quite what capacity we never discerned. His review of the second stage on the Friday included a brisk – indeed, brusque – dismissal of the performance of The Flaming Lips. Subsequent to publication, a few of our more pedantic readers wrote in to remind us that The Flaming Lips had in fact cancelled several weeks previously. They made outrageous insinuations that our man had simply read the running order off the back of a T-shirt and invented his entire report. We replied to the effect that they didn't know Paul like we did – and that if he said he'd seen The Flaming Lips, there was, at least as far as he was concerned, every chance he had.

I continued to accept any and every opportunity to see the world on someone else's dime. I was sent by *Vox* magazine to Sweden to write about an allegedly burgeoning Scandinavian pop scene – an assignment which, largely thanks to the appetites of my hosts and guides, The Wannadies, and my naive attempts to keep up with them, descended into shambles. I retain precisely three memories of this trip. One, myself and fellow Woodstock veteran Ed Sirrs being thrown out of the comedy tent at some festival somewhere in the north of the country for repeatedly shouting 'Jamaica?' every time one of the performers paused in their (Swedish) monologue. Two, waking on the couch of my Stockholm hotel room, fully clothed except for one shoe, which I later discovered by the lift in the hall. Three, having to cancel one of the major interviews for the piece on the grounds that I just couldn't face the morning, and having to do it on the phone from London a few days later.

Many of us were also crisscrossing the Atlantic regularly. Gripped by inevitable hubris, the groups who'd sold a revivified English pop tradition to the British assumed they'd find an equally responsive audience in the United States – or at least those handling the groups did. The artists themselves tended to have a better understanding of the daunting requirements of breaking America, as well as an understandable reluctance to put themselves through such a grind of interminable and repetitive touring, after-show glad-handing and sighing their way through station idents for WKRAP-FM in Fucknut, Arkansas.

American rock groups pay their dues. British people form rock groups as a means of avoiding paying theirs. I spent a few days in New York City with Sleeper. They had been baffling Americans. 'Much as I love Beavis and Butthead,' said Louise Wener, 'I didn't enjoy playing to a crowd of them. You just think, "Fuck off, you're wankers, and we're here to educate you, so sit down and listen."' America had also been baffling Louise Wener, who had been to see Sleeper's label-mates, The Grateful Dead, at New Jersey's Meadowlands Stadium. 'I now have no hope for humanity,' she declared, 'after seeing 60,000 people standing in the baking heat waiting for these old, old guys to come on, and then when they did you had all these young kids on acid freaking out to this music which was just total, total rubbish.'

Examining anything up close is rarely as glorious or giddying as revering it from afar; ask the guy who cleans the pyramids. Sleeper were excited to be playing CBGB, the legendary Bowery dive whose stage had shaken to the beat of early Blondie, Ramones, Television, Patti Smith and Talking Heads. I was nearly as excited to be going to a gig at CBGB. Said excitement was not, however, sufficient to flatteringly fog a view of indolent staff and toilets like hell's basement, or prevent the forming of the opinion that a visit from some civic-minded arsonist wouldn't be altogether a bad thing. Either the fates are cruel, or I was just ungrateful, or possibly both, but where music journalism was concerned, I was increasingly nagged by that exhausting, querulous conundrum of reacting to getting the things I'd always wanted by wondering why I'd ever wanted them.[3]

This was a lonely place to be. Or, given the clip at which Radiohead's new album was selling, perhaps not. *The Bends* was a primal howl of disillusionment – and, not coincidentally, my favourite album of 1995. Radiohead were, at this point, caught between being cultishly adored indie rock wunderkind and stadium-rocking radio favourites, and unsure whether they really wanted to be either, and if neither, then what? Their – admittedly enviable – dilemma was illustrated by seeing Radiohead play consecutive shows opening for R.E.M. in some fathomless arena in Hartford, Connecticut, and headlining a much cooler, yet much sweatier, dive in New York.

Despite an already established popular image as sulking Grinches, Radiohead turned out to be capable of a certain amount of incredulous elation at what was happening to them – although, tellingly, they seemed more excited about

---

3 Louise's memoir of her time in Sleeper, variously published as *It's Different For Girls* and *Just For One Day* is a smart, funny elucidation of the bracing process of demystification that is life in a semi-successful pop group. CBGB closed in 2006. Good.

their proximity to their idols than by any validation of themselves. During R.E.M.'s set in Hartford, Radiohead bassist Colin Greenwood shepherded me onto the stage, to a vantage point just behind Peter Buck's amplifiers. 'I can't believe I'm watching this,' he said, like a man who hadn't been occupying the same spot as R.E.M's guitarist an hour earlier. But most of what Radiohead told me was anxious, cautious, the fretting of men shining a thin beam of light around a singularly forbidding cave as they inched forward, fearful of what lurked in the shadows.[4]

'The thing that's really freaked me out about doing a tour with a band as big as R.E.M.,' said Thom Yorke, 'is seeing how being so famous can change the way everybody, and I mean absolutely everybody, behaves towards you.'

Thom wasn't that famous yet, but was beginning to get the idea that he could be if he wanted to be.

'I find it . . . fuck, you know, I don't want it to happen. But that's presuming we're even going to make another record that people like.'

Radiohead's circumspection shouldn't have been surprising. The life of a successful rock musician is potentially glorious for someone generally lacking brains, conscience or manners. This is obviously a major part of the appeal for many young men, at least the type who regard the music they make in between parties and groupies as a necessary but tedious drawback of the job, to be knocked off with as little expenditure of time and effort as possible. For those attempting to create worthwhile art, these temptations are a twofold pitfall: it's not just that the temptations are temptations in and of themselves,

---

4 There's more of this trip, and of another to Paris with Radiohead about a decade later, in *Rock & Hard Places*, a book described as 'Sharp, witty and sarcastic' by the *Chicago Tribune*, a verdict with which it would seem churlish to quibble.

but that getting your work done, and distributed and written about, is dependent to a large extent on people who are busy giving in to them.

Thom, unusually for a young man, and extremely unusually for a young rock star, did not claim to know everything. He had, he said, learnt a great deal from R.E.M.

'To some degree,' he said, 'you do find yourself in the same boat, having gone through the same experiences, and they're quite a limited set of experiences, and they can turn you into quite a limited personality. So, I think, it's a shock when you discover that there other people who have gone through that, who are a few years ahead of you in the time machine, and have come back and said it's okay, you know, they're still alive.'

*

I confess that I expected little in the way of such self-aware humility from Green Day. The Berkeley brats had become suddenly ludicrously famous in the previous eighteen months. If one had wanted to do that music critic's thing of divining subtext from probably unrelated occurrences, one could have surmised that Green Day had been inadvertent beneficiaries of Kurt Cobain's suicide. Green Day shared with the grunge acts of the north-west a fondness for punky guitar rock, but propounded little of grunge's morose fury, instead affecting an attitude of bug-eyed cartoon angst. Green Day were a band whose misery you could enjoy, secure in the knowledge that the singer wasn't about to ruin anyone's vicarious thrill by doing anything so human and messy as shooting himself. Green Day's album *Dookie* had sold something in the vicinity of ten million copies.

Stephen Sweet and I flew to Halifax, Nova Scotia, to see Green Day play, and then on to Fredericton, New Brunswick, to interview them. We undertook this expedition with little optimism. Green Day's management, like the management of many famous American groups, had already laid down a list of conditions only slightly less onerous than those adumbrated in the Treaty of Nanjing. And then, at some point during our Atlantic crossing, Green Day read *Melody Maker*'s review of their new album, *Insomniac*. This had been composed by Neil Kulkarni, who tended to write like he was signalling from a warship under fire. He had denounced *Insomniac* as the work of 'quacks and mountebanks peddling placebo enervation which is in fact tranquiliser to kids stupid enough to know what they want and how to get it', before concluding, as if afraid that anyone may had failed to catch his drift, 'Green Day suck for real'. I admired both Neil's gusto and deployment of the word 'mountebank', but doubted Green Day would share these sentiments.

Sweet and I arrived at the appointed time and place, the Fredericton hockey arena where Green Day were playing that evening, entirely prepared to be informed that our names weren't down, that we weren't coming in, and that if we departed with appropriate haste, the tour manager might see his way clear to just firing the first few rounds over our heads. Green Day did not, after all, have all that much to gain by speaking to us. If, I grimly pondered, I'd sold ten million or so albums, and some hack from some rag which had dissed my new record wanted an hour of my afternoon, I might make him do a little dance for my amusement before I told him to piss off, but that would be about the limit of my hospitality.[5]

---

5   A more detailed account of this trip appears in *Rock & Hard Places*, a book described as 'The most important critical anthology on popular music in a long time,' by KEXP Seattle, which I think is a radio station.

Green Day turned out to better mannered than that. They were – eventually – affable, accommodating and happy to let us help polish off their disappointingly monkish backstage catering (they were, they explained, all about keeping costs, and therefore ticket prices, down). To an extent that verged on self-parody, they seemed to want to use the – eventually very long – interview to reassure readers, and perhaps themselves, that nobody thought it more ridiculous than they did that Green Day were now plausibly the biggest band in the world. (*Dookie* was outselling all of The Cure's *Wish*, U2's *Zooropa*, R.E.M.'s *Monster*, Pearl Jam's *Vitalogy* and, come to that, Nirvana's *Nevermind*.) They were aghast at persistent rumours that they hailed from prosperous backgrounds, and so eager to stress the humility of their upbringings that large stretches of the interview tape sounded like Monty Python's 'Four Yorkshiremen' sketch with one too few cast members, and in the wrong accent. Green Day were, of course, Americans, and therefore eternally petrified that some metaphorical bailiff would kick in their door brandishing an invoice confirming that their dues had not been paid.

'I don't want to sit here and complain about being a rock star,' said Billie Joe Armstrong, after spending an hour or so doing exactly that. 'I don't want to be whining and moaning. Fuck that, you know. I'm not gonna take for granted the fact that I have the ability to play music for the rest of my life if I want to. That's all I've ever wanted. For one or two or a few people to understand what the hell I'm talking about in my songs, that's more than I've ever asked for, for people to fuckin' get it.'

Most music fans will have experienced the mixed feelings inspired by seeing some group they loved early on hitting the big time, and confronting the compromises pressed on them by success. We rarely quell our snobbish dudgeon long enough to ponder how very much weirder it must be when the band in question is the one you play in.

*

The Britpop thing was – with still another eighteen months to go before Tony Blair welcomed Oasis to Downing Street – getting daft.

There is a downside to inspiring a generation to believe that their day has dawned, their time is now, and that the world is perched on the edge of its seat, holding deliriously on to its hat, agog to hear what they have to say – which is that the spotlight swiftly becomes crowded with the approximate artistic equivalent of those attention-seeking cretins who hover behind television news reporters, gurning stupidly and waving to their mates. Blur and Oasis in particular had inspired phalanxes of timewasters, who'd nonetheless managed to acquire followings and record deals and to whom *Melody Maker* was therefore obliged to pay attention. The Blur-ites generally came from London, sang in exaggerated cockernee accents and sounded like The Rezillos playing 'Knees Up Mother Brown' (Thurman, Powder, Menswear). The Oasisesques mostly came from somewhere further north, sounded like Oasis, and looked like they were about to menacingly ask you for a tenner to watch your car during the match (Cast, Northern Uproar).

A couple of *Melody Maker* writers, Simon Price and Taylor Parkes, made a valiant attempt at forging something new by inventing Romo – a scene which consisted of a few dozen pale young men encumbered by elaborate haircuts and makeup who posed at each other in London clubs, occasionally taking time out from their busy schedules of pouting and flouncing to make records which sounded like the works of the world's first all-chimp Spandau Ballet tribute group. We put representatives of four of these troupes – Orlando, Plastic Fantastic, Sexus, Dexdexter – on the front of the 25 November issue. This immediately entered *Melody Maker* lore as the 'God help us if there's a war' cover, and while the music created by the groups concerned faded from the collective consciousness quickly, it was at least an attempt to educate – even goad – the readers.

My real problem with Romo – aside, obviously, from the patent uselessness of almost all the groups concerned – was that I felt myself getting too old for this stuff. Though I wouldn't turn so much as twenty-seven until December, I was plagued by an idea that this rock journalism lark might already have been as good as it was going to get, that there were other things I might want to write about, and that I was starting to care less than enough about it. It was telling that two of the interviews I enjoyed doing most in 1995 were with musicians in a similar position; they had been around the block often enough to grow tired of the view, but were unable or unwilling to turn off in the direction of new horizons.

I spent a June afternoon with Mudhoney as they whiled away the pre-show hours backstage at the Empire in Shepherd's Bush. They refused to take any of my questions seriously, on the grounds that they – still – couldn't imagine why anybody was interested in what they thought about anything. 'I don't know how anyone who actually makes money out of playing music could think any other way,' said Mark Arm. 'It's absurd.'

The same month, I took The Jesus & Mary Chain's William and Jim Reid out to dinner at Sticky Fingers, the Kensington restaurant-cum-rock'n'roll museum then owned by former Rolling Stones bass player Bill Wyman, a venue deliberately chosen – either by me or the Mary Chain's press officer, I can't recall – to annoy them.

The interview yielded what may be the only proper scoop of my career in rock journalism. The Mary Chain's foundation myth, circa the release of *Psychocandy* in 1985, cast them as pair of surly, solvent-abusing, delinquent teenagers. At some point during our largely liquid dinner, William or Jim became muddled about the date of some or other milestone, prompting me to vent a suspicion that they may have been fibbing about their ages this last decade. William looked meaningfully at Jim, who shrugged. William then announced, 'Aw, fuck it. I can't be bothered anymore. I'm thirty-six, Jim's thirty-three.'

The Reids were not inclined to reflect on their – incalculably influential, justly acclaimed and reasonably profitable – career to date with serene gratitude.

'It has fucked with my soul,' snarled William, slurping margaritas with a relish that noticeably distracted other diners. 'It has fucked with me since day fuckin' one. I'm disenchanted, disillusioned, disenfranchised, disengaged, disconnected. I think when you're fourteen and you want to go on *Top of the Pops* you're seeing everything as . . . poetry. Being in a band, making music. Then when you actually get there you see it in all its . . . tat. And that's what the music business is, it's tatty. It's fine if you're willing to be produce, but it's not so nice a place when you genuinely believe that rock'n'roll isn't only rock'n'roll, that it's an art form.'

This soliloquy was at least in keeping with the theme of the Mary Chain single William was supposed to be promoting. It was called 'I Hate Rock'n'Roll'. There were people, I said – and I'd been one of them, once, as had he – who'd have been profoundly dispirited by this survey of the view from the revered position he occupied, as surely as if Neil

Armstrong's first words upon disturbing the dust of Tranquility Base had been, 'Well, this is rubbish. Don't know why I bothered.'

'I'm not in the business of writing fairytales for twelve-year-old kids,' William said. 'I'm in the business of writing about me and my life. That's what I'm here for. And if it sounds disillusioning to other people, so be it. Big fuckin' deal.'

*

At the end of 1995, I cast my votes for the following albums. *Melody Maker* wouldn't ask me again.

Pulp, *Different Class*

Melody Maker's Album of the Year, and quite rightly ('Common People' was *Melody Maker*'s Single of the Year, also quite rightly). It seemed for much of 1995 that Jarvis Cocker did little with his time but give interviews to *Melody Maker*. I got my turn at John Peel's farmhouse, where Cocker and Peel were recording a special on Pulp's first Peel session, recorded back in 1981. Jarvis's first memories of hearing Peel's show were a perfect summation of the lonely outsider convincing himself that here was news from somewhere better, a 'place where you could hear this kind of music that other radio stations wouldn't play. Probably at a great cost to my social life, I stayed in most nights, and taped stuff off the radio.' Cocker would scarcely have been alone among his generation in this desperate tuning in of signals from more interesting worlds than the one he was damned to inhabit: the obliteration of provincial boredom by the internet's all-day, on-demand, no-cost universe of entertainment is likely to have devastating long-term consequences for rock'n'roll.

ANDREW MUELLER

Blur, *The Great Escape*

The popular narrative of Britpop holds that the work of epoch-ending decadence that embodied the terminal decline of the phenomenon was Oasis's third album, 1997's *Be Here Now*. While *Be Here Now* is indeed wretched – overblown, inane and more or less exactly what you'd imagine a rock'n'roll album by Colonel Gaddafi would have sounded like – in this as in many respects, Blur did it before Oasis, and with greater panache. *The Great Escape*, like *Be Here Now*, is the sound of young men who believe themselves incapable of doing wrong. *The Great Escape*, like *Be Here Now* – and like all ventures undertaken by young men who believe themselves incapable of doing wrong – is a showcase of the least appealing qualities of the young men involved. However, unlike *Be Here Now*, *The Great Escape* did have moments of redemption, specifically the perfect 'The Universal' and the mournful 'He Thought of Cars', a foretaste of the much more interesting records Blur would subsequently issue. At the time, the time being what it was, I thought *The Great Escape* nearly as marvellous as Blur did.

Oasis, *(What's the Story) Morning Glory?*

If anyone asked me to make the choice – and if you worked for a music paper in 1995, they did – then I was always very much Team Blur. And I was/am aware that if you're supposed to extend grudging admiration to one Oasis album, it's the previous year's swaggering debut, *Definitely Maybe*. But *Morning Glory* was as close as anyone had got in twenty years to recreating the preposterous hubris of imperial-period Rolling Stones, and was therefore an immense, vicarious, foolish, guilty thrill. Indeed, I'd be prepared to argue that *Morning Glory* is hobbled short of a sort of barmy flawlessness only by the inclusion of the ghastly – and, in 1995, oppressively ubiquitous – 'Wonderwall', a miserable, maudlin drone that sounds like it was written to be bellowed through letterboxes by drunk boyfriends at women who have quite sensibly grown tired of waiting for them to return from the pub, and have locked them out.

Elastica, *Elastica*

Elastica – and *Elastica* – arrived so perfectly formed that an awful lot of people wasted an awful lot of time regarding them with prissy suspicion. Indeed, one of the many reasons I liked Elastica – and *Elastica* – as much as I did was that they were precisely what you'd have come up with if you'd wanted to come up with something which would most enrage the most boring of rock'n'roll camp followers, i.e. those who are grimly obsessed with authenticity and credibility. Elastica possessed all the qualities that such dunces detest most pedantically: they were predominantly female, somewhat posh, and displayed a jaunty insouciance about helping themselves to dusty old post-punk riffs that the authors of same were no longer doing terribly much with. The many, many letters we received decrying Elastica were, without exception, from dreary trainspotters, all of whom have by now hopefully dropped dead.

Teenage Fanclub, *Grand Prix*

I shuffled along to somewhere in West London to interview Teenage Fanclub shortly before this came out, having heard nothing from it but the single, 'Mellow Doubt' – an amiable but insubstantial semi-acoustic shamble with a whistling solo. I may, over lunch, have essayed a concern that it was all getting a bit Crosby, Stills & Nash. 'Aye,' said Norman Blake, 'listen to this,' and planted a pair of headphones on me, before cueing a song I now know to have been 'Sparky's

371

Dream'. It's a wonderful thing to hear for the first time a song which you know instantly will stay with you, will become a tool you reach for time and again to make a bad time feel okay or a good one feel better. It's an extremely eerie thing to hear such a song for the first time when the people who wrote and recorded it are peering intently at you across a table in Pizza Express. 'If it's any consolation,' said Blake, noting my astonishment, 'that's kind of how we felt the first time we heard it, as well.'

Radiohead, *The Bends*

A meticulous cataloguing of Thom Yorke's disgust set to a backdrop of exuberant guitars and malevolent keyboards. As a rejection of the fripperies of fame, *The Bends* was a worthy companion to, say, Elvis Costello's *This Year's Model* or The Byrds' *Younger Than Yesterday* – which, ironically, only encouraged lazy casting of Yorke as the tormented ombudsman of a generation's despair. The tone of the coverage of Radiohead around this time, especially in the wake of the suicide of Kurt Cobain and the disappearance of Richey Edwards, became unhealthily carnivorous. *Melody Maker* – and we should have known better – was among the outlets who took it upon themselves to play circling vulture to Thom's limping cowboy. A strapline on one 1995 Radiohead cover asked the crashingly tactless question 'Another Rock Martyr in the Making?' over a photo of Yorke. Happily, the rule about newspaper headlines which end in question marks demonstrated its infallibility once more.

Tindersticks, *Tindersticks*

Listening to this, never mind admiring it, necessitated overcoming a massive personal prejudice. I've always taken against self-titled albums, even ones as good as *Elastica*, at the best of times, on the grounds that it bespeaks a lazy, indifferent attitude to words – you rarely catch authors doing it ('So, Fyodor Dostoyevsky, tell us about your new novel, *Fyodor Dostoyevsky.*') But Tindersticks compounded the affront by releasing two eponymous albums in a row, which would have been annoying enough even if the conceit had been original, but it wasn't – The House Of Love had performed the same tedious trick with their first two albums, 1988's *The House of Love* and 1990's *The House of Love.* Anyway, *Tindersticks* was – much like *Tindersticks* – a sublime, maudlin masterpiece, crested by the perfect ballads 'Travelling Light' and 'Tiny Tears', and the priceless monologue 'My Sister', which suggested Flannery O'Connor trying to get Simon Bates to read her letter on *Our Tune.*

Bruce Springsteen, *The Ghost of Tom Joad*

In a priceless illustration of both the Britpop-induced solipsism engulfing the music press, and the disregard into which Springsteen had lapsed following the underwhelming *Lucky Town/Human Touch* twinset of 1992, neither *Melody Maker* nor *NME* admitted this to their Top 50 albums of 1995 – lists which were dominated by exactly who you might imagine, i.e. the artists who dominated my own list, among many, many others much, much less eminent. Springsteen, in the unlikely event that he troubled to read either our Christmas issue or theirs, might well have wondered what more he had to do to dislodge the likes of Wagon Christ, Spring Heel Jack, Blumfeld, Telstar Ponies, Whipping Boy, Whale and Labradford.

Steve Earle, *Train a Comin'*

I don't know how I happened across *Train a Comin'*, still less how Earle's four previous albums had escaped my attention.

I do know, however, that one of the greatest pleasures available to a music fan is discovering an artist who, while new to you, has a history waiting to be discovered. Again, possibly perversely, this is less fun now that it's something you can do at whim, rather than having to schlep around record shops asking if they have *Copperhead Road* or *Guitar Town* in stock. At some level, even consumers have a need to suffer for their art.

Emmylou Harris, *Wrecking Ball*

Emmylou Harris sings songs by Steve Earle, Neil Young, Bob Dylan, Rodney Crowell, Jimi Hendrix, Gillian Welch and Daniel Lanois. This album should therefore have made everyone's end-of-year lists just in theory.

26

IN WHICH THE AUTHOR IS HANDED THE REGIMENTAL REVOLVER AND INSTRUCTED TO TAKE A WALK INTO THE WOODS

Paul Simon once warbled to the effect that there are fifty ways to leave your lover. He was wrong. There are really only two – but, speaking as a hack who has more than once had to desperately pad out some spurious list conceit, I sympathise. Your pair of options for departing a relationship which is thwarting, troublesome, dysfunctional or has just run its course are as follows: i) be honest with yourself and whoever else is concerned, explain yourself clearly but kindly, walk away with dignity, and permit the other party to do the same; ii) behave with increasing self-indulgence, discourtesy, twattery and/or bellendery until they finally lose patience and ditch you – this tack, often pursued semi-wittingly by people not entirely certain what they want, has the bonus of subsequently allowing one, once the heave-ho has been administered, to feel and act self-righteously aggrieved at the sundering, almost as if it wasn't all your fault for behaving like a self-indulgent, discourteous twat and/or bellend.

And this – spoiler alert – was what I did. I wanted to leave *Melody Maker*, but lacked the courage to go, and so I got myself fired. This makes the process sound like the result of coherent and conscious planning, which it wasn't, and sound not like a series of the sort of dopey and counter-productive decisions one makes when one is past caring, which it was. *Ikon* magazine had closed, owing me a little over £3000, which was a little over £3000 more than I had (this debt was eventually settled by *Ikon*'s owners, thanks to an obdurate stand on principle by the editors, Chris Roberts and Ian Gittins, who refused to come to terms until everyone had been paid). I believed that I was assimilating this with exemplary equanimity, under the circumstances, serenely untroubled by anything except this constant, eye-watering pain in my lower jaw which felt something like my face was on fire.

'Stress can do that,' explained the doctor, and prescribed some painkillers which I think were normally used as local anaesthetic to enable the performance of dental surgery upon whales, but which numbed me to the agony in my mandible and to much else besides, like the consequences of doing really stupid, insensitive things. It was at this point that Laura Lee Davies, then editor of *Time Out*'s music section, asked me to write a column ruminating on the failure of *Ikon* and what this said about the state of the British music press as a whole.

So, really, it was all her fault.

*

The last things I wrote for *Melody Maker* could not have been said to resonate with valedictory portent. In the new year issue, I couldn't even find it in myself to tip anybody for the top, however risible or unlikely or recently they'd been staying on my couch.

My penultimate[1] feature for *Melody Maker* was a reunion with Paul Barker and Al Jourgenson of Ministry at the Warners office in South Kensington; Jourgenson, swaddled in leather and hidden behind sunglasses, swigged champagne by the bottle throughout. Near the end of our allotted hour, he leant meaningfully towards me and asked if I ever wore nappies. I replied that it had been a while. 'I do,' Jourgenson enthused. 'And I'll tell you. There is no better damn feeling in the world than sitting on a nice comfortable chair pretending to be carrying on a sensible conversation with someone while all the time you're pissing in your trousers. I'd recommend it to anyone.' I left without shaking his hand. My final feature was an interview with Dubstar, a St Etienne-ish pop concern who probably should have been bigger: a story which focused untowardly on the merriment we derived from looking up double-entendre surnames in a directory by the phone booth which served as a photo location probably didn't help.

And the last line of my last ever singles page was written as a throwaway chuckle, but in hindsight I perceive somewhere in its glib arrogance a muted cry for help: 'I'm off down Soho,' I announced, 'to flog this lot before the bloke in the shop reads this and realises what rubbish he's buying.[2] Toodle pip.'

---

1 There isn't really a footnote here, merely an observation that while 'penulti-mate' is in itself a satisfyingly orotund way of denoting 'second-last', I spend too much time trying to think of ways to insert the related terms 'antepen-ultimate' (third-last) or – even better – the majestic 'preantepenultimate' (fourth-last) into everyday conversation.

2 The offloading of unwanted CDs to a well-trodden circuit of second-hand record shops in Soho was a widely availed source of supplementary income. You're not really a rock writer if you've never reacted to the arrival of a gas bill by ringing around every press office you know, floating entreaties varying on the theme of 'I've been hearing good things about Whichever Desperate Act It Is You're Spruiking This Month – can you send me a copy of their album? And, er, all the singles – I'm told the b-sides are well worth hearing.'

This would have been a pleasingly if unintentionally apposite signoff. As it was, the last words ever published above my by-line in *Melody Maker* appeared a couple of weeks later in the 27 January 1996 issue, on the cover of which leered the lamentable Northern Uproar, looking as usual like a group mugshot. Said words were arranged in the form of a brief review of *Scars From Falling Down*, a dull album by Steel Pole Bath Tub,[3] listening to which was, I assessed, 'approximately like waiting for a derailed train to leave the station.'

Those who believe that whatever a writer is writing about, he's writing substantially about himself, are not entirely wrong.

*

I suspect that at this point the reader – and thanks, incidentally – is imagining that I'm taking my time revealing the heresy that got me excommunicated in order to build suspense. I'm not. I'm putting off revisiting the one piece of my writing I would most like to strike from the record.

The column on the state of British rock journalism that I wrote for *Time Out*, and which ran under the title WRITE

---

3   There's always someone worse off. My name appeared in *Melody Maker* twice more that I know of. The first, in August 1996, was in a caption beneath a photo of myself, Feargal Sharkey and a couple of others racing luggage trolleys in Exeter Airport, during a farcical helicopter-borne press junket to Dartmoor to witness the firing-up of a tank-mounted sound-system owned by The KLF's Jimmy Cauty. The second, later that year, was in the context of a feeble but nevertheless gratifying snippet I passed along to whoever was writing *Melody Maker*'s gossip column at the time. I had been invited to Damon Hill's book launch party. By the buffet, I perceived motor racing enthusiast George Harrison. Believing – at time of writing correctly – that this might be my only opportunity for conversational interaction with a Beatle, I made for the canapes nearest him. 'Excuse me,' I ventured. 'Whoops, sorry,' replied the composer of 'While My Guitar Gently Weeps' and 'Here Comes The Sun', and moved aside. 'Cheers,' I said.

OF PASSAGE:[4] ANDREW MUELLER VERSUS THE MUSIC PRESS in the 17–24 January issue, wasn't entirely misguided. I do not, at this distance, perceive much fault with my assertion that the reason such flash-in-the-pan music titles as *Siren, Indiecator, Lime Lizard* and the Jonathan King brainchild *Revvolution* had flashed and then gone down the pan was that they were terrible and, therefore, nobody had wanted to read them. And I don't think I was alone in expressing weariness with the fact that the general opinion of the music press was still intractably mired in the late 1970s, due largely to the veterans of that period – Julie Burchill, Paul Morley, Danny Baker, Tony Parsons et al – using their subsequent domination of the proper papers to bang on and interminably on about how bloody marvellous they used to be.

But I was crashingly, smugly, thoughtlessly wrong about everything else, even when I was right. It was not inaccurate to state that *NME* and *Melody Maker* freelancers were 'demoralised' because they were stingily remunerated – or, as I joshed insufferably, paid 'a wretched pittance that hasn't increased in six years. Many now survive by selling unwanted CDs to shops in Soho, and their own internal organs through a mafia contact in Bialystok, who supplies Russian military hospitals who aren't too fussy about the quality of the livers and kidneys they buy.' And it was certainly true that the

---

4 Whoever wrote the column headlines for *Time Out* was a genius. They rarely had the space that allowed we *Melody Maker* and *NME* types to indulge our more rococo contrivances – my 1994 feature on Sleeper, for example, had been graced with I'M A-SLUMBER, JACK, AND I'M OKAY. A year or so earlier, I'd written a *Time Out* music column expressing distaste at the sentimental cult that had developed around the unctuous schlock of The Carpenters, positing that had Karen Carpenter not died in such gruesome and tragic circumstances, The Carpenters would possess the approximate cachet of The Nolan Sisters. *Time Out*'s subs topped that with the appalling but perfect WEARING THIN.

lousy money, which was indeed lousy, had been a staple of gallows humour in *Melody Maker*'s own pages for as long as I'd been working for it. But just as one defends, outside the home, the parents and siblings one might tease when among friends and family, one does not traduce one's publication in the pages of another.

Still less does one get haughty in such a context with one's comrades – or even, really, one's immediate rivals, who are, after all, toilers at the same parsimonious coalface. I could probably just about have gotten away with scoffing at the straitlacedness of the *NME*, as I did, or even – at a very long stretch – dismissing IPC's monthly *Vox* as 'the only still-birth ever to reach adulthood', and noting that it had become even duller since being placed under the editorial control of the *NME*, a transformation I appraised as akin to 'making water wetter',[5] but I've no idea what I was thinking when I described *Melody Maker*'s own writers as 'either unmissable or patently unreadable.' I mean, I'm sure I thought that was true – and I'm sure there were some who thought highly of me, etc – but I cannot overstate the urgency with which I wish to plunge backwards through time, hover like a slightly greyer ghost behind the shoulder of my younger self as he taps righteously away at one of *Time Out*'s terminals, and whisper, 'Seriously, kid. There's a time and a place, and this is neither.'

The daftness of what I'd done was measurable, the day of publication, by the frequency with which my phone rang – and the manner in which everyone seemed to feel obliged to whisper their support. I really knew I was done for when

---

5 At the risk of picking at time-smoothed scars, *Vox* was eventually delivered into the editorial oversight of Everett True, who appeared – at least to me – to be on the verge of turning it into an interesting and idiosyncratic title, at which point it was closed.

even a couple of *NME* writers, who didn't much care for me professionally or (I supposed) personally, called to tell me how much the column had amused them. When Allan rang to confirm that he was going to choose to interpret it as a sort of open letter of resignation, he didn't even sound angry, and I couldn't find it in myself to confect sufficient pharisaical outrage to play the martyred messenger. I'd sown it, and I was reaping it: it's the way the world is supposed to work. I put the phone down, made a cup of coffee, picked the phone up, and began cold-calling newspaper editors, looking for work.

*

Years later, when touring various portions of the world attempting to interest people in purchasing one of my books – and seriously, Bill Bryson has enough money; buy another one of mine – I'd often field the stock question regarding my biggest break as a writer. I developed a stock response, in two parts: being hired by *Melody Maker*, and being fired by *Melody Maker*. The benefits of the former will be clear to anybody who has read this far. And the latter was about as well-timed a sacking as one could wish for.

I think I knew, even if I hadn't admitted it to myself, that it was time to go. I was twenty-seven. I didn't want a full-time editorial position on a music magazine, still less a career in magazine publishing (or, really, any sort of 'career' in anything, if it might involve offices and meetings and getting up at the same time to do the same thing every day). I was feeling the first twinges of the creeping malaise that afflicts music fans as they grow older, as they listen to the strummings of subsequent generations and react, even despite themselves, not with empathy and excitement but querulousness and spite. It's the inevitable progress – unless it's decline – from

'We're the young generation, and we've got something to say,' to 'What do you know about anything, you born-yesterday, wet-behind-the-ears wanker? Get a haircut.' I suspected that there might be more to life than a place on the guest list at the Town & Country, and I wanted to find out what.

But it would have been a good time to be leaving even if I hadn't wanted to. Measuring the state of the music press now against the state of the music press then, I feel something of the gratitude of the mutinous seaman cast adrift in a longboat shortly before the vessel upon which he served struck a reef. Allan left *Melody Maker* in 1997 to found *Uncut*, a fine journal to which I am proud to contribute to this day. *Melody Maker*'s publishers declined to do the obvious and sensible thing and put Everett True in charge, and instead awarded the position of editor to a former *NME* sort, who reduced the *Maker* to a doleful hybrid of *Smash Hits* and *Loaded*, committing the strangely common error of alienating the readers the paper already had in a quest for new readers who probably didn't exist. *Melody Maker* folded in 2000, by then a pitiful parody of the paper which had changed my life.

There were two reasons why life for the music press became difficult in the late 90s. The Britpop bubble deflated, and nothing really swelled in its place. And there was what a feature in the 26 August 1995 issue of *Melody Maker* had referred to, with the sort of hesitantly respectful capitalisation that might once have been bestowed by cultural periodicals upon Rock And Roll, as The Internet. Paul Lester's story about a fledgling iTunes called Cerberus Sound & Vision promised a world in which we would be able to order music from our computers. It's not a phrase I type lightly, but we should have paid more attention to Paul. 'You can see where all this is heading,' he wrote. 'Retailers made obsolete. Manufacturers run out of town. Distributors sat on their arses with bugger all to do.' He concluded by tempting fate, asking one of the geniuses behind Cerberus what this would mean for *Melody Maker*. 'Oh, that'll be alright,' was the reply. 'People are still going to want something to read on the train.'

Ah, well.

ANDREW MUELLER

27

IN WHICH THE AUTHOR TOYS WITH THE 'AND THEN I WOKE UP, AND DISCOVERED IT HAD ALL BEEN A DREAM' CLOSING GAMBIT

Every so often, among the usual flotsam in my email inbox, I'll find an enthusiastic entreaty from some rosy-cheeked, twinkle-eyed stripling who has read something I've written about music – one of my other books, perhaps, copies of which may be found in all good bargain bins, or something in a recent issue of *Uncut*, or perhaps a yellowing review from *Melody Maker* they disinterred while stripping wallpaper. The correspondent will state that he – and it is almost invariably a he – wishes to follow in my footsteps, and seek his fortune as a rock journalist. Depending on my mood, my response will vary in tone somewhere between 'It's too late for me, but you're young, you're healthy – save yourself,' and 'That ship has long since sailed and sunk, kid, but I had my fun, and that's all that matters.'

This will usually ruin my day. I don't miss working for the rock press myself, and nor should I. I'm forty-four years old, and possess items of gardening equipment, some of which I know how to operate; I have opinions about wine, some of them informed. But, speaking as someone who still consumes (if largely inadvertently) popular culture and as someone who tries (if intermittently successfully) not to begrudge the young their youth, I miss the rock press being there in the way it once was. When I look at the early twenty-something in those photo albums I mentioned at the outset of this volume, I find it difficult to imagine what he would have done without *Melody Maker*. There are many like him now, I'm certain, who would benefit incalculably from having their Wednesday mornings – Tuesday afternoons, if they were really keen and lived in London – enlivened by a publication which prodded their assumptions so vigorously in the ribs, and was so keen for them to learn, to think, to explore.

I'm familiar with the counter-argument – that the cloistered cartel of the music press has been replaced by the exuberant free market of the internet. But to bound gaily between metaphors, I'd argue that it's more like the difference between watching an organised soccer match between teams of top-flight professionals, and being a spectator at a fixture of one of those unruly primordial predecessors of the game in which hundreds of straw-hatted yokels tussled up and down the cobbled streets of their village, using a greased pig as a ball. Which is to say that figuring out what is going on is difficult and tiresome, and because almost nobody is getting paid or is operating much in the way of quality control, the field is open to any bozo who fancies their chances – which constricts the space in which the skilful performers can operate, and makes them harder to spot amid the hurly-burly.

Also, rock'n'roll has pretty much had it. Granted that people have been saying that since, probably, about five minutes after Elvis Presley knocked off 'That's All Right' at Sun Studio in Memphis one summer day in 1954 ('Well,' you can imagine some pompadoured pundit harumphing, 'It's no "Rocket 88" by Jackie Brenston and the Delta Cats, is it?').

And granted that one of the consolations of middle age is telling young people that what they're doing now was way more fun back when you were doing it. But rock'n'roll really has pretty much had it.

The decline of rock'n'roll is not solely attributable to the decline of the music press, and nor is my personal perception of that decline entirely down to the fact that I'm a forty-something grouch. The diminishment of rock'n'roll's returns is actually mathematically quantifiable. It's now fifty years since The Beatles released 'Please Please Me'; fifty years before that, nobody in the world owned an electric guitar. The summer of punk was over thirty-five years ago; thirty-five years before that, World War II had barely got under way. Grunge was twenty years ago, and not many of those groups were doing much that Led Zeppelin hadn't done twenty years before that. It is altogether arguable that since that heady decade and a half in which rock'n'roll soared from the cheerful skiffle of, say, Bill Haley's 'Rock Around the Clock' to the engorged sonic immensities of, for example, Jimi Hendrix's 'Electric Ladyland', everybody has just been playing dress-up. There are, and there will be, great rock'n'roll bands. There is just no chance – none whatsoever – that any of them will make an album as audacious, resonant, influential and upsetting as *Sticky Fingers*, never mind *Nevermind*.

None of which should be interpreted as a statement of regret of my service in this lost cause. I have no way of knowing what my adult life to this point would have been like had Everett True taken the entirely reasonable decision, one morning in 1990, to crumple my review of Straitjacket Fits and toss it in the direction of the nearest dustbin. But I'm pretty certain it would have involved going to fewer interesting places, meeting fewer interesting people, and a general paucity of inebriated camel-riding lessons in Morocco with Def Leppard.

Which is why, even and ever since I got canned by *Melody Maker* back in 1996, I've kept writing about music and the people who make it for various newspapers and magazines. The interviews, when they're good, remain an extraordinary pleasure: discussing the ambiguities of southern American culture with Randy Newman, the focusing effects of mortal illness with Holly Johnson, the seductive banality of the tortured artist cliché with Polly Harvey, the difference between *Smash Hits* and *Melody Maker* with Neil Tennant ('At *Smash Hits* we did depth through surface. At *Melody Maker* you did surface through depth').

The occasional tour stories are still a pleasingly surreal way to see the world: desecrating Moscow with The Bloodhound Gang, perplexing Beirut with The Prodigy, brunching in northern California with Merle Haggard, rolling across Georgia and Florida with The Drive-By Truckers, joining U2's circus in the US, Australia, Europe or the Balkans. And every so often I'll get to make a call to a given number at an appointed time, and be answered by a voice so intimately familiar that it seems implausibly remote: 'Hello, it's Keith Richards/Mick Jagger/Jimmy Page/Michael Stipe/Mike Scott/ Charlie Louvin/Paul Westerberg.'

These assignments remain rewarding miles above and beyond the ammunition they provide for subsequent name-dropping – which, at any rate, becomes an emptier pleasure the more you realise how little chance there is that any of your subjects remember the encounter at all, still less are boasting about it at dinner parties. Each is an opportunity to sit down with someone who created a thing which has taken up residence in your head, and in the heads of others, and ask them to explain themselves. Sometimes, they know what they're doing and why they're doing it. 'I mean,' erupted an exasperated Steve Earle, circa his persecution for writing a song about Californian mujahid John Walker Lindh, 'this idea that artists are not qualified to comment on society . . . that's our job!' Much more often, they're less confident. 'If you're genuinely talented,' fretted Nick Cave, 'and stay true to your talent, and don't start doing things for the wrong reasons, you'll be able to continue to do what you do, to continue to be given songs. I do know that if I started to abuse this, if I started to just do stuff for money, there's a good chance that my abilities would be taken away from me.'

It doesn't really matter whether you find yourself liking and admiring them as much off record as on. They all do an interesting job, distilling the mysteries which baffle, enrage and inspire us most into just a few dozen words and a hummable tune. One day, I'm going to interview Smokey Robinson, and I'm going to start by asking 'Right then. "My Girl". How on Earth did you do that?'

*

If you do anything repeatedly, especially if you do it professionally, it gradually grows less exciting. Somewhere above us right now, an orbiting astronaut is yawning irritably at his thousandth view of the sun erupting from the fathomless darkness of space and splashing life-giving light across our lonely, fragile blue bauble, and thinking: 'Christ. How many more fucking laps do I have to do in this godforsaken bean tin? They might at least have given us a magnetic Monopoly set.'

Twenty years ago, I used to go to three or four gigs a week. My yearly average now isn't quite down to that, but it's getting there. I grew tired of being treated like livestock – albeit livestock assumed to possess the wherewithal to spend a fiver a time on a small, crinkly plastic cup half-full of undrinkable zinfandel – by venues. And though I was never one of those people who went to gigs to sing or clap along – and if you are one of those people, incidentally, please shut up; you're nearly as annoying as people who chant during the cricket – I no longer have any need or desire to have my choices validated by gatherings of like-minded people. An unexpected redeeming liberation of middle age is finding yourself ever more serenely uninterested in what anyone thinks of you.

This renders you more or less useless as a music fan, at least for the purposes of the music business, but it reinvigorates you as a music lover. When you're young, you listen to – or, in further-gone cases, write about – music at least partially for an imagined audience of peers and/or acolytes who you imagine will be impressed – even, perchance, aroused – by your choices (I have, yes, made mix tapes for girls, and will forever think fondly of those who pretended to listen to them). While you may well enjoy the works of Artist X on their merits, you also wish, at some level, to be perceived as the kind of person who appreciates the works of Artist X. This is why young people wear T-shirts with the name of Artist X on them (there are middle-aged people who also do this, but they should be arrested). By the time a man reaches my age, he has – ideally – something to say for himself that he hasn't cribbed from a lyric sheet or an interview in a music magazine; this frees him to listen to music purely and simply because he likes it.

Whether or not this makes you a better music journalist is a judgement only readers can make. But just as my feelings about music have changed – one would prefer to think matured – so have my feelings about music journalism. I'm at once more sceptical and more forgiving a critic than I once was. Even were the opportunity that *Melody Maker* once provided still available, I don't think I'd be as quick, these days, to declare a given record a more worthwhile expenditure of household budget than food, or to defame a given artist as a talentless mountebank who should be enthusiastically upholstered with tar and feathers and heaved into the canal by an exultant mob (though I'm always happy to make an exception for Sting). I recognise that a record, however great, is still only – well, 'only' – words and music, and that most records are made by fallible people who have worked hard and sacrificed much to pursue a dream and/or a muse as best they can. Even while acknowledging that a critic is principally responsible to the reader, not the artist, I don't derive the rush of smug hauteur I once did from announcing that the perpetrator of a sub-standard pop album should be shot, conscripted or boiled in the urine of goats before having their head impaled on a spike at the gates of the city. (Although, again, as long as David Byrne continues to make records, I reserve the right to excuse myself from this generalisation.)

But somewhere, by somebody, music should be being discussed and dissected in such absolutist terms. For the proper – for which, perhaps, read 'tragic' – music fan, anger and rage are crucial components of the experience. To deny that, to be cosy and complacent with music, means collaborating in the process by which music has become cosy and complacent. This is no longer my department, nor my problem, but someone should get on it. Annoyed though I am that it's now perfectly possible to conduct reasonably intelligent conversations with people born in the 1990s, I'd trade their infinity of options in a blink for what I was supremely fortunate to have as a listener and reader – and writer. I dislike profoundly the idea that there are twenty-two-year-olds who are scrimping through barely paid internships at dismal, decline-managing consumer rags when they should be drunk on their favourite band's tour bus, somewhere between two places they've never been before.

*

The great American reporter H.L. Mencken died as rock'n'roll was being born. He'd have hated rock'n'roll, but he'd have made a fine rock journalist – irreverent, iconoclastic, delighted at the way words can dance. His summation of his career in newspapers is often invoked by his fellow hacks, with either or both a hoisted glass or rolled eyes: 'As I look back over a misspent life, I find myself more and more convinced that I had more fun doing news reporting than in any other enterprise. It is really the life of kings.'

Rock journalism was like that, but with free T-shirts.

ANDREW MUELLER

EPILOGUE

The *NME* still totally blows.

ANDREW MUELLER

ACKNOWLEDGEMENTS

Fulsome gratitude for contributing to a singularly fortunate early adulthood and/or this telling of it are due to the following.

First and foremost, the *Melody Maker* Wrecking Crew, past, present and honorary. We should really all have got tattoos, probably featuring the face of Mr Abusing above whatever the Latin is for 'All Rock Stars Are Tossers' (still, there's always the next reunion). Particular thanks to those in positions of (relative) responsibility circa my arrival at King's Reach Tower, who encouraged me most when I probably deserved it least: Everett True, Allan Jones, Steve Sutherland, Mat Smith, Carol Clerk, David Stubbs, Chris Roberts, Ted Mico.

Back in the old country, all who tolerated my presence in the office and on the pages of *On The Street*, 1987–1990, especially Margaret Cott, Michael Smith and Sharon O'Connell.

Astrid Williamson for, among and amidst a great deal else, the conversation which prompted me to realise exactly which Todd Snider lyric I should steal the title from.

Todd Snider for graciously declining to press charges when informed of the theft.

Patterson Hood, Mike Cooley and Drive-By Truckers, my favourite 21st century rock'n'roll group, for agreeing to accept payment in beer for the use of a couplet from one their many fine songs as an epigraph.

Gen Matthews, Jeremy Jones, Lara Pattison and Norman Levene, i.e. all who presently sail in The Blazing Zoos, a band who don't really feel we're part of any sort of 'scene', y'know, it's not really something you can categorise, we just sort of make music for ourselves, really, and if anyone else likes it, it's a bonus.

Luke Haines, Cathal Coughlan and Audrey Riley, my fellow interpreters of *The North Sea Scrolls*.

Chloe Combi, for goading me along during the period I was writing this book by writing a book of her own that was much better.

Everybody at the print and radio incarnations of Monocle.

My friends, who are just great.

And my family, especially my kind, funny, brilliant, brave and much-missed mother, Gweny, who would have liked this book more than she did the ones full of angry foreigners with guns.

Lightning Source UK Ltd.
Milton Keynes UK
UKHW02f2327170818
327401UK00004B/160/P